ABERFAN

Government and Disaster

'The research is outstanding ... the investigation is substantial, balanced and authoritative ... this is certainly the definitive book on the subject ... Meticulous.'
John R. Davis, Kingston University, *Contemporary British History*

'Definitive ... authoritative ... anyone who wants to understand the process of government and its obsession with secrecy should read this book.'
Ron Davies, Secretary of State for Wales 1997-1998

'Intelligent and moving.'
Planet

ABERFAN

Government and Disaster

Iain McLean and Martin Johnes

welsh academic press

Published in Wales by Welsh Academic Press, an imprint of

Ashley Drake Publishing Ltd
PO Box 733
Cardiff
CF14 7ZY

www.welsh-academic-press.wales

First edition (Aberfan - Government and Disasters) - published 2000
Second, revised and updated, edition (Aberfan - Government
and Disaster) - published 2019

ISBN
978-1-86057-0336

British Library Cataloguing-in-Publication Data.
A CIP catalogue for this book is available from the British Library.

Typeset by Prepress Plus, India (www.prepressplus.in)
Cover design by Welsh Books Council, Aberystwyth
Cover image © Media Wales

Contents

I'r rhai a garwn, ac yn galarwn o'u colli
To those we love, and miss so very much

Foreword

We were very pleased to be asked by Iain McLean and Martin Johnes to contribute a few words to this important new work, *Aberfan: Government and Disasters*. Professor McLean has aided the cause of the bereaved of Aberfan and Merthyr Vale previously through several newspaper articles, which led to the reparation by the Government of £150,000 taken after the disaster from charity funds to clear the tip. This book is a meticulous examination of the documents and media reports relating to the disaster and, as such, is a landmark as the first serious lengthy academic treatment of Aberfan. Professor McLean and Dr Johnes have conducted their research with sensitivity and sympathy, and remained committed to uncovering the truth throughout. Their findings are as shocking as they are illuminating, and are a lesson to this and future governments as to how disasters should be handled. The bereaved of Aberfan and Merthyr Vale hope that such gross mismanagement and injustice is never again meted out to this community in the most dire and unthinkable of circumstances.

H. Clifford Minett
Chairman of the Aberfan and Merthyr Vale Cemetery
and Memorial Garden Committee.
September 2000

Introduction
to the Second Edition

'Of recent years the houses in the valleys and on the lower slopes are still further overshadowed by the huge coal-tips which are being piled on the breasts and upper slopes and which, besides making the landscape hideous, will in time endanger the very lives of those dwelling in the valleys below.'

1917 Commission of Enquiry into Industrial Unrest; No. 7 Division, Wales and Monmouthshire, Cd 8668

This is a completely revised edition of *Aberfan: Government and Disasters* published by Welsh Academic Press in 2000. The first edition was widely cited and used extensively, among others by television programme makers who made hard-hitting documentaries on both the 40th and the 50th anniversaries of the disaster. The book had been out of print for some years, and we were delighted to be invited to revise and reissue it while memories of Aberfan have been freshly stirred by the events surrounding its 50th anniversary, on 21 October 2016.

The focus of this second edition has been tightened so that it is much more exclusively about Aberfan than the first edition, which is still available in libraries for people who want to read about our research and conclusions on other disasters. Some of its findings, including those about the *Titanic* disaster, were published separately.[1]

The remainder of the Introduction is a revised and updated version of the Preface from the first edition.

---

1. Iain McLean and Martin Johnes, '"Regulation run mad": the Board of Trade and the loss of the *Titanic*', *Public Administration*, 78 (2000), 729-49.

If you are over 70, you probably remember exactly what you were doing on two days in the 1960s. One was 22 November 1963 when President Kennedy was assassinated. The other, also a Friday, was 21 October 1966, the day that 109 children were killed in their classrooms at Pantglas Junior School, Aberfan, near Merthyr Tydfil in south Wales, when a waste tip from Merthyr Vale Colliery slid down the mountain and engulfed their school. The total death toll was 144. Aberfan horrified the nation like no other British event since 1945, except the mass murder of schoolchildren in Dunblane in 1995.

On the evening of 21 October 1966, like the rest of the nation, one of us (IM) stood transfixed in front of the TV to hear Cliff Michelmore, in tears, saying, 'Never in my life have I seen anything like this. I hope I shall never ever see anything like it again. For years of course the miners have been used to ... disaster. Today for the first time in history the roll call was called in the street. It was the miners' children.'[2] Like everybody else, I wanted to do something. I did not have the courage to go and dig, so I started to raise money. The funds I raised went with thousands of others to the Disaster Fund announced by the Mayor of Merthyr on the evening of the disaster. As related below, some of that money ended up by paying for the removal of the National Coal Board's dangerous tips from above Aberfan.

The thirtieth anniversary of the disaster not only brought renewed media attention; it also meant the opening of governmental papers under the UK's 30-year rule. These papers revealed new information, especially about the behaviour of the National Coal Board, the Ministry of Power, the Welsh Office and ministers in the Wilson government, in the aftermath of the disaster. Some of the injustices of the handling of Aberfan were widely known, or at least suspected, at the time. The new evidence confirmed and elaborated this knowledge.

This evidence led to an academic paper and a number of newspaper articles by IM.[3] In August 1997, when Ron Davies, then Secretary of State for Wales, repaid the £150,000 taken from the Disaster Fund

---

2. A clip replayed by several radio and TV stations on 21 October 2016.
3. 'Heartless bully who added to agony of Aberfan', *Observer*, 5 January 1997. 'It's not too late to say sorry', *Times Higher Education Supplement*,

to help pay for the removal of the tips at Aberfan, he cited IM as one of the people who had influenced his decision. From this research sprang a grant from the British Academy (APN 6714) to preserve and catalogue the archives held by Merthyr Central Library. The results of that work can be found online at www.nuffield.ox.ac.uk/politics/aberfan/home.htm. This book builds on the foundations of that earlier work. Funded by a grant from the Economic and Social Research Council (ESRC: grant no. R00022677), it revises some of the earlier conclusions, widens the scope of the study of the disaster and places it in the fuller and comparative context of developments since 1966.

The book begins with an account of the Aberfan disaster and its aftermath. This is based entirely on first-hand accounts with no editorial intervention. Chapter 2 is a revised version of the original academic article. It explains how and why the disaster happened. It documents the National Coal Board's (NCB) evasion of responsibility for the disaster in the face of the condemnation of it and its senior management in the Tribunal Report. It explains how nobody was sacked, demoted, sued, or prosecuted; and the roles of the Welsh Office, George Thomas, Harold Wilson and Lord Robens in the political aftermath.

Chapter 3 explores the relationship between the NCB and Merthyr Tydfil County Borough Council. A small local authority whose citizens depended on the coal industry was unable to challenge a large corporation. In the aftermath of the disaster, this unequal relationship continued to cause problems for the council, whose resources were almost overwhelmed by the tasks that it had to confront. While other parts of south Wales were witnessing a rise in support for Plaid Cymru, in Merthyr, and particularly in Aberfan and Merthyr Vale, anti-government feeling was channelled into independent resident groups and the local MP, S.O. Davies, who had been expelled by the Labour Party.

Nothing like Aberfan had happened since the Second World War, and nobody realised quite how large a task counselling the survivors would be. Chapter 4 documents what services were made available to

---

17 January 1997. 'On moles and the habits of birds: the unpolitics of Aberfan', *Twentieth Century British History*, 8 (1997), 285-309.

help Aberfan in its recovery. It locates this within the contemporary understanding of traumatic stress and shows how there was some misunderstanding of the needs of the bereaved, survivors and community. Our understanding of the traumatic impact of disasters has increased significantly. Yet the kind of long-term problems suffered in Aberfan have continued to be witnessed after other disasters. Despite the advances in knowledge, there remains no clear consensus on how to help disaster victims while the misguided actions (and inaction) of different authorities continue to deepen the trauma that disaster creates.

The press labelled the Aberfan Disaster Fund 'the second Aberfan disaster'. The question of how to spend the huge sum of money donated caused arguments and further distress in the village. Chapter 5 investigates how the Charity Commission, which felt itself duty-bound to uphold an outdated and inflexible law, intervened and obstructed payments by the charitable Disaster Fund to individual victims and for the cemetery memorial. It did not intervene to protect the Fund from a government raid on its money to pay for the removal of dangerous coal tips above Aberfan – a raid that seems dubiously justifiable in charity law. The failures of regulation relating to the Fund are discussed; some of them have since been remedied, some not. The chapter reviews why people donate to disaster funds and how their administration has changed since Aberfan.

The three final chapters of the original edition have been replaced by a completely new chapter 6, which explores what has changed and what has not since 1966. We discuss legal, institutional, and social change all under the shadow of the question 'Could it ever happen again?'

Academic rigour and ethical concerns demand that this book be as dispassionate and as objective as possible. Nonetheless, the history of disasters in Britain is littered with emotion, anger and injustice. It is unavoidable that we comment on such matters. Some believe that it is best to put the past behind us and 'leave the dead to rest in peace'.[4] However, for many survivors and bereaved families it is impossible to

---

4. See, for example, letter from Geoffrey Morgan, formerly secretary of the Aberfan Disaster Fund, discussing Aberfan and Hillsborough in *The Times*, 19 April 1999.

achieve this until they have seen justice for their losses. The failures of the legal system have meant that closure is impossible for many. Even when justice is done, the painful memories of disasters remain for the bereaved and survivors. After 50 years, Aberfan is still sometimes a place of tears. The cardinal principle of our research has been not to intrude where we were not wanted nor where we could cause harm. We do not name individual victims of any disaster, even where such information is now in the public domain. It is hoped that this work will help highlight injustice rather than perpetuate grief.

Acknowledgements

This book was written with the help of a great many people. The Economic and Social Research Council funded the bulk of the research through a generous grant while the British Academy and the Glamorgan County History Society financed earlier stages of the work. Without these grants none of what follows would have been possible.

Carolyn Jacob, Geraint James and the staff of Merthyr Central and Dowlais Libraries kindly provided research facilities in the early stages of the work and continuing help throughout. Malcolm Todd assisted with access to the Charity Commission's records. The staff at Cardiff University libraries, Nuffield College library, the Bodleian Library, the National Library of Wales, the Glamorgan Record Office, the South Wales Coalfield Collection (University of Wales, Swansea), and the Public Record Office (now the National Archives) all provided valuable research assistance, as did Alistair McMillan at the outset of the work. Friends and family in London and Aberystwyth provided hospitality on what otherwise would have been lonely research trips.

For the first edition, Desmond Ackner, Kenneth Barnes, Alan Blackshaw, Bryn Carpenter, Barbara Castle, J.M. Cuthill, Alun Talfan Davies, Ron Dearing, Geoffrey Holland, Geoffrey Howe, Cledwyn Hughes, Gaynor Madgwick, Richard Marsh, Cliff Minett, Geoffrey Morgan, Cyril Moseley, Colin Murray Parkes, C.H. Sisson, John Taylor, Margaret Thatcher, Harold Walker, Hugh Watkins and Tasker Watkins all kindly took time, in letters or discussions, or both, to share their memories of the disaster and its aftermath with us. Less formally, a host of people from across the world have kindly shared with us their memories of Aberfan and other disasters, both before and since the first edition of this book.

The following kindly provided details on the work of their respective organisations or other information: Air Accident Investigation Branch, Catherine Alderson, Jenny Bacon (Director

General, HSE), Barrie Berkley (Disaster Action), A. Cooksey (HM Railway Inspectorate), Emergency Planning Division (Home Office), Hillsborough Families Support Group, Peter Hodgkinson (Centre for Crisis Psychology), Maureen Hughes (*Headway*), Peter Jones, John Lang (Chief Inspector of Marine Accidents), B. Langdon (HM Chief Inspector of Mines), Lynton Tourist Information Centre, National Mine Health and Safety Academy (US Department of Labor), David Pendleton, Deborah Perkin, Owen H. Prosser, Peter Spooner (Herald Charitable Trust) and Philip Stephens.

The following all kindly shared the benefit of their expertise in their respective fields; without such assistance the inter-disciplinary approach of this book would have been impossible: David Baldwin, Peter Bartrip, David Bergman, Fiona Bickley, Dave Billnitzer, Camilla Bustani, Richard Colbey, Alan Dalton, Simon Deakin, Dominic Ellis, Andrew Evans, Anne Eyre, Frances Gardner, John and Rhiannon Goldthorpe, Paul Johnson, Nicola Lacey, Stephen Lloyd, Laurence Lustgarten, Andrew McDonald, James Mallinson, Ross Manning, Richard Mayou, Derek Morgan, Ken Morgan, Michael Moss, Michael Napier, Morgan R. O'Connell, Clive Payne, Nick Roberts, Ted Rowlands MP, Patrick Schmidt, Phil Scraton, Celia Wells, Chris Williams, Stewart Wood, Charles Woolfson, William Yule, and a safety officer of a railway company. Those present at various papers given by us at Cardiff, Oxford and Southampton Universities also provided useful comments and observations.

For the new edition we wish to record our thanks to Celia Wells (again!), Scot Peterson, Elaine Carter, and Rob Jago for legal updating. Following a lead from Keith Sanders (whose father-in-law remembered RAF reconnaissance photographs of the dangerous Aberfan tips being tossed aside contemptuously by an NCB area manager), we located some, with assistance from Martin Evans, Emmett Sullivan, and the Royal Commission on the Ancient and Historic Monuments of Wales (RCAHMW).

We had many discussions with programme makers leading up to both the fortieth (2006) and fiftieth (2016) anniversaries, and wish to thank especially Max Boyce, Iwan England and Huw Edwards for their superb work in 2016. We renewed acquaintance with many friends in Aberfan during the preparation of this edition, and feel honoured at our mention in Gaynor Madgwick's recent book

Aberfan: a Story of Survival, Love, and Community in one of Britain's Worst Disasters.[1] We are sorry that her father, Cliff Minett, did not live to see the minute's silence throughout Wales on 21 October 2016, but we recall his generous support as we reprint his Foreword to the first edition. Another important book published for the 50th anniversary, *Surviving Aberfan*[2], presents 27 moving interviews with survivors, bereaved parents, and rescuers. It draws on our work for background, but, like Gaynor's book, brings the disaster home with an immediacy that our trawling through the archives cannot.

We helped the *Life* photographer I.C. Rapoport with the deposit of his Aberfan pictures in the National Library of Wales,[3] and acknowledge his generosity in ensuring that they will be kept in perpetuity as another memorial.

Extracts from *I Can't Stay Long* by Laurie Lee (Penguin Books, 1977, copyright © Laurie Lee, 1975), pp. 90, 94, and 96, are reproduced by permission of Penguin Books Ltd. Interviews first published in the *Daily Mail*, 5 October 1996 are reproduced by kind permission of the *Daily Mail* and Solo Syndication. Extracts from Gaynor Madgwick's *Aberfan: Struggling Out of Darkness, A Survivor's Story* (Valley and Vale, 1996) are reproduced by kind permission of the author. Extracts from interviews first published in Melanie Doel and Martin Dunkerton's *Is it Still Raining in Aberfan? A Pit and its People* (Logaston Press, 1991) are reproduced by kind permission of the authors. Grateful acknowledgement is made to Philip Stephens (producer) and to Swansea Sound (part of the Wireless group) for kind permission to quote interviews recorded for the radio programme *Aberfan: an Unknown Spring*.

Earlier versions of some of the chapters in this book appeared in *Twentieth Century British History, Legal Studies, Disasters* and *Welsh History Review*. We thank the editors and publishers of these journals for permission to reuse this material. Our publishers have

1. Talybont: Y Lolfa, 2016.
2. Sue Elliott, Steve Humphries, and Bevan Jones ed., *Surviving Aberfan: the people's story* (Guildford: Grosvenor House Publishing Ltd in association with the BBC), 2016. A documentary of the same title based on the testimonies was broadcast by the BBC in October 2016.
3. See https://www.llgc.org.uk/blog/?p=12739, accessed 28.11.2016.

shown great personal commitment and enthusiasm for this project. We are delighted to have such enthusiastic colleagues. On a more personal note – our families have been a source of love and support throughout.

For the second time, the people of Aberfan, past and present, have shown us incredible forbearance in the course of this research. They have welcomed us into their homes, and taken the time and pain to share with us their memories and thoughts. Only those who have personally experienced a disaster can possibly hope to understand fully what they have been through. This book is dedicated to Aberfan and the memory of those it lost on the morning of 21 October 1966. The authors and publisher are giving a proportion of the royalties from this book to the Aberfan Memorial Charity, which exists for the maintenance and repair of the memorial garden and cemetery memorial at Aberfan, and for the relief of all those in need who have suffered as a result of the Aberfan disaster.

Iain McLean, Oxford
Martin Johnes, Swansea
May 2019

Abbreviations used in the text and footnotes

AAIB	Air Accident Inquiry Branch
ADA	Aberfan Disaster Archive, Merthyr Tydfil public libraries
ADF	Aberfan Disaster Fund
APRA	Aberfan Parents' and Residents' Association
CMCH Act	Corporate Manslaughter and Homicide Act 2007
CPS	Crown Prosecution Service
DPP	Director of Public Prosecutions
EPD	Emergency Planning Department, Home Office
FWA	Free Wales Army
GA	Glamorgan Archives
HM	Her/His Majesty's
HMI	Her/His Majesty's Inspector(ate)
HMRI	Her Majesty's Railway Inspectorate
H&S	Health and safety
HSC	Health and Safety Commission
HSE	Health and Safety Executive
HSWA	Health & Safety at Work (etc.) Act 1974
MEP	Member of the European Parliament
MP	Member of Parliament
MTCBC	Merthyr Tydfil County Borough Council
nd	No date
NCB	National Coal Board
ORR	Office of Rail and Road
PTSD	Post-Traumatic Stress Disorder
RAIB	Rail Accident Inquiry Branch
RPI	Retail Price Index
TNA	The National Archives
SWCC	South Wales Coalfield Collection, Swansea University
WRVS	Women's Royal Voluntary Service

1

The Last Day Before Half-term

On the mountain

I told him [Vivian Thomas] what I told him before, that the tip was sinking pretty bad and what were they going to do about it. ... He told me to go up to the tip, take a burner with me, and get the crane back as far as I could for we were to start another tipping site later on in the week. ...

[Q. When you got to the front of the tip, did you see how far it had sunk?] I should say about 18 to 20 feet. ... [The crane rails] had broken off and fell down into the hole. ... I told the boys that we would get the rails up from there and start and put the crane back. I said before we start we have a cup of tea, and we went back into the shack. We were not there five minutes ...

Tip gang chargehand[1]

I was standing on the edge of the depression, sir, I was looking down into it, and what I saw I couldn't believe my eyes. It was starting to come back up. It started to rise slowly at first, sir. I still did not believe it, I thought I was seeing things. Then it rose up after pretty fast, sir, at a tremendous speed. Then it sort of came up out of the depression and turned itself into a wave, that is the only way I can describe it, down towards the mountain ... towards Aberfan village, sir. ... And

---

1. Leslie Davies, *Transcript of Tribunal of Inquiry into the Aberfan Disaster Proceedings*, Day 5, pp. 265-68.

I

as it turned over, I shouted: 'Good God, boys, come and look at this lot'. ... I was looking down in the crevice, sir, down at the drop, and it seemed to me like as if the bottom shot out.

Tip worker[2]

We were not in there more than five minutes when I heard a shout. ... We all got out in a matter of seconds. ... We all stood there, sir, on the front of the tip. ... I saw the tip going in ... all I can tell you is it was going down at a hell of a speed in waves. I myself ran down the side of Number 3 tip, all the way down towards Number 2 and Number 1 tip on the side. As I was running down I heard another roar behind me and trees cracking and a tram passing me. I stopped – I fell down in fact. All I could see was waves of muck, slush and water. I still kept running. ... I kept going down shouting. I could not see, nobody could. ... I was stumbling and I got stuck in a bit of the slurry. I could hear a rush behind me and all I could see was soaking wet slurry like waves coming down, more water than muck itself coming down.

Tip gang chargehand[3]

I never expected it would cross the embankment behind the village which I could not see because of the mist which covered the whole of the village. There was nothing I could do. We had no telephone to give an alarm or any warning device. I shouted, but it was no good.

Tip gang chargehand[4]

It never dawned on me or came to my thoughts, sir, that it had gone as far as the village.

Tip worker[5]

---

2. Gwynfor Elgar Brown, *Tribunal Transcript*, Day 7, p. 364.
3. Leslie Davies, *Tribunal Transcript*, Day 5, pp. 268-70.
4. Leslie Davies' statement to Treasury Solicitor. Quoted in *Tribunal Transcript*, Day 6, p. 316.
5. David John Evans, *Tribunal Transcript*, Day 8, p. 413.

In Aberfan

I heard a noise, a big rumbling noise. ... I saw a tree and a telegraph pole coming towards me first, then I saw a big black mass of stuff. ... A black wave of muck.

Schoolboy, age 13[6]

As I was walking up the hill where it turns left, I saw a big wave of muck coming over the railway embankment. It was coming straight towards me and I ran. ... I saw trams, trees, trucks, bricks and boulders in it.

Schoolboy, age 14[7]

[It sounded] Like a jet plane. ... and two or three seconds later I could hear stones and rubble, so I ran back down the hill. I thought it was the tip. ... I said 'I don't think it is a jet, it is the tip,' and I shouted at them [two boys] to run, and they ran down behind me. ... I remember in Moy Road I could see the front windows crashing in, and the front doors; it was like a pile of dominoes coming down. ... I went into that lane for shelter; I didn't know what to do. ... I had only got in about a yard and this top of the garage was down and a sheet of zinc came down and hit me on the head, hit me down. ... I could not force it off me. There was a lot of bricks on it; it protected me. ... [The noise] was suddenly cut off, just like the wireless being turned off. ... It stopped as it hit the last house down, Number 1 Moy Road, and there was a terrible silence.

Aberfan resident[8]

In that silence you couldn't hear a bird or a child.

Aberfan resident[9]

---

6. Gareth Groves, *Tribunal Transcript*, Day 3, pp. 110-11.
7. Howard Rees, *Tribunal Transcript*, Day 3, p. 107.
8. George Henry Williams, *Tribunal Transcript*, Day 4, pp. 190-2.
9. George Henry Williams quoted in *Tribunal Transcript*, Day 4, p. 192.

Pantglas Junior School

Mr Davis, our teacher, got the board out and wrote our maths class work and we were all working, and then it began. It was a tremendous rumbling sound and all the school went dead. You could hear a pin drop. Everyone was petrified, afraid to move. Everyone just froze in their seats. I just managed to get up and I reached the end of my desk when the sound got louder and nearer, 'til I could see the black out of the window. I can't remember any more but I woke up to find that a horrible nightmare had just begun in front of my eyes.

Pupil, Pantglas Junior School[10]

I was standing in front of the class and the thing I remember the most was what I thought was a couple of slates dropping off the roof; because they had been repairing the roof. And with that I looked up through the fog and I could see this enormous spinning boulder and there was a black line alongside it. And I had time to realise that that spinning boulder wasn't heading for me. I immediately looked at the class and with that it crashed into the room at the speed of a jet aeroplane and I was hurled from the centre of the room to the corner by the door. ... I could feel the room shaking and I could see the room filling up. I'm afraid my life didn't flash in front of me. What was happening I just didn't know. And then it stopped. And there was such an eerie silence I remember. From ... a tall old classroom ... with echoes and sounds, there was nothing, there was just this deadness. And I had a chance to reassess the situation. I was trapped up to my waist in desks and rubble and goodness knows what else. And I looked up to the roof and I could see a young lad in my class right up at the roof and climbing down what was then a tip inside my classroom. And I could hear all the children, they weren't screaming, they were trapped amongst their desks. And mercifully in my classroom no one was injured badly as far as I can remember, they were trapped but no one was injured badly. And I remember this boy climbing down and he climbed to the door, and I was trapped near the door, and he started kicking the top half of the door in. So I said to him 'What are

---

10. Gaynor Madgwick, *Aberfan: Struggling out of Darkness, A Survivor's Story* (Blaengarw: Valley & the Vale, 1996), p. 23.

4

you doing?' And he said 'I'm going home.' And the reality still hadn't come home to me I don't think because I felt like giving him a row for breaking the glass. So he kicked the top half of the door and then he went out. And I thought well I better try and get out of here.

Teacher, Pantglas Junior School[11]

I was about to start marking the register when there was a terrible noise like a jet plane and I was afraid it was going to fall on the school. So I said to my children 'Get under your desks quickly and stay there.' And there was one little boy in front of me ... and he kept poking his head out, 'Why Miss? Why have I got to do that?' And I said, 'Because I'm telling you to, get under your desk,' and I had to go and put his head under and stand by him. As it happened nothing happened in our classroom, just this dreadful noise. It seemed like ages but it must have been only a few minutes and there was silence.

Teacher, Pantglas Junior School[12]

Pandemonium then, children rushing around and screaming. When it hit the school there was a tremendous crashing and next I felt being lifted up, desk, everything, pushed on top of the tidal wave. I didn't realise what was happening, it was all black. I thought it was the end, basically. I was knocked unconscious for maybe seven minutes. There were rocks and stone and plants and trees and everything coming in.

Pupil, Pantglas Junior School[13]

My abiding memory of that day is blackness and dark. I was buried by this horrible slurry and I am afraid of the dark to this day.

Pupil, Pantglas Junior School[14]

I went to the door of the classroom and tried the door of the classroom, the children were still under their desks, the door opened, some

11. SWCC Interview with Howell Williams, 1986, AUD/522.
12. SWCC Interview with Hetty Williams, 1986, AUD/523.
13. Sue Elliott, Steve Humphries and Bevan Jones, *Surviving Aberfan: The People's Story* (Guildford: Grosvenor House, 2016), p. 26.
14. Susan Robertson quoted in *Daily Mail Weekend*, 5 October 1996, p. 13.

rubble fell but when I looked out all I could see was black and large lumps of concrete which were parts of the cloakroom. But when I looked I could see there was enough room for us to crawl through sort of a tunnel. So I went back to the children and I said we had a fire drill and I wanted them to walk out of class quietly. That I'd go to the school door and open it and then I'd come back and they were to go out one at a time. They weren't to talk, they were to go out and stand in the yard and wait for fire drill. And every one of the children did as I asked them. They went out quietly and stood in the yard. I came out then at the end and Mair had come down from the room and we didn't know what had happened. We went round the corner and when we looked around the corner well it just looked as if the end of the school had just vanished, there was just a black tip.

Teacher, Pantglas Junior School[15]

... when I got outside I looked at what was to become a famous picture of where the school, where three classrooms had been ... the school was smashed over with this rubble. And I remember standing looking at that and thinking, well, the reality of it, I just couldn't believe it. And from where there were, at least to my calculations, a hundred children, there wasn't a sound.

Teacher, Pantglas Junior School[16]

I remember being thrown across the classroom when the stuff hit us, then I must have blacked out. I woke to the sound of rescuers breaking a window, then I saw [my friend]. I will never forget the sight. There was blood coming out of his nose and I knew he was dead. If I close my eyes I can still see his face as plain as that moment.

Pupil, Pantglas Junior School[17]

I was there for about an hour and a half until the fire brigade found me. I heard cries and screams, but I couldn't move. The desk was

---

15. SWCC Interview with Hetty Williams, 1986, AUD/523.
16. SWCC Interview with Howell Williams, 1986, AUD/522.
17. Gerald Kirwan quoted in *Daily Mail Weekend*, 5 October 1996, p. 12. Name of deceased friend withheld.

jammed into my stomach and my leg was under the radiator. The little girl next to me was dead and her head was on my shoulder.

Pupil, Pantglas Junior School[18]

The rescue

We are so used to having coal tipped near the school and this noise sounded just like coal being tipped only much more noisy than usual; it was a heavy sound. ... I was going towards the school, and I suddenly realised the sound was coming nearer all the time, and the feeling it was the tip came to my mind straight away; so I ran back to the house; my little girl was in bed, so I got her and the wife outside and I went back to the school.

... The north side of the school was completely down, and the tip had come right down the road, Moy Road. I went straight into the boiler house of the junior school and raked out the fire. ... I came out of the boiler house and saw in the classroom next to the boiler house some children there and they were unable to get out, so I tried to smash the window to get the children out, but there was not enough space to get them out that way. The teacher managed to open the door somehow. ... I went in through the door and the children came out past me, out to the yard. Then I went round to the front of the school where Mrs Williams' class was. I saw she was in there and she could not breathe – she shouted she could not breathe. So I went in through the window, the window was that height from the yard, you know. I climbed in through the window. There was some children trapped in the masonry; I got those children out, passed them out through the window. After that I went outside again and saw a little girl on top of the tank above Miss Jennings' classroom. She was right up and wanted to come down. How she got there I do not know. But I got up on the tank and got her down. Then I saw Mrs Williams, a teacher, and went to the assembly hall and started digging them out.

---

18. Jeff Edwards quoted in *Daily Telegraph*, 18 October 1996.

After that I do not know, I cannot remember anything; all I know is
my two boys were buried in the rubble.

School caretaker[19]

Then the next thing I remember was seeing a mass of men coming
up from the colliery still with their lamp lights on. That was really
moving because they were black, they'd just come off the shift and
they'd been sent straight up. And they had their lights on. And after
that they just took over from us.

Teacher, Pantglas Junior School[20]

I went down to work, changed, went down the pit and I hadn't been
down the pit ten minutes when they sent for everybody to come up,
that the tip had slid. Well we came up, I couldn't fathom it out; I'd
never seen anything like it. The front of the school was there but
there was no back. We went there and we dug and dug all day.

Miner and bereaved parent[21]

We had to break the front windows and then climb in. ... We had no
tools – we used our bare hands and anything we could find. But there
was nothing anyone could do, between the slurry and the water
coming down. That was the worst, not being able to do anything.
There's nothing as bad as that.

Bereaved parent[22]

The women were already there, like stone they were, clawing at the
filth – it was like a black river – some had no skin left on their hands.
Miners are a tough breed, we don't show our feelings, but some of
the lads broke down.

Miner[23]

---

19. Stephen David Andrew, *Tribunal Transcript*, Day 4, pp. 193-194.
20. SWCC, Interview with Hetty Williams, 1986, AUD/523.
21. SWCC, Interview with Emlyn Richards, 1986, AUD/519.
22. Cliff Minett quoted in *Daily Mail Weekend*, 5 October 1996, p. 10.
23. Gwyn Davies quoted in *The Times*, 17 October 1986, p. 14.

I have been asked to inform you that there has been a landslide at Pantglas. The tip has come down on the school.

Emergency call received by Merthyr Tydfil police,
9.25 a.m., 21 October 1966[24]

We didn't know what to expect. I had no idea of the scale of the thing. It was a great shock. There was absolute chaos and somehow I had to organise that chaos.

Assistant Chief Constable[25]

I left by car for the scene of the incident. ... and I arrived at Moy Road ... at about 10 o'clock. That was near the infants' school. With the co-operation of the chief inspector I set up an incident post at a police car on the colliery side of the incident to maintain communications with police headquarters by radio telephone. ... I then made a reconnaissance of the whole area above the school, and I managed to get round to the streets to the other side, the north side of the incident at the Mackintosh hotel. This reconnaissance revealed that not only was the Pantglas junior school buried under approximately 20 to 30 feet of debris, but a large number of houses in Moy Road and Pantglas had been demolished and submerged under a pile of debris and liquid mud.

... at 10.30 a large quantity of water was still pouring into the disaster area, and I was informed that it was coming from the mountain springs and two large water mains which had been fractured when the disused canal and disused railway embankment had broken.

Chief Constable of the County Borough of Merthyr Tydfil[26]

They [the vehicle and rescue workers] had to retire a little to avoid being swamped by the new rush of water and slurry. ... It certainly hindered the rescuers from the end that I was working and had

---

24. Quoted in *Tribunal Transcript*, Day 3, p. 100.
25. John Parkman, quoted in *Wales on Sunday*, 16 June 1991, p. 25.
26. T.K. Griffiths, Chief Constable of the County Borough of Merthyr Tydfil, *Tribunal Transcript*, Day 3, pp. 101-103.

that water not come quite a number of properties would have been saved.

Chief Inspector in Merthyr Tydfil County Borough Police[27]

As I was in the shop there was dirty black water coming down the hill, and as I was waiting my turn to be served I shouted out that we were going to be flooded. As I dashed back to the house with my little baby Alan, who was just one, in my arms, I fell over the milk bottles.

With that my friend Glenys from a few doors away arrived with her daughter Sian who was dirty. She said Sian had come home from class all covered in dirt, and she had thrust her into my arms before running back up to the school. I asked Sian what had happened and she said that the school had fallen down.

I didn't know what to do, so I went round to Glenys' house where the door was wide open and a stream of dirty water was just rushing through.

I ran up to the top then and when I saw the school had fallen down, my legs just turned to jelly. I couldn't walk. I just stood there dazed as all the time water flooded my home. Glenys came past and said she hadn't seen [my daughter].

Aberfan resident[28]

As I was being carried out I realised I had lost my jumper. It was a mustard-coloured one that my mother had knitted. There were five children in our family and you couldn't afford to lose a jumper, so I tried to go back and look for it because I thought I would get into trouble. I was taken straight to hospital and my parents did not come to see me until evening. They must have spent the whole day not knowing where I was, not knowing if I was alive or dead. But we never talked about it.

Pupil, Pantglas Junior School[29]

---

27. Chief Inspector R. Wilson, Chief Inspector in Merthyr Tydfil County Borough Police, *Tribunal Transcript*, Day 3, pp.113-114.

28. Jessie Meredith quoted in Melanie Doel & Martin Dunkerton, *Is it Still Raining in Aberfan? A Pit and its People* (Little Logaston: Logaston Press, 1991) p. 47. Name of daughter withheld.

29. Gerald Kirwan quoted in *Daily Mail Weekend*, 5 October 1996, p. 12.

I could hear men's voices but I didn't know what they were doing or where they were. I heard someone crying and then this voice was asking me if I could see daylight and I could put my finger through it and then I was dug out.

I was passed through a chain of men, out through a window and into the yard and handed to the policeman, who carried me to the side of a wall where he placed me on the ground. ... I looked back at the school and I just couldn't believe what had happened. It was completely flat.

Pupil, Pantglas Junior School[30]

At that time I'd bought felt pens and they were rather a new thing. They cost 2/6 at the time. And I had these three felt pens, a red one, a blue one and a mauve one. And I was more interested in getting these felt pens out. And the fire officer said to me, 'Forget those bloody felt pens and let's get you out.'

Pupil, Pantglas Junior School[31]

Men, women and children were tearing away the debris in an effort to reach the trapped children. As the men shovelled debris from spade to spade, children's books appeared. An odd cap was seen. A broken doll.

Mothers gathered around the school steps, some weeping, some silent, some shaking their heads in disbelief. ...

The slurry had piled up 25 feet against the school, smashing its way through the building, filling the classrooms.

Teams of 50 men and boys worked in long rows from the school building, handing buckets of slurry up the mountainside from the classrooms.

On each side of the school mechanical shovels and bulldozers gouged the debris out. An endless line of lorries carried it away. ... At regular intervals everything would come to a halt – the roar of heavy machinery, the shouts, the scraping of shovels. Not a murmur would be heard among the thousand workers. Time stood still. And rescuers listened tensely for the slightest sound from the wreckage – for a

---

30. Susan Robertson quoted in *South Wales Echo*, 21 October 1996, p. 2.
31. Jeff Edwards, *Timewatch: Remember Aberfan*, BBC2, broadcast on 15 October 1996.

cry, a moan, a movement – anything which would give hope to the mothers and fathers.

First journalist on the scene[32]

Nobody told me what had happened at the time. I asked somebody next to me, it must have been a couple of hours later, he said "What is this stuff?"; I did not know myself what it was, and I was under the impression it was an explosion of gas. I did not think the tip had slipped; I did not realise anything about the tip. It must have been a good two hours when somebody said 'it's the tip that has slipped.' I did not know; I was just knocked for six; I did not realise that it was that.

Bereaved parent[33]

It's like a blitz – as though a bomb had been dropped on the whole school.

We can only work in small groups, and gas is leaking. Progress is slow, as we have to prop up the beams and wall as we go in.

The chances of survival are negligible, but I hope I'm wrong.

Rescue worker[34]

You only have to mention what you want and it comes. We've had no trouble at all to get anything.

Civil Defence worker[35]

The really incredible thing was that you couldn't walk five yards without a member of the WVRS or the Salvation Army or the Red Cross putting a cup of soup, a cup of coffee or a cup of chocolate into your hand.

Detective constable[36]

---

32. Sam Knight, *Merthyr Express*, 28 October 1966, p. 6.

33. Robert Michael Minney, *Tribunal Transcript*, Day 5, pp. 247-8.

34. Eric Hughes, quoted in *Merthyr Express*, 28 October 1966, p. 6.

35. Mrs Elizabeth Ingram quoted in *Merthyr Express*, 28 October 1966, p. 10.

36. Bob Evans quoted in *Western Mail*, 12 October 1996, Arena supplement, p. 3.

We cut up cotton sheets for bandages, and gave blankets and pillows for the children as they were brought out on stretchers. Rescuers came in for everything, and we gave all we could. All we thought of was that children's lives were at stake. Everything lost its value in comparison with those children.

Aberfan resident[37]

No one was brought out alive after 11 o'clock.

Chief Constable of the County Borough of Merthyr Tydfil[38]

... the roads leading to the incident both from Merthyr Vale and from Troedyrhiw were blocked with vehicles with rescue workers and helpers, both official and voluntary, and similarly the A470 road between Pentrebach and the Travellers Rest was becoming congested, and in a number of places it had become completely blocked. ... The mortuary was set up in the early stages at Bethania Chapel, and I appointed an officer of the regional crime squad to take over the identification and handling of the bodies, and by 11.30 at night on the first day 67 bodies had been brought in and identification was then in progress.

Chief Constable of the County Borough of Merthyr Tydfil[39]

I reached the tragic village of Aberfan on Saturday morning. The initial panic and hysteria had died and now there was a well-ordered rescue operation underway. But it was still a grim sight. There was a greyness everywhere. Faces from the tiredness and anguish, houses and roads from the oozing slurry of the tips. The grey-black mass seemed to have penetrated everywhere and all around were evacuated houses.

Merthyr Express[40]

Heavy rain started at 2.30 p.m. Saturday, causing immense anxiety and fear that the huge tip would slide again and engulf the rescuers. ...

37. Mrs Francis Smith quoted in *Merthyr Express*, 4 November 1966, p. 3.
38. T.K. Griffiths, quoted in *Merthyr Express*, 28 October 1966, p. 6.
39. T.K. Griffiths, *Tribunal Transcript*, Day 3, pp. 101-3.
40. *Merthyr Express*, 28 October 1966, p. 10.

By this time about 2,500 workers were on the scene. Extra police were called in because inexperienced rescuers would not leave the scene.

Merthyr Express[41]

... no less than 144 men, women and children lost their lives. 116 of the victims were children, most of them between the ages of 7 and 10 ...

Report of the Tribunal appointed to inquire into the Disaster at Aberfan[42]

Bereavement

Up until then [Friday, 7 p.m.] I had hoped that the chapel was a hospital, but as I went into Bethania people were coming out who had been told their children had gone. Until I went in I still had hope that they were just lost. When I went all the pews were covered with little blankets and under them lay the little children. They picked up the blankets and showed me every girl until I came to [her] and said she was mine. There wasn't a mark on her except a little scratch over her mouth, even her clothes were clean.

What I missed most was the noise and fun around the house. [My daughter] was boisterous and full of fun. Our house was as quiet as a mouse after she'd gone.

Bereaved mother[43]

As soon as the word swept around Aberfan that the bodies were being taken to Bethania Chapel, parents and relatives arrived at the front door. They waited in a long patient line to be permitted in, to try and

---

41. *Merthyr Express*, 28 October 1966, p. 11.
42. *Report of the Tribunal appointed to inquire into the Disaster at Aberfan on October 21st, 1966*, Chairman Lord Justice Edmund Davies, HMSO 1967, p. 26. (Hereafter *Aberfan Report*).
43. Jessie Meredith quoted in Doel & Dunkerton, *Is it Still Raining in Aberfan?*, p. 48. Name of daughter withheld.

identify the daughter, son, wife, husband, mother or father. Because of the cramped conditions in which we were operating we could only deal with two sets of relatives at a time.

When we established the age and sex of the person they were seeking they were shown all the bodies that matched. The task was not made easier by the fact that most of the boys wore grey short trousers and the girls a standard dress and cardigan.

Policeman working at the mortuary[44]

In the night we had to go to see if we could identify her in this chapel. I've never forgotten that. It comes back to me every day. There's some part of the day that that picture comes back to me and I can never forget that. ... All these little bodies wrapped in blankets.

Bereaved father[45]

So they went back, my daughter Angela, and my husband and her husband as he is now, to look and search for the child. Someone had said that the child was taken down to Church Village. So they went down to the hospitals there but no they couldn't see the child. I knew that when Emlyn came in the early hours of the morning that [she] was not going to be found. His face was grey and Angela was terrible, we knew then that the little one was gone.

Bereaved mother[46]

The streets were silent but for the sound of shuffling feet. Some mourners wept while others pent up their emotions until they reached the cemetery.

As the funeral singing began, hymn singing drifted down to the village below where everyone shared in the sorrow. All shops were closed; the doors of the public houses were bolted and normal life ceased.

---

44. Charles Nunn, 'The Disaster of Aberfan', *Police Review*, 16 October 1987, p. 2069.
45. SWCC, Interview with Emlyn Richards, 1986, AUD/519.
46. SWCC, Interview with Elaine Richards, 1986, AUD/520. Name of daughter withheld.

At the graveside above, three thousand people gathered to pay their last respects.

The burial took place in the shadow of the now depleted tip.

Merthyr Express[47]

... all those little coffins in the grave. It was terrible, terrible. There was hundreds of people up there. Some screaming, some crying ...

Bereaved father[48]

Please use this small amount in any way you wish. I was saving it up for a new coat, O God I wish I had saved more. Yours sincerely, A Mother.

Letter to the Aberfan Disaster Fund[49]

Anger and determination

I was helping to dig the children out when I heard a photographer tell a kiddie to cry for her dead friends, so that he could get a good picture – that taught me silence.

Rescue worker[50]

During that period the only thing I didn't like was the press. If you told them something, when the paper came out your words were all the wrong way round.

Bereaved father[51]

The brave front of the people of Aberfan cracked on Monday at an inquest on 30 of the children.

---

47. *Merthyr Express*, 4 November 1966, p. 5.
48. SWCC, Interview with Emlyn Richards, 1986, AUD/519.
49. Quoted in Benedict Nightingale, *Charities* (London: Allen Lane, 1973), p. 178.
50. Anonymous quote in *The Times*, 17 October 1986, p. 14.
51. SWCC, Interview with Emlyn Richards, 1986, AUD/519.

There were shouts of 'murderers' as the Coroner of Merthyr, Mr Ben Hamilton, began reading out the names of the dead children.

As one name was read out and the cause of death given as asphyxia and multiple injuries, the father of the child said 'No, sir, buried alive by the National Coal Board.'

One of the only two women among the 60 people at the inquest at Sion Primitive English Methodist Chapel at Aberfan, shouted out through her tears, 'They have killed our children.'

Then a number of people called out and got to their feet. The coroner tried to restore order and said: 'I know your grief is such that you may not be realising what you are saying.'

The father repeated: 'I want it recorded – "Buried alive by the National Coal Board." That is what I want to see on the record. That is the feeling of those present. Those are the words we want to go on the certificate.'

Merthyr Express[52]

It was impossible to know that there was a spring in the heart of this tip which was turning the centre of the mountain into sludge.

Rt. Hon. Lord Robens of Woldingham, Chairman of the National Coal Board, to a TV reporter[53]

A man who lost his niece at Aberfan broke through a police cordon to talk to Lord Justice Edmund Davies – the man who is to head the inquiry into the disaster – as he toured the stricken village on Tuesday.

The man, 61-year-old Mr Philip Brown, a disabled miner, told the judge: 'Don't let strangers pull the wool over your eyes.'

The judge spoke to Mr Brown for a couple of minutes and then moved away to continue his tour.

Afterwards Mr Brown said 'I asked him if I could speak to him for five minutes. He told me, "Most certainly." He is a real gentleman.

'I said, "Don't let strangers take you up the mountain and pull the wool over your eyes. If you must go up, go up with a local man who knows the real facts."

---

52. *Merthyr Express*, 28 October 1966, p. 18.
53. Quoted in Lord Robens, *Ten Year Stint* (London: Cassell, 1972), p. 251.

... 'I told him the spring at the head of the mountain had always been there.

'It was not a hidden spring. The National Coal Board must have known about it because everyone in the village did.'

Merthyr Express[54]

I was tormented by the fact that the people I was seeking justice from were my people – a Labour Government, a Labour council, a Labour-nationalised Coal Board.

Bereaved husband and parent[55]

The Aberfan disaster was very much a disaster of the Valleys; it could have happened in any part of them. It was the crowning disaster of a dangerous industry, and its victims were the innocent.

Aberfan community worker[56]

Why there is bitterness

'During my childhood I played on that monstrous mountain of slag, and in my youth I rummaged coal from it. Everyone knew that one day – some day – this hideous scar on the landscape, this indiscriminate dumping of colliery refuse, would bring disaster. But little did we think that when it did happen, it would leave such devastation and heart-breaking sorrow in its wake.'

These words are written by a native of Aberfan, an ex-pupil of Pantglas school. They are contained in a letter to the editor expressing heartfelt sympathy to all those people who are suffering in this hour of indescribable tragedy.

---

54. *Merthyr Express*, 28 October 1966, p. 24.
55. John Collins quoted in unaccredited press clipping in ADA, Merthyr Collection, D/17.
56. Erastus Jones, 'Working in Aberfan and the Valleys', *Social and Economic Administration*, vol. 9, no. 1, Spring 1975.

There is today sadness in the hearts of everyone who lives in a mining valley. But there is bitterness too.

The coal mining communities of south Wales have lived so long with death as a companion that they reconcile themselves to accepting the peril that hangs over them.

Everyone knows that coal tips move. Everyone fears that one day the tip above their village will come rumbling down into the valley, but it is a possibility that they accept.

Without the tip above Aberfan the Merthyr Vale Colliery could have closed down. Without the colliery the village would itself have died.

This is the terrible fear that ate into the minds of the people of Aberfan.

Now the worst has happened. Tragedy of the most devastating kind has struck. A village has lost its children. Is not the bitterness, therefore, understandable?

Merthyr Express editorial[57]

My first impression of Aberfan was terrible. I couldn't imagine, I never imagined that it was like that. The village was dirty, my house was dirty, everything was dirty. The tip had left mud and slurry everywhere. I was fortunate in one way because I had no conception what this tip had done to us at Aberfan. It wasn't until a long time after that I came to terms with this. Then, instead of being a passive person as I was before, I became a fighter for Aberfan. I felt that we had a duty to the children who were left and those who were yet to be born. And it was a duty that we must build a better Aberfan for the children that were coming.

Bereaved parent on returning to Aberfan after the disaster[58]

The villagers had done admirably in rehabilitating themselves with very little help. A Government gesture was needed to restore confidence and only complete removal of the tips would do this. Many people in the village were on sedatives but they did not take

57. *Merthyr Express*, editorial, 28 October 1966.
58. SWCC, Interview with Elaine Richards, 1986, AUD/519.

them when it was raining because they were afraid to go to sleep. Children did not close their bedroom doors in case they should be trapped.

Official note of Aberfan social worker's comments at meeting with Welsh Office[59]

They took the money out of the Disaster Fund to pay for the removal of the tips, which was to me shocking. Absolutely unbelievable. And that's always been in me. I think they [the NCB] owe us. They owe the people of Aberfan a debt. Call it a debt of conscience if you like. I don't think we should beg for this. And we need the money. There's the Memorial Garden to be maintained. And the cemetery. For many, many years to come. Where is it going to come from in later years when we're gone ...?

Bereaved parent, speaking in 1996[60]

Recovery

I tried to rescue people but I realised it could be dangerous just digging, not knowing what you were doing, and I was getting in the way of people so I immediately switched over to pastoral work. ... The end of Chapter 8 of Romans is a great summary of faith – *What can separate us from the love of God?* – It's a passage I always use when there's a personal tragedy or disaster and that's a message we always try to emphasise – I am certain that nothing can separate us from the love of God, neither death nor life, neither angels nor other heavenly rulers or powers, neither the present nor the future.

Bereaved Baptist minister, speaking in 1996[61]

---

59. Meeting with Aberfan Deputation at Welsh Office, London, 12 Noon, Wednesday 7 February 1968. TNA: BD 11/3804.
60. Chris Sullivan, *Timewatch*, 15 October 1996.
61. Rev. Kenneth Hayes, in 1966 Minister, Zion English Baptist Church, Aberfan, *Timewatch*, 15 October 1996.

My work afterwards was more like that of a pastor. People had to face not only grief but bitterness, anger and even guilt. The first real thing that happened were the terrible nightmares people suffered, reliving the event time and time again. That went on for months. There was a terrible worry and pressure on people while the tip was still there, and every time there was a row over what was to be done about the tip my surgery would be full the next day. The stress and anxiety triggered off by what to do would affect people's health.

It was predicted at the time that a lot of people might suffer from heart attacks brought on by the stress and grief, but that didn't happen. Other experts predicted that there would be a number of suicides, but that didn't happen either. These people hadn't allowed for the resilience of the families involved. It was psychological problems that hit worst.

One thing that did happen within a short time afterwards was that the birth rate went up. Also many people were drinking a lot more and for some time after I had to deal with people who had serious drink problems, and for people who already had health problems, those problems increased.

From the time of the disaster for about the following six years I dealt with people who suffered breakdowns. There was no set pattern or any time when it could be expected to happen. It happened at different times for different people.

After the disaster I warned the community would have to come to accept its guilt. This guilt came out in many ways. There were the so-called guilty men who were blamed for what happened; they suffered themselves and were the victims of a hate campaign. But it wasn't only them. Women who had sent their children who hadn't wanted to go to school that day suffered terrible feelings of guilt. ... Grief and guilt came in many different ways. There was a strange bitterness between families who lost children and those who hadn't; people just could not help it.

Aberfan doctor[62]

---

62. Dr Arthur Jones quoted in Doel & Dunkerton, *Is it Still Raining in Aberfan?*, pp. 49-50.

I kept asking myself why I hadn't died and I blamed myself for allowing my brother and sister to die.

Pupil, Pantglas Junior School[63]

I've got to say this again, if the papers and the press and the television were to leave us alone in the very beginning I think we could have settled down a lot quicker than what we did.

Bereaved father[64]

[W]e were a community that were not used to being exposed on television or in papers. We are a community that wears our hearts on our sleeves. We're quite open and we were only doing in the time after the disaster, as far as I'm concerned, what we've always done for years, thrashing out, and the press exploded it. The other thing I always felt was that many of the facts that they reported were, if they kept to the facts, fairly accurate. But it did remind me of a scientist who has got a theory and then forces the facts to prove it. But what I wanted them to do was to take the facts and then decide what it told them. And the result was that they were coming in, and I remember more than one interviewing me, wanting me to give certain answers.

Bereaved father[65]

We weren't prepared for it. We weren't geared up for what was happening. Like the people from the press. They came in. We hadn't seen any of this, ever, we didn't know, it's a different world to us. And they came from all over the place. ... They were round with their notebooks and their pads and asking all these questions, 'How are you getting over it?' You can't ask me that now, never mind 30 years ago.

Bereaved parent, speaking in 1996.[66]

---

63. Gaynor Madgwick, quoted in Doel & Dunkerton, *Is it Still Raining in Aberfan?*, p. 43.

64. SWCC Bryn Carpenter, Interview with Bryn Carpenter, Rev. Kenneth Hayes & Doug Pearson, 1986, AUD/528.

65. SWCC Kenneth Hayes, Interview with Bryn Carpenter, Rev. Kenneth Hayes & Doug Pearson, 1986, AUD/528.

66. Chris Sullivan, *Timewatch*, 15 October 1996.

Fragments of the school itself still lie embedded in the rubbish – chunks of green-painted classroom wall. ... Even more poignant relics lie in a corner of the buried playground piled haphazardly against a wall – some miniature desks and chairs, evocative as a dead child's clothes, infant-sized, still showing the shape of their bodies. Among the rubble there also lie crumpled song-books, sodden and smeared with slime, the words of some bedtime song still visible on the pages, surrounded by drawings of sleeping elves.

Across the road from the school, and facing up the mountain, stands a row of abandoned houses. This must once have been a trim little working-class terrace, staidly Victorian but specially Welsh, with lace-curtained windows, potted plants in the hall, and a piano in every parlour – until the wave of slag broke against it, smashed the doors and windows, and squeezed through the rooms like toothpaste.

Something has been done to clear them, but not very much. They stand like broken and blackened teeth. Doors sag, windows gape, revealing the devastation within – a crushed piano, some half-smothered furniture. You can step in from the street and walk round the forsaken rooms which still emit an aura of suffocation and panic – floors scattered with letters, coat-hangers on the stairs, a jar of pickles on the kitchen table. The sense of catastrophe and desertion, resembling the choked ruins of Pompeii, hangs in the air like volcanic dust.

... Prettily dressed and beribboned, riding expensive pedal-cars and bicycles, they [surviving children] are an elite, the aristocrats of survival, their lives nervously guarded and also coveted by those who mourn. By luck, chance, and by no choice of their own, they are part of the unhealed scar-tissue of Aberfan.

Laurie Lee, writer, on Aberfan one year on[67]

Of course, we could have lost the boy too. He was on his way up Moy Road when he saw the houses falling towards him. He ran off home; and I couldn't get a word out of him for months. He had to go to the psychiatrist. ... Just wouldn't talk about it, and wouldn't mention his

67. Laurie Lee, 'The village that lost its children' in *I Can't Stay Long* (Harmondsworth: Penguin edn, 1977), pp. 90, 96.

sister either. And the two of 'em worshipped each other. They was always together; slept in the same room, holding hands. ... He used to hide when we went to the grave. ...

Then one night – about four months later it was – we was round at our brother's place. The boy went outside to the lavatory and I heard him call Dad! Ay, what is it, boy? I said. Come out here! he said. Sure, I said, what's the matter? It was a beautiful frosty night. He said, Look at that star up there – that's our Sandie, Dad. Sure, I said, that's our little Sandie.

The boy's all right now, and I'm going to see he's all right. ... And I'll make damn sure he never goes down the pit. He's not going to grow up daft like me.

Bereaved father talking to Laurie Lee in the pub, 1967[68]

We were a generation that lost out. We lost out on our education and on our futures. I can't think of any of us who ever did really well and most of just stayed and grew up in the village. We haven't gone far at all.

Pupil, Pantglas Junior School[69]

In Mount Pleasant school, which was a similar school, I remember vividly the first day going in, I took the remains of the upper part of the school, going into the classroom and sitting down there and outside was a railway line coming from the colliery and a diesel rumbled past, very very slowly, and I can see the looks on the children's faces and mine. But it turned out all right but the actual shock of getting back to school was enormous and eventually everything went off all right and the children returned to normality.

Teacher, Pantglas Junior School[70]

There was none of the discipline we used to have ... We didn't go out to play for a long time because those who'd lost their own children

---

68. Quoted in Lee, 'The village that lost its children', p. 94.
69. Gaynor Madgwick quoted in Doel & Dunkerton, *Is it Still Raining in Aberfan?*, p. 42.
70. SWCC, Howell Williams interview, AUD/522.

couldn't bear to see us. We all knew what they were feeling and we felt guilty about being alive.

Pupil, Pantglas Junior School[71]

As children we never got any sympathy. We were always told we were lucky to be alive. I suppose everybody in the village was so badly affected that nobody had the time to give us any sympathy. At school, though, the teachers treated us differently. It was as if they could not bring themselves to be strict with us. We lost a lot of schooling after the disaster anyway, and most of us never really made it up.

Pupil, Pantglas Junior School[72]

What happened in Aberfan that day was the dark little secret when we were young and it still is. We knew we must not speak out. We have been quiet for the sake of the other people, those who lost children and those who did not want to hear about what happened, especially from the mouths of their own children. ... What's more, the survivors have never spoken to each other about it. Most of us live in the same small village and have grown up together, yet we all kept everything locked away inside ourselves. ... I think that, in some ways, it is harder for a man to deal with, especially around here. Here I am, a grown man, tough ex-miner and all that, yet since that day I don't like the dark. Down the pit was all right as long as I was in company. I made sure I was never alone down there. Even being at home on my own at night makes me uneasy. I don't like being alone anywhere. ... When we were young there was almost nobody left. We wandered streets like lost souls.

Pupil, Pantglas Junior School[73]

In those days talking of your emotions was an embarrassment. As a child you felt ashamed to tell someone what you were feeling, even if you were crying. You didn't want them to know you were crying. I only cried when I'd gone to bed in the evenings. If my mother heard me she would come in to see me. But I couldn't talk to her about how I felt – and in the morning I would feel embarrassed. In my family we never

71. Gaynor Madgwick quoted in *Daily Mail Weekend*, 5 October 1996, p. 11.
72. Janet Smart, quoted in *Daily Mail Weekend*, 5 October 1996, p. 13.
73. Gerald Kirwan quoted in *Daily Mail Weekend*, 5 October 1996, p. 12.

discussed what had happened. Nothing was said. Just tears and very quiet. It's the same round here today – people don't want you to see they're upset. I've never seen my dad cry, never. When I went to bed I would speak to God. He was the only one I could speak to at the time. You don't get an answer back but you could feel there's somebody there. And that's a comfort. ... My dad was very bitter for years. It was his only son, you see. My mother still won't talk about that time. She doesn't want to know. She's blanked it out. It was the only way she could cope. We always went to church and she turned atheist for a while, which was bad because it meant she had no comfort anywhere. But she started to believe again and I think it has given her back her strength.

Pupil, Pantglas Junior School[74]

We couldn't talk about the loss for some time. Our boy was only seven. It threw our family life completely off-balance. [My wife] was breaking down all the time. What can you say? You feel so helpless. You sit there and you can't do a thing.

Bereaved father[75]

It gives you a respect for living. You're thankful just to be here and all my friends seem to be very placid, I never argue with people. We seem to be different, for I never discuss the disaster with friends – I think you do tend to wipe it out.

Pupil, Pantglas Junior School[76]

Today, when a disaster happens, you bring in people who are trained counsellors to help the victims' families cope. But the counselling in Aberfan then was done by the community itself. That true Welshness, the sense of belonging and togetherness, came to the fore then.

Detective Constable[77]

---

74. Gaynor Madgwick quoted in *Daily Mail Weekend*, 5 October 1996, pp. 11-12.

75. Cliff Minett quoted in *Daily Mail Weekend*, 5 October 1996, p. 12.

76. Gaynor Madgwick quoted in Doel & Dunkerton, *Is it Still Raining in Aberfan?*, p. 42.

77. Bob Evans quoted in *Western Mail*, 12 October 1996, Arena supplement, p. 3.

By every statistic, patients seen, prescriptions written, deaths, I can prove that this is a village of excessive sickness. And the cause is obvious. ... Psychiatrists came and wrote 'Aberfan needs no help.' Now they come to study what grief did to us. Nowhere else has grief been so concentrated. Lockerbie, Zeebrugge, King's Cross – everywhere they used the lessons this place taught them.

Aberfan doctor[78]

For many years after the disaster if I was sitting in an enclosed room and a jet aeroplane would approach I would absolutely quake and shiver until it had gone and actually feel the nerves running through my body. I think it also affected my driving as well. I was very aware of the environment and dangers in the environment. But gradually over the years it sort of disappeared and now I'm all right, I can rationalise a jet aeroplane.

Teacher, Pantglas Junior School[79]

As far as we're concerned now, we've still got two boys. We're only separated for a time. One day we're going to meet. The parting and the loneliness and being without him is terrible, but it's not for ever.

Bereaved Baptist minister, speaking in 1996[80]

78. Dr Arthur Jones quoted in *Daily Mail*, 15 October 1991.
79. SWCC, Howell Williams interview, AUD/522.
80. Rev. Kenneth Hayes (1930-97), *Timewatch*, BBC2, 15 October 1996.

2

On Moles and the Habits of Birds: The Unpolitics of Aberfan

'We found that many witnesses, not excluding those who were intelligent and anxious to assist us, had been oblivious of what lay before their eyes. It did not enter their consciousness. They were like moles being asked about the habits of birds.'

Lord Justice Edmund Davies, Chairman,
Tribunal into the Disaster at Aberfan

At 9.15 a.m. on Friday, 21 October 1966, a waste tip from Merthyr Vale Colliery slid down a mountainside onto the mining village of Aberfan, near Merthyr Tydfil in south Wales. It first destroyed a farm cottage in its path, killing all the occupants. At Pantglas Junior School, just below, the children had returned to their classes. It was sunny on the mountain but foggy in the village, with visibility about fifty yards. The tipping gang up the mountain had seen the slide start, but could not raise the alarm because their telephone cable had been repeatedly stolen. (The Tribunal of Inquiry later established that the disaster happened so quickly that a telephone warning would not have saved lives.) The slide engulfed the school and about twenty houses in the village before coming to rest. One hundred and forty-four people died at Aberfan; 116 of them were children.

So horrifying was the disaster that everybody wanted to do something. Hundreds of people stopped what they were doing, threw a shovel into the car, and drove to Aberfan to try to help with the rescue. It was futile; the untrained rescuers merely got in the way of the trained miners. Nobody was rescued alive after 11 a.m. on the day of the disaster, but it was nearly a week before all the bodies were recovered. A disaster appeal quickly raised the unprecedented sum of £1.75 million (worth approximately £29.4 million in 2015).

A Tribunal of Inquiry was immediately set up under Lord Justice Edmund Davies, a native of Mountain Ash, another mining community in south Wales. The Tribunal reported in August 1967, finding that

> Blame for the disaster rests upon the National Coal Board ... The legal liability of the National Coal Board to pay compensation for the personal injuries (fatal or otherwise) and damage to property is incontestable and uncontested.[1]

These dry conclusions belie the passion of the preceding text. The Tribunal was appalled by the behaviour of the National Coal Board (NCB) and some of its employees, both before and after the disaster. One Coal Board engineer's 'unreliability as a witness proved as great as his manifest self-satisfaction'. 'Does it really lie in the mouths of the members of the National Board to say that they ... are ... to be excused for having paid no attention to tip stability? They cannot be so excused.' On the Coal Board's refusal to make concessions: 'this will not do. It will not do at all'.[2] It rejected accusations of 'callous indifference' on the part of the NCB but instead concluded

> there are no villains in this harrowing story. In one way, it might possibly be less alarming if there were, for villains are few and far between. But the Aberfan disaster is a terrifying tale of bungling ineptitude by many men charged with tasks for which they were totally unfitted, or failure to heed clear warnings, and of total lack of direction from above.[3]

Colliery engineers at all levels concentrated only on conditions underground. In one of its most memorable phrases, the Report

---

1. *Aberfan Report*, p. 131.
2. *Aberfan Report*, pp. 68, 84, 88.
3. *Aberfan Report*, p. 25.

described them as 'like moles being asked about the habits of birds'.[4] While the Tribunal was being set up, the Cabinet decided that it was important for the Aberfan parents to be properly represented and thus provision was made for their legal costs to be recouped. They would not otherwise have been eligible for legal aid. Their solicitors looked for a QC not from the south Wales bar, as they felt that every south Walian QC was constantly appearing for or against the Coal Board, and liable to be influenced by it. Their contacts recommended Desmond Ackner QC (later Lord Ackner), who became counsel for the Aberfan Parents' and Residents' Association. In his closing speech, Ackner said that Coal Board witnesses had tried to give the impression that 'the Board had no more blameworthy connection with this disaster than, say, the Gas Board'.[5]

The Tribunal concluded that the Board's defence, until a very late stage in the inquiry, was that 'the disaster was due to a coincidence of a set of geological factors, each of which in itself is not exceptional *but* which collectively created a particularly critical geological environment'. It called aspects of the Board's post-disaster behaviour 'nothing short of audacious'.[6] Lord Robens, the Board's chairman, had said soon after the disaster that 'it was impossible to know that there was a spring in the heart of this tip'. The Tribunal had ignored this on the grounds that it was based upon hearsay and decided that Robens could not help the Tribunal. However, when Ackner attacked Robens for this comment, the Tribunal offered Robens the opportunity to reply. Under questioning by Ackner, Robens admitted that it was known that the disaster was foreseeable by the time the inquiry began. Yet this was inconsistent with the geological argument put forward by the NCB at the inquiry. The NCB counsel asked the Tribunal to ignore Robens' evidence. The Tribunal chose to do so but maintained that if the Board had known that it was to blame then it should have made this clear at the outset.[7]

---

4. *Aberfan Report*, p. 11.
5. Ackner's appointment: TNA CAB 128/41 CC 52(66). All archival references in this chapter are from The National Archives (TNA) unless otherwise specified. Gas Board: *Aberfan Report*, p. 86.
6. *Aberfan Report*, pp. 85, 87.
7. *Aberfan Report*, pp. 89-92.

Despite the searing findings of the Tribunal, nobody was prosecuted, dismissed, or suffered a pay cut. Initially the Board postponed a decision on the seven Coal Board employees who still worked for it and had been identified as in some degree blameworthy until the Director of Public Prosecutions had announced whether he would be instituting criminal proceedings or not. When it was announced that he was not, the seven were interviewed by Lord Robens and W.V. Sheppard CBE, his Director of Production. Five of the seven were moved to 'jobs of smaller compass' without reduction of pay. The other two were left in comparable or more senior posts, despite the statements to the contrary in Robens' memoirs and in Parliament.[8] The NCB's internal memorandum on the Tribunal Report noted that, in dealing with the individuals criticised, it was not motivated by the desire to punish; they had already suffered severely. It went on to note that the board might have considered 'others in the chain of command' at least 'equally blameworthy' and that those who were singled out were 'but links in a chain of responsibility. ... [There was n]o suggestion that in their work as a whole they showed bungling ineptitude but they did not realise how dangerous an unstable tip could be.'[9] The Board's desire not to further punish the individuals concerned was also influenced by a feeling that the Tribunal should not have named names, and if it had felt that it had to, then it should have at least got the right names. Robens and Sheppard interrogated Thomas Wright, the Area General Manager for the area including Merthyr Vale. They treated Wright very differently to the seven blamed employees. To them, Robens had been friendly and considerate (something he was not always behind their backs). The hapless Wright bore the full brunt

---

8. POWE 52/212 Richard Marsh to Harold Wilson, 3 August 1967. Lord Robens, *Ten Year Stint* (London: Cassell, 1972), p. 259. The local lodge of the NUM petitioned the Board for Vivian Thomas to be retained in employment at Merthyr Vale Colliery. COAL 73/5 W.R. King to Lord Robens, 10 September 1968. BD 521154, 'Brief for Aberfan Debate', unsigned [October 1967]. COAL 73/3, Staff Memo, 4 August 1967; COAL 73/4 Staff Administrative Branch Memo, 5 January 1968. POWE 52/215, 'Harry' (Ministry of Power, Office for Wales) to R. Dearing, 18 August 1967.
9. POWE 52/212.

of their fury. Robens' private office thought that Wright had escaped blame at the Tribunal only because 'Edmund Davies took a shine to him'.[10] Robens and Sheppard accused Wright of failing to deal with a personality clash between civil engineer R.E. Exley and mechanical engineer D.L. Roberts that caused a lack of communication and co-operation between the two. The ramifications of this became serious when both were instructed to inspect the disaster tip in 1965. Exley did not; Roberts claimed to have done, but the Tribunal was sceptical of his claim. They did not work together on the issue and neither reported on its obvious instability.[11] Wright lamely replied that the standard of area officers was not up to that in his native Midlands:

> It was his experience in Wales that he could not make people do as they were told nor make them work. ... As regards Mr Roberts, he was an unreliable character but a good engineer. ... Generally, he [Wright] had thought long and hard about the events which had happened and could offer no explanation except that it was Wales and Welshmen.[12]

The Minister of Power accepted that the seven had suffered enough and did not request the board take further action.[13]

---

10. Interview, MJ and John Taylor, 28 May 1999. Examination of Thomas Wright, Transcripts of Hearings, Days 42 and 43. Various sets of these transcripts exist. We use the two sets in Merthyr and Dowlais Libraries, which we conserved in the first part of our work, funded from a British Academy Small Grant. A catalogue of the transcripts with an index is at our website at http://www.nuffield.ox.ac.uk/politics/aberfan/home.htm, accessed 31 October 2016.
11. Wright's reported statements here are not consistent with his statements at the tribunal. *Aberfan Report*, pp. 98-100; Transcripts, days 42 and 43.
12. COAL 73/3 Meeting, Lord Robens, W.V. Sheppard, C.A. Roberts, T. Wright, 30 August 1967.
13. POWE 52/212 Aberfan Disaster: Report of the Tribunal of Inquiry – Memorandum by the National Coal Board & The Report of the Tribunal appointed to inquire into the Disaster at Aberfan – A [draft] note by the Minister of Power. John Taylor interview.

Robens and Sheppard were themselves among the people most sharply criticised in the course of the inquiry.[14] Between the date of the disaster and publication of the Report, but after Sheppard's evidence had been described as 'astounding' by HM Chief Inspector of Mines and Quarries for South Wales, Robens nominated Sheppard for appointment to the main Coal Board. The Minister duly appointed him to the Board but refused Robens' 'strong representations' that Sheppard be made a deputy chairman.[15]

On publication of the Tribunal Report, 'Government sources' told the press that the question of Robens' resignation had been considered; however, he did not offer to resign until four days later.[16] Richard Marsh, the responsible minister, asked him to stay for at least a month while the Coal Board responded to the inquiry's recommendations. At the end of the month, Marsh rejected Robens' resignation offer. Public opinion was heavily in favour of Robens staying. One dissenter was the Labour MP Leo Abse, who called the Robens-Marsh exchange a 'graceless pavane' and a 'disgraceful spectacle'.[17] However, all the other Labour MPs who spoke in the Aberfan debate in October 1967 supported Robens and the Coal Board. Opposition speakers (including the new Conservative front bench spokesman on power, Margaret Thatcher) complained about the failure of anybody to take responsibility, and about Coal Board headquarters' unsustainable argument that there had been no warning signs of impending disaster. She later wrote: 'Someone, I thought, should have resigned, though I held back from stating this conclusion with complete clarity.'[18] The briefing notes for Richard Marsh's speech in reply to the debate show that the Ministry of

---

14. Robens: *Aberfan Report*, pp. 89-92; Sheppard: *Aberfan Report*, pp. 84-5.
15. POWE 52/212 The Report of the Tribunal appointed to inquire into the Disaster at Aberfan – A [draft] note by the Minister of Power.
16. *The Times*, 4 August 1967, p. 1, subhead 'I Have Not Offered to Resign'; *The Times*, 8 August 1967, p. 1.
17. *Hansard*, Commons, 5th series, vol. 751, col. 1978. POWE 52/212 The Report of the Tribunal appointed to inquire into the Disaster at Aberfan – A [draft] note by the Minister of Power.
18. Margaret Thatcher, *The Path to Power* (London: HarperCollins, 1995), p. 143.

Power expected calls in the debate for the dismissal of Robens and/or Sheppard. In Sheppard's defence, the best the note could say was that 'he had more excuse than some for failing to realise the dangers', on the grounds that he did not come from south Wales.[19] Plaid Cymru was the only party to call for not only Robens' resignation but also Marsh's. Gwynfor Evans, the Plaid Cymru MP for Carmarthen, told the Commons that this was 'not a matter of having heads roll. This is a central matter for any social democracy. After all, to say that no one is responsible ultimately for the culpability of a State industry is an absurdity.'[20]

When Lord Robens neared the end of his contract as Chairman of the Coal Board, he was made chairman of a committee to review the law on health and safety at work. This committee reported that it was generally inappropriate to make negligence of health and safety at work a criminal offence, except in cases where the imposition of 'exemplary punishment would be generally expected and supported by the public'.[21]

Fifty years have passed since Aberfan. The papers made available in 1997 at the National Archives[22] and elsewhere show that the Coal Board spin-doctored its way out of trouble, controlling the

---

19. BD 52/154, 'Brief for Aberfan Debate'. Another copy is in POWE 52/68. Overall responsibility for the note rested with R.E. Dearing (later Lord Dearing), the head of the economic section of the Coal Division of the Ministry of Power (POWE 52/68, briefing note cover sheet, 9 September 1967, telephone interview with Sir Ron Dearing, 13 January 1997). On Robens, the briefer wrote, 'It is suggested that the Minister should not seek to defend Lord Robens' evidence.' He did not: *Hansard*, Commons, 5th series, vol. 751, col. 2004: 'It is not for me to defend Lord Robens' conduct at the Tribunal.'
20. *Hansard*, 5th series, vol. 751, col. 1959-60. POWE 52/212 The Report of the Tribunal appointed to inquire into the Disaster at Aberfan – A [draft] note by the Minister of Power.
21. *Safety and Health at Work, Report of the Committee*, Chairman Lord Robens, Cmnd 5034, 1972, para. 263.
22. Especially classes BD 11, BD 50, BD 52, CAB 164, COAL 29, COAL 73, POWE 52, and PREM 13. All Aberfan papers at the National Archives were opened on 2 January 1997, although many of them would not normally have been opened until 1998 or later as they include documents from 1967

public agenda from the day of the disaster until the tips were finally removed. The second section of this chapter documents that process. The records show that Robens was able to control the agenda while ministers decided it was unnecessary to accept his resignation. The third section considers the 'unpolitics of Aberfan'. It is rare to be able to document why things one might have expected to happen did not;[23] however, the records in the National Archives and elsewhere facilitate it in this case.

Apportioning blame: October 1966 – August 1968

The Coal Board was in session as news of the disaster arrived in London. Lord Robens decided not to go to the scene immediately, but to put the Divisional Director of Production in overall charge of rescue and stabilisation operations. This was an entirely defensible decision and the normal policy in the aftermath of a disaster. However, he proceeded with his planned installation as Chancellor of the University of Surrey on the Friday evening and Saturday, an event which produced news photographs of a smiling Robens in grand chancellarial robes. Meanwhile, somebody wrongly told the Secretary of State for Wales, Cledwyn Hughes, that 'Lord Robens ... has been personally directing this work.' (In his closing speech to the Tribunal, counsel for the NUM, defending his clients against the charge that they should have realised that the tip was unsafe and alerted their managers, pointed out that if Coal Board officials could mislead the Secretary of State for Wales, they could also mislead the Merthyr Vale lodge of the NUM.)[24] With Harold Wilson and the Duke of Edinburgh both having visited Aberfan on the Friday afternoon,

---

or later. Class BD 52 (records of the Tribunal of Inquiry) was opened in 1996.

23. The canonical example, whose title we borrow, is Matthew A. Crenson, *The Unpolitics of Air Pollution: a study of non-decisionmaking in the cities* (Baltimore: John Hopkins University Press, 1971).
24. *Hansard*, Commons, 5th series, vol. 734, col. 643; *Tribunal Transcripts*, Day 71, p. 3973.

Robens' failure to attend, and his subsequent presence in Guildford, exposed him to public criticism.

Robens had not attended university but was surrounded by members of his staff who all had degrees. Thus the ceremony at Guildford was personally important to him and he was keen for it to go ahead. For a man usually adept at public relations, this proved to be an uncharacteristic mistake. Nonetheless, the visits of Wilson and Prince Philip, complete with aides and security, temporarily blocked the roads to Aberfan. This did not cost lives but, in retrospect, it did perhaps vindicate Robens' decision not to visit Aberfan immediately.[25]

Robens left Guildford at lunchtime on the Saturday, pausing to condemn the 'ghoulish' media coverage,[26] and went to Aberfan. Satirist John Bird said,

> Perhaps someone should have been there on that Friday to exercise some good taste but the Chairman of the NCB himself had a more pressing engagement to keep – he was at Guildford for the ceremony installing him as the University of Surrey's first Chancellor, so it wasn't until that night that he was able to get away to Aberfan and announce that he'd been sickened by the work of the TV reporters who'd been there for the previous day and a half.

Once arrived in Aberfan, Robens told two television and several newspaper interviewers about a 'natural unknown spring' in the

---

25. John Taylor interview. Similarly, Richard Marsh recalls how a telephone line between a meeting of the heads of the rescue services and the disaster site was taken off the hook because it rang while Wilson was speaking. Richard Marsh, *Off the Rails* (London: Weidenfeld & Nicolson, 1978), pp. 114-15. Wilson did, however, tell rescuers to carry on work after they were stopped in order for the Prime Minister to be introduced. The Queen did not visit the scene immediately for fear of disrupting the rescue. Tony Austin, *Aberfan: The Story of a Disaster* (London: Hutchinson, 1967), pp. 62, 69. She visited six days afterwards, and on 21 October 2016, she sent a message via Prince Charles, who attended the 50th anniversary commemoration in Aberfan.
26. COAL 29/378, 'Radio and TV Transcripts: Aberfan'. Bird: BBC TV, *The Late Show*, 5 November 1966.

tip. It was a statement based upon hearsay rather than considered opinion. Robens told a member of his private office that he had made the statement in attempt to protect members of the tipping gang who he understood to be the target of severe local criticism.[27] Whatever the motive, the statement was to haunt the NCB at the Tribunal of Inquiry.

Several Aberfan villagers immediately contradicted the 'unknown spring' story. One of them was Leslie Davies, the tipping gang chargehand, who was interviewed by Fyfe Robertson for BBC TV's *24 Hours*. The most relevant section is:

LD: Well, I don't know about an unknown spring, that spring has been there ever since I've known it.
FR: Did you get instructions to tip on top of the spring?
LD: No, all the instruction I got was tip, that's all. My instruction's to tip muck, isn't it?

At the end of the interview, Robertson turned to camera and said that in previous pit disasters he had reported on, the final report had nearly always been 'a frustrating exercise in official whitewashing'.[28] It turned out that Davies' statement was entirely true (and that the Tribunal report was not a frustrating exercise in official whitewashing). Nevertheless, the interview infuriated politicians. Sir Elwyn Jones, the Attorney General, issued a Commons statement to the effect that unauthorised comment or speculation on the causes of the disaster could constitute contempt of the Tribunal, which might be punishable as if it were contempt of court.[29] It is perplexing

27. John Taylor interview. Cf also letter from G. Morgan, D. Powell, C. Jones, D.L. Roberts, R.N. Lewis, R.V. Thomas and T.J. Wynne (i.e., the seven NCB employees blamed by the Tribunal) to Lord Robens 10 August 1967: 'We were all very conscious that your comments to the press and on TV during the first days of the incident were designed to assist the local officials as much as possible. We are so sorry that this effort created so many difficulties for you at a later date.' COAL 73/3.
28. Austin, *Aberfan*, pp. 150-3. A less coherent transcript is in PREM 13/1280.
29. *Hansard*, Commons, 5th series, Vol. 734, cols 1315-20.

that Davies' entirely truthful statement, which he later repeated to the tribunal, should be so described. Elwyn Jones' statement was fiercely criticised. Edward Heath, leader of the Opposition, said it was a threat 'to the freedom of us all'.[30] Jones later conceded that it was 'badly drafted'.[31] Although we have found no evidence that it was made with the intention of shielding the NCB, it had that effect. Newspapers reported the Tribunal proceedings very sparingly, and always in the studiously neutral tone of court reports, ending with a phrase such as 'The tribunal continues today.'

Several of the Sunday newspapers (notably *The Sunday Times* and *Sunday Mirror*) had managed to get the cause of the disaster approximately right in their issues of 23 October 1966, which went to press only 36 hours after the disaster. After that, accurate information went underground like an Aberfan spring, to emerge only in August 1967. Disinformation continued to flow, despite the Attorney General's warning. Three days after the 'gag', Robens was quoted in *The Sunday Times* as saying 'The Aberfan disaster has produced a new hazard in mining about which we knew nothing before.' This line was repeated by other NCB officials, including Geoffrey Morgan, the senior engineer in charge of stabilisation.[32] Given the history of tips sliding in south Wales, such a comment was clearly false, as well as defying the Attorney General's warning.

---

30. Quoted in Austin, *Aberfan*, p. 148.
31. Lord Elwyn-Jones, *In My Time: An Autobiography* (London: Futura, 1988), p. 234. An interdepartmental committee later recommended that 'The law of contempt in its application to Tribunals of Inquiry should not prohibit or curtail any comment at any time about the subject-matter of the inquiry.' The government of the day (1973) stated that it accepted this recommendation. Cmnd 5313/1973, Appendix C. Lord Howe of Aberavon, who as Geoffrey Howe QC, was counsel for the British Association of Colliery Management and the National Association of Colliery Managers, was one of those who criticised Jones' warning: Geoffrey Howe, 'The Aberfan Disaster', *Medico-Legal Journal*, 38 (1968), 107-21.
32. Quoted in Austin, *Aberfan*, p. 159. Also see *The Sunday Times*, 30 October 1966. Cf. also interview with Geoffrey Morgan, the engineer in charge of stabilisation, in *The Times*, 26 October 1966: 'The tip had been properly inspected, he said ... "It is our opinion that the spring responsible for this incident [sic] was a recent eruption." '

The Sunday Times of 26 February 1967 carried a remarkable piece, which Ackner accused Robens of planting or inspiring:

> On most of the 48 days of the Aberfan inquiry so far the Coal Board has been under attack. The Board's main case for its defence will ... be ... that the disastrous slide of a waste-tip which buried alive 144 people was 'unforeseeable' because its root cause was 'a coincidence of geological factors', each of which in itself was not exceptional. No surface observation, the Board will claim, could have detected this particular danger. The attack by counsel on Coal Board employees [is] now almost over.[33]

The story goes on to give a mostly accurate account of the weaknesses and failures which Coal Board witnesses had admitted. In fact, the Board had already started its 'unforeseeability' defence. On the second day, the NCB's counsel had said 'The prime cause of the disaster was therefore geological ... it would be unreal and unjust to credit any individual with foresight of this danger that only hindsight has revealed.'[34] Further references to a 'coincidence' of geological factors continued this line.[35] This defence was not finally abandoned until its counsel's closing speech on Day 74 of the inquiry. But it already knew, and Ackner forced Lord Robens to admit, that the 'unforeseeability' argument was untenable.[36] The springs over which waste was tipped are on an Ordnance Survey map of 1919 and a Geological Survey map of 1959. There had been a tip slide in 1939 of comparable magnitude to Aberfan just

---

33. *The Sunday Times*, 26 February 1967, p. 5; *Aberfan Tribunal Transcripts*, Day 70, p. 3926. In the Tribunal's cutting of this story the passage above is sidelined and the word 'unforeseeable' underlined: BD 52/109. Lord Howe did not share Lord Ackner's belief that the article was NCB inspired (interview and correspondence with IM, 1999).
34. Tribunal of Inquiry, transcript of evidence, Day 2, pp. 88, 90.
35. See *Aberfan Report*, pp. 85, 86.
36. *Aberfan Tribunal Transcripts*, Day 70. Cross-examination of Lord Robens by Desmond Ackner, p. 3924: Q: 'Does it come to this, that by the time the inquiry started on 29 November you were then satisfied that the causes were reasonably foreseeable?' A: 'That is so.'

down the road. This led to a detailed memorandum on preventing 'The Sliding of Colliery Rubbish Tips'. The Powell Memorandum, as it was known, was reissued in 1965 after another large slide in south Wales. Local engineers were told to inspect their tips to see if they met the memorandum's recommendations. The Aberfan tips did not. But the personality clash between two local engineers meant they were not inspected or, if they were, their condition was not reported. The Aberfan tips themselves had slid in 1944 and 1963; the unstable shape of the tips is obvious even to the untrained eye in photographs taken between 1963 and 1965 by parties other than the Coal Board.[37] Reportedly, the air reconnaissance branch of the RAF had written to the Coal Board warning it that the Aberfan tips were unstable. When the letter was forwarded to the local Divisional Manager, Thomas Wright, he reportedly dismissed it with contempt.[38]

Not all prior tip slides in south Wales were reviewed by the tribunal, despite its exhaustive work. On 4 February 1909, at Pentre in the Rhondda, a colliery spoil heap collapsed. Witnesses claimed that the 'moving rubbish flung itself onward with the speed of an avalanche'. The noise was 'as if the whole mountain were moving'. Four houses were buried, while a fifth was 'severed in twain', killing a young boy, James Williams.[39] The Aberfan Tribunal missed the Pentre slide, which is very unfortunate as the report from the Pentre coroner's inquest suggests close parallels with Aberfan, albeit with 143 fewer fatalities:

> Mr C. Edmunds, manager, explained that the tip had not been in use for 12 months, as they were now operating on another above it. Although the ground was rather loose he was unaware that any stream of water ran under the tip. A retaining wall, 6ft. in thickness, which had been built at the rear of the three demolished houses, was

---

37. *Aberfan Report*, Fig. 1, Fig. 2, Plate 1, and Plate 3.
38. Recollections of Evan Bryant, statistical clerk and secretary to Thomas Wright, No. 4. Area, forwarded by his son-in-law Keith Sanders, 26 October 2016.
39. *Cardiff Times*, 13 February 1909. H.J. Siddle, M.D. Wright & J.N. Hutchinson, 'Rapid failures of colliery spoil heaps in the South Wales Coalfield', *Quarterly Journal of Engineering Geology*, 29 (1996), p. 105.

swept away by the slide. They had had trouble [with] the roadway moving, but it was never anticipated that the whole body of the tip would give way. He should say that hundreds of thousands of tons of rubbish were involved in the slide. Questioned as to the cause of the accident, witness expressed an opinion that it was due to the stormy weather and rain which had percolated the ground. The Coroner observed that the same thing happened at Cwtch, Wattstown, years ago, but then it was discovered that a stream had loosened the debris.[40]

That incident may not have been discussed at the Aberfan Tribunal but numerous other tip slides were. The inquiry was a catalogue of warnings unheeded. Tip slides were neither unknown nor unforeseeable.

We interviewed the last surviving member of Robens' 1966 private office, John Taylor, in 1999. Mr Taylor felt that the NCB had never tried to evade its blameworthiness, pointing to the fact that Robens had told reporters on 22 October 1966 that the Board accepted responsibility for the disaster. Instead, the NCB had fallen back upon a defensive position as a result of Desmond Ackner's confrontational approach to the Tribunal, which the Board felt was essentially turning the whole proceedings into a trial. He summarised the attitude of the NCB towards the Tribunal as 'not a conspiracy but a cock-up'.[41] But this does not clearly explain the lack of any clear initial acceptance of responsibility by the Board at the outset or the NCB's counsel, Philip Wien's use of the unforeseeability argument

---

40. *Cardiff Times*, 13 February 1909. Mr Edmunds' failure of imagination was echoed by Thomas Wynne, manager of Merthyr Vale Colliery from 1963 to 1967. He reported to a colliery consultative committee in 1963 that a 'very big banking' formed by the disused railway and canal would protect the Pantglas schools from any slide. Aberfan Disaster Archive, Dowlais Library, F001; *Aberfan Report* para 136.

41. John Taylor interview. Howe felt that his role at the inquiry was 'acting as an insulator between those accused and the avenging fury of the public'. Geoffrey Howe, *Conflict of Loyalty* (London: Macmillan, 1994), p. 41. The only newspaper that reported Robens' acceptance of responsibility was the *Observer*. See Robens, *Ten Year Stint*, p. 249.

on Day 2. Robens' initial comments about an unknown spring may be excused on the grounds that they were ill-informed; but not only did the NCB not recant them, it added to them with its arguments about geological conditions. If the 1909 coroner's report on Pentre had been unearthed, the nonsensical stand of the NCB could have been dismissed at the outset.

The NCB's memorandum on the Tribunal Report claims that its experts had not made their final conclusions on the causes of the disaster when Wien opened the defence on day 2. It goes on to state that it was wrong for the Tribunal to take the evidence of individual officials (who refused to accept they were to blame) as being submissions by the Board itself. The memorandum also maintains that the board had done its utmost to help the Tribunal throughout but that it was not its role to 'make concessions and thus to anticipate the conclusions on matters which ... cannot fail to have an impact on other parties similarly represented.'[42] If this is all accepted, then the Board appears to be condemning the behaviour of its chairman (whom the memorandum did not defend) and its officials. The Coal Division of the Ministry of Power commented on the memorandum that the evidence, for whether the NCB knew that the disaster was foreseeable before the Tribunal began, was conflicting:

> Lord Robens' own evidence on this point is confused and whilst it is clear that the Board's Chief Divisional Surveyor had concluded before the hearing began that a slip could clearly have been foreseen, it is far from clear that he had so advised the Board. Indeed from the minutes of a meeting in Hobart House two months after the hearing started it seems that Mr Sheppard still thought that the conditions at Aberfan were rare.[43]

Whoever was to blame, the attitude of the NCB and its officials towards the Tribunal was confused, defensive and contradictory. The essence of the disaster is perfectly clear. Tip 7 was built on top of

---

42. Aberfan Disaster: Report of the Tribunal of Inquiry, Memorandum by the National Coal Board. POWE 52/212.
43. Aberfan: Coal Division's comments on the NCB memorandum, 25 August 1967. POWE 52/212.

springs which were marked on the map and obvious on the ground. Other tips in south Wales had slid before, including those at Aberfan. There can hardly be a clearer case of a disaster waiting to happen.

'He may feel bound to resign': the position of Lord Robens

A draft of the inquiry report reached ministers in July 1967. Richard Crossman, then Leader of the House of Commons, is the most candid witness:

> *Tuesday, July 15th [1967]*
> At Cabinet this morning we started with Aberfan. I'd had a row with the PM about this on Saturday when he told me he intended to release a statement before the publication of the report, which is immensely damaging. ... When Cledwyn [Hughes, Secretary of State for Wales] came to me yesterday to discuss publication I suggested that he shouldn't hurry it but let the preparation run on, with maps and diagrams until, say, the middle of August [i.e. after Parliament would have risen]. I would just announce this in our adjournment debate. Cabinet agreed that I should make the announcement this afternoon and meanwhile appointed Gordon Walker chairman of a Committee of Ministers to consider the implications of the Report.[44]

Harold Wilson wrote on his copy of this memorandum, 'I have now looked at the Report. It is devastating. Pl ask S/S Wales whether he should not make a statement to the House *before* publication. ... While it is exceptional to make a statement before publication, the fact that the House is adjourning – combined with the deep public concern and the devastating nature of the Report makes this desirable.'[45]

---

44. R.H.S. Crossman, *The Diaries of a Cabinet Minister. Vol. 2: Lord President of the Council and Leader of the House of Commons 1966-68* (London, 1976), pp. 440.
45. BD 11/3810, G. Daniel to B. Trend, 19 July 1967. PREM 15/1280, MS note on this memo in Wilson's hand. Original punctuation.

The Cabinet rejected the idea of delaying the Report. The Deputy Secretary at the Ministry of Power was sufficiently shocked by the Report to abandon the Ministry's customary protection of the Coal Board. He wrote to Marsh's private secretary that the Report

> calls in question his [Robens'] character and sense of proportion. In view of the tribunal's strictures, he may feel bound to resign. If so, his resignation should, in my view, be accepted but I do not think there is occasion to require his resignation. He is responsible for the organisation and efficiency of the industry. If there is a major failure anywhere in it, he must have some responsibility – wrong men in big jobs, inadequate overall direction from HQ.[46]

Gordon Walker's ministerial committee decided that since the Report did not blame Robens for the disaster, it was not sufficiently damning to require his dismissal but the Government should not press him to stay if he offered his resignation.[47]

The Cabinet met again to decide on a course of action. Crossman noted:

> *Tuesday, August 1st*
> There was a big meeting about the presentation of the Aberfan Report. ... [The Prime Minister] decided to take the chair ... and he called a lot of people to it. Patrick Gordon Walker had felt we should accept Alf Robens' resignation or even force it on him but without apparently realising that we should then have all the problem of the pit closures being sabotaged by Alf from outside. On the other hand it was equally dangerous to say, as Dick Marsh did, that we must on no account let him resign. I finally said to the PM, 'We ought to spend three weeks playing it out and request a report from the National Coal Board before we decide whether any resignations are accepted or not.'[48]

---

46. POWE 52/94, R.B. Marshall to A. Blackshaw, 31 July 1967.
47. CAB 130/328, MISC 157(67) 1st meeting, 27 July 1967.
48. Crossman, *Diaries of a Cabinet Minister, Vol. 2*, pp. 440, 453.

Ministers agreed to avoid detailed public discussion of the Report and to request the Board's observations before deciding whether to accept any resignations that might be offered.[49]

Marsh was therefore sent to confront Robens on 3 August with two statements authorised by the Prime Minister in his pocket: one to use if Robens offered his resignation, the other if not. The minutes of his meeting with Marsh give a very rare glimpse of raw passion behind Civil Service prose:

5. Lord Robens said he hoped the Government would never again set up a Tribunal of this nature ... It has been an inquisition into the Board's affairs without the Board having the normal protection of the law ... The Tribunal had shown their bias in their criticism of his own evidence as not being consistent.

7. Lord Robens said that ... the Tribunal Report was a conspiracy of silence as a result of which only the Board had been accused. The real cause of the failure of the Board ... was a breakdown of communication in that ... Mr Roberts ... and Mr Exley were not on speaking terms.[50]

9. The Minister said that any criticism of the Tribunal by the Board would be liable to misinterpretation and it would be best for the Board to confine itself to a factual statement.

10. After a good deal of further discussion, Lord Robens agreed that this was so and undertook to exclude any such comment from his Statement.

11. The Minister asked Lord Robens if he had come to any firm view on his own position. ... Lord Robens said that ... he intended to give his resignation to the Government next Tuesday morning, 8 August. He could not possibly continue as Chairman of the NCB unless the Government expressed their confidence in him.

---

49. CAB 130/328, MISC 157(67) 2nd meeting, 1 August 1967. For the Board's self-exculpatory report, in POWE 51/212, see n. 45 above. Cledwyn Hughes later said that Parliament should have extended to allow a Commons debate. *Western Mail*, 1 January 1998.
50. Roberts and Exley: *supra*. Transcripts, Days 32-6 (Roberts); 36-7 (Exley).

13. The Minister said that it was not inconceivable that at the end of the day the Government might have to announce the resignations of Mr Sheppard, Mr Kellett and Mr Morgan.[51] Lord Robens said ... that it would be hateful if people were to go round with long knives looking for victims.

15. Lord Robens reiterated that the Tribunal had been a conspiracy of silence for the benefit of the local people. They had even accepted that a man who had been tipping waste for over 20 years could not be expected to know anything about tip safety, whereas much of this was common sense. The Tribunal had cleared everybody in Aberfan other than Board officials, and equally had cleared the Civil Engineers of Merthyr Tydfil.[52]

Robens' general demeanour is clear from these minutes. Whoever was to blame, senior Coal Board people were not. On 8 August 1967, an emotional Robens informed a full meeting of the Board of his decision to offer his resignation. No one tried to dissuade him.[53]

Robens had had a copy of the Report since 31 July 'on a very confidential "Privy Councillor" basis'.[54] On 4 August, Robens visited

---

51. A. H. Kellett was Chairman of the South Western Division of the Coal Board. G. S. Morgan was Production Director for South Wales. There was some feeling within the NCB that it was unfair that certain individuals had escaped censure when others had been named. MJ interview with John Taylor. Cf William Ashworth, *The History of the British Coal Industry, Vol. 5, 1946-1982: The Nationalized Industry* (Oxford: Clarendon Press, 1986), p. 287. Marsh expressed surprise at the above meeting that Kellett and Collins (the Board Member for Production) were not interviewed by the Tribunal. Marsh thought that Kellett would have been responsible for the liaison between division and HQ and that he might have reasonably been expected to know of the dangers of the Aberfan tips from the complaints in the local press. Paul Foot claimed that Kellett and Collins were told by Robens to stay at a conference in Japan 'which effectively prevented either man losing his head'. 'Footnotes', *Private Eye*, 28 April 1967.
52. POWE 52/94. The Aberfan Report and the NCB: note of a meeting held in the Minister's room, 3 August 1967.
53. John Taylor interview.
54. A. Blackshaw to R. Marshall, 31 July 1967. Earlier, Robens had complained to his Board about the 'difficulties encountered in obtaining

pits in Scotland, and pointedly criticised the Government decision to build a nuclear power station at Hunterston in Ayrshire. In making such a speech Robens was following his usual programme and agenda. Nonetheless, it helped cement his popularity within the industry: 'Lord Robens has had massive support from miners all over the country, who feel that he has done a fine job in standing up for their interests.'[55] Most areas of the National Union of Mineworkers (NUM) urged that he should stay, although its south Wales area executive was 'not unanimous'.[56] Robens' office drafted three form letters 'To Outsiders', 'To Unions', and 'To Management', to use in reply to incoming messages of support.[57] Details of the numbers of letters of support Robens had received were released to the press by the NCB, including one from former Prime Minister Harold Macmillan, who had appointed Robens to the Coal Board. Macmillan complained that he had not intended it for publication. The press clearly perceived a 'Robens must stay' campaign, orchestrated from Coal Board headquarters. The *Guardian*, which on the whole thought he should stay, nevertheless commented that 'Over the last few days the Coal Board's behaviour has ... been rather unseemly, in the circumstances.'[58] A Coal Board eyewitness maintains that while they and the NCB press office may have been trying to demonstrate public support for Robens, they were not doing so under his instructions.[59] In contrast, Richard Marsh believed that Robens had been personally manipulating the press 'the whole time ... He was a highly political animal and he was extremely good at it. It was quite natural because it was ... ongoing'.[60]

Robens' 'resignation' letter was issued on 8 August. A draft of the letter in his office papers, dated 3 August, was almost threatening:

advance copies ... it was essential that they should have access to the document well in advance of publication'. COAL 73/2, Secret Minute of the Board, 28 July 1967.
55. *The Times*, 7 August 1967, p. 1.
56. *The Times*, 9 August 1967, p. 2.
57. COAL 73/3, 8 August 1967.
58. Leader, 'Is it a Resigning Matter?' 7 August 1967.
59. John Taylor interview.
60. Lord Marsh interview with MJ.

'In going now I would be leaving it [viz. the reconstruction of the coal industry] incompleted [sic]. But without the confidence and support of the Government I cannot stay.'[61] The published letter omitted this, and referred only to the doctrine of ministerial responsibility. Robens had been a Labour politician before becoming Chairman of the Coal Board and those close to him at the time maintained that he valued this traditional doctrine.[62] Yet Robens must also have known that nobody had ever tried to claim that the chairman of a nationalised industry was liable, under the doctrine of ministerial responsibility, for the failings of his subordinates. The letter was published to the accompaniment of heavy hints from the usual sources that the resignation would be refused.[63]

Marsh complained about comment in the press relating to the resignation issue but did not actively try to prevent it.[64] He waited and watched, using the Coal Board's impending comments on the Tribunal Report as an excuse not to take action on Robens' 'resignation'. He saw that public as well as industry opinion was in favour of Robens staying. Gallup found that those it polled in August 1967 believed that Robens should not resign by a margin of 74 per cent to 15 per cent.[65] The national press, meanwhile, was divided on whether he should resign or not.[66] The NCB submitted its comments on the Tribunal Report to the Minister on 23 August. Robens'

---

61. COAL 73/2, draft resignation letter, 3 August 1967.
62. John Taylor interview.
63. For example, E. Silver, 'Lord Robens' Offer to Resign Not Accepted Yet', *The Times*, 8 August 1967: 'Although Mr Marsh is still keeping his own counsel, it is now thought unlikely in Whitehall that he will accept Lord Robens' offer.' Marsh claimed in his memoirs (*Off the Rails*, p. 116) that Robens had offered his resignation before the Tribunal reported, but that he then rejected it.
64. POWE 52/94. R. Marsh: 'Note for the Record Lord Robens', 9 August 1967.
65. Letter from The Gallup Organisation to IM, 7 November 1996. POWE 52/93, letters from NOP and Government Social Survey to Press Office, Ministry of Power, giving poll results, 6 September 1967 and 11 September 1967.
66. See, for example, the summaries of press opinion given in the *South Wales Echo*, 4 August 1967.

private secretary described them as 'not too pugnacious and not too contrite'.[67] On 30 August, Lord Robens left for New York on board the *Queen Mary*. He left behind a tantalising hint that he might be prepared to resign in March 1968. Sir David Pitblado, the Permanent Secretary at Power, minuted,

> There are timing complications. The Minister would not be able to talk this over with Lord Robens until September 29th, since he will be in USA until September 14th, and at sea until September 20th. It will be impossible to postpone a public statement of the Government's attitude to his resignation until then. If this course of action commended itself to the Minister and the PM, it would be necessary to write to him (or to get him to fly back which might be dramatic).[68]

On 5 September, Marsh and Wilson decided, in the light of the public and industry support for Robens, to reject his resignation. Marsh telegraphed a draft letter saying so to Robens in New York, using the British Ambassador to the UN, Lord Caradon, as a go-between. Robens went to see Caradon, having already been informed by the NCB Deputy Chairman that Marsh was probably going to reject his resignation offer.[69] Caradon reported:

> I saw Lord Robens this afternoon and conveyed your message to him. He asked me to make the following reply. Begins. Provided the sentence 'It is the whole board, not the Chairman alone, which is appointed by the Minister and responsible to him for the operations of the industry' is deleted, my reply would be as follows. Thank you for your letter about my offer of resignation. In view of what you say I willingly agree to continue as chairman of the NCB. Ends.

---

67. COAL 73/3, A. Alderson to Lord Robens, 17 August 1967. The comments (POWE 52/93, 'Aberfan Disaster: Report of the Tribunal: Memorandum by the NCB', 23 August 1967) pugnaciously rebut some statements in the Tribunal Report. There is little sign of contrition in them.
68. POWE 52/93. Memo from D. Pitblado to A. Blackshaw, R. Marshall, and C. Thorley, 31 August 1967.
69. John Taylor interview.

Marsh's private secretary complained that the disputed sentence was there for constitutional reasons – namely to explain that, if the doctrine of ministerial responsibility implicated anybody, it implicated the entire Board. Nevertheless, Marsh issued the letter without it, as instructed by Robens. It is indeed a powerful politician who can dictate the letters he receives, as well as the letters he sends.[70]

Robens was able to do this because, in general, the Coal Board under his chairmanship was managing decline competently. It was for this purpose that the Macmillan government had appointed Robens, a trade unionist and former front bench Labour politician. Robens succeeded in raising productivity per man-shift, in reducing underground casualties, and in sharply cutting employment all at the same time. This was no mean achievement. But it was one that Robens wished to manage on his own terms. These terms involved carrying mineworkers, and their powerful union, the NUM, with him whenever he could. As a former Labour politician, he knew exactly how and where to apply political pressure. He seems to have mesmerised ministers. Richard Marsh, who thought Robens must stay at all costs, nevertheless complained that in 1967 'Labour Members of Parliament were being openly briefed, on Alf Robens' direct instructions, at the Coal Board headquarters.'[71] Barbara Castle, who complained that somebody 'already rivalling Robens in megalomania' might 'do a Robens on us by leaking to the press', was nevertheless the minister who appointed Robens to chair the health and safety committee.[72] In the summer of 1967, relations between Robens and ministers were at their lowest point. Ministers correctly saw that natural gas was about to become a cheap and clean fuel. They also believed, incorrectly, that nuclear power was about to do the same. These two beliefs necessarily implied that British coal production must decline more rapidly than previously unless it could

---

70. POWE 52/93. Draft of Minister's Reply: Telegram from Lord Caradon (both 5 September 1967); A. Blackshaw to R. Marsh, 6 September 1967.
71. Marsh, *Off the Rails*, p. 111.
72. Barbara Castle, *The Castle Diaries 1964-70* (London: Weidenfeld & Nicolson, 1984), p. 370 (7 February 1968); cf. also p. 313 (25 October 1967). For comparably hostile comments on Robens see Wilson, *Labour Government*, p. 625; Crossman, *Diaries, 11*, p. 751 (13 November 1967).

find new product or export markets. Nobody seems to have attempted this, perhaps because it was common, but unspoken, ground that British coal was uncompetitive on world markets. Both Robens and Marsh, in their memoirs, perceived the main row of 1967 to have been not Aberfan but the government White Paper on Fuel Policy.[73] Although it promised to keep the coal import ban in being, and mentioned in passing that the pithead price of coal in the USA was less than half its price in the UK, Robens felt that its projections for future coal demand in the UK were too low, and fiercely lobbied against them. (In fact, demand for UK coal has fallen much faster than the 1967 projections. The last deep mine closed in 2016.[74]) Consequently he was an extremely popular figure with the NUM.

Why then were ministers so determined to keep Robens? As already noted, Crossman feared: 'we should then have all the problem of pit closures being sabotaged by Alf from the outside.'[75] Marsh was in no doubt that Robens would have pursued a campaign of attacking government fuel policy if he left the NCB. He also maintained that Robens' friendship with Cecil King, chairman of the Mirror Group, would have meant public backing for any attack from the *Daily Mirror*. The bitterness Robens felt towards the government, Harold Wilson and the Labour Party would have added to his zeal to criticise them publicly. To Marsh the whole issue of whether to keep Robens

---

73. Cmnd 3438/1967. Robens, *Ten Year Stint*, pp. 178-222; Marsh, *Off the Rails*, pp. 109-11.
74. Department for Business, Energy, and Industrial Strategy, *Digest of UK Energy Statistics 2016*, Charts 2.1 and 2.2. At https://www.gov.uk/government/uploads/system/uploads/attachment_data/file/552060/DUKES_2016_FINAL.pdf, accessed 12 November 2016.
75. Crossman, *Diaries*, II, p. 453. Whether or not Robens actually would have sabotaged the pit closures from outside is of course debatable. His obituary in the *Independent* (29 June 1999) notes that upon leaving the NCB in 1971 Robens deliberately kept a low profile on coal and energy matters. However, it also notes that by 1974 he was publicly attacking government energy policies. Nor does Robens' flirtations with Cecil King's plot for a *coup d'état* suggest any particular inclination to ease the Government's path.

was nothing to do with Aberfan but everything to do with his intense dislike of the government's policy on fuel.[76]

Not only would there be the problem of an angry Robens outside the NCB tent but there was also the question of the lack of any suitable successor. It was then an axiom of British politics that no politician should ever be foolish enough to take on the NUM. It remained so until 1984. Robens alone, ministers felt, could shield them from the wrath of the NUM. Marsh noted

> If it were decided to accept the resignation it is relevant to bear in mind that Lord Robens' successor would appear to have been appointed in opposition to the wishes of the industry ... His successor might therefore encounter some hostility. With the many serious difficulties that lie ahead of the coal industry, hostility between the chairman and unions would be a severe handicap.[77]

The monopoly power of the NUM, which made it so feared, was conferred by British governments themselves, notably in the bipartisan policy of banning coal imports. Ministers felt that Robens, however much he infuriated them, was indispensable.

There was also little parliamentary pressure on the government to do otherwise, including at the Commons debate on the report. The Labour MPs for Welsh valley constituencies were, with the sole exception of Leo Abse, intimately connected with the mining industry. Like other Labour Party members, they regarded the nationalisation of coal as a crowning achievement of the 1945-51 government. Therefore, they were uncomfortable with the notion that the NCB could do anything wrong. In contrast, S.O. Davies, a former miner and the constituency MP for Aberfan, claimed that the remaining tips were unsafe. Marsh forcefully rebutted the allegations. Meanwhile, Gwynfor Evans, the new MP for Plaid Cymru, claimed that had the tips slid on to 'Hampstead or Eton', the Government response to the disaster would have been stronger, and went on: 'The odds are that if Wales had had her own Coal Board ... this disaster

---

76. Lord Marsh interview.
77. Draft note by Minister of Power, 1 September 1967. POWE 52/94. Also see letter from James Callaghan to Harold Wilson, 31 July 1967.

would never have occurred.' This was scarcely borne out by the Tribunal Report. He was on firmer ground when he claimed 'the right thing, the decent thing, the just thing and the dignified thing for the Chairman to do was to resign and stay resigned'.[78] David Gibson-Watt, the Conservative spokesman for Welsh affairs, highlighted the criticisms made of Robens and stressed that while he was not calling for a resignation he wanted to know why it had been refused.[79] Leo Abse, the Labour MP for Pontypool who was not from a mining background, Margaret Thatcher, the shadow minister for power, and Colonel Claude Lancaster, a former colliery owner, also raised telling questions about Robens and Sheppard. However, many of the criticisms anticipated in the briefing note compiled for the Minister of Power were not made and there was little in the debate to change the government's position over Robens. *The Times* of 27 October called it 'a bitter and unpleasant debate with a sense of pointlessness'. The *Western Mail* referred to it as 'disappointing' and complained that it dwelt upon the past rather than the future.[80]

Why was there no legal action against the NCB or any of its employees?

A reader today of the Tribunal Report might have difficulty in understanding how Robens, Sheppard, and Morgan could have kept their jobs. But outside Aberfan itself (and, in relation to those low down the NCB hierarchy, not even there), there was little demand for individuals to be punished. The press magnate Cecil King noted that press comment on the Report itself was 'more hostile' than he expected.[81] Yet the disaster was still generally viewed as an accident. After more recent disasters, there have been persistent calls for heads to roll. After Aberfan, there were not. The nine named individuals were

78. House of Commons Debate, 26 October 1967, vol 751, cc.1956, 1958.
79. House of Commons Debate, 26 October 1967, vol 751, cc.1922-3.
80. *Western Mail*, 28 October 1967, editorial.
81. Cecil King, *The Cecil King Diary, 1965-70* (London: Jonathan Cape, 1972), p. 138.

treated sympathetically by the press and there was even a local petition for the two still working at Merthyr Vale colliery to keep their jobs. The NCB's refusal to castigate them in public, and the private disquiet within sectors of the coal industry over the Tribunal's findings, also strengthened their position, just as it had for Lord Robens.[82] In Aberfan itself, given the publicity given to what was portrayed as bitter argument and division within the community, there may also have been a quiet desire amongst some to avoid the further acrimony of sackings.

The question of criminal proceedings however was more complicated and, even if the Coal Board and ministers had behaved quite differently when it came to people's jobs, the broader legal outcome might not have been very different.

At the parliamentary debate on the Aberfan Tribunal Report, Gwynfor Evans MP, said,

> If one drives a car dangerously and has the terrible misfortune to hurt somebody, proceedings can be instituted. It is possible for a driver to be convicted of manslaughter. But it is not possible to take any sort of action against a public board. There seems to be one law for the private person and another for the public board. I am not suggesting that action should be taken against personal members of the Coal Board. I would not suggest that. But there should be some way of bringing a public board to justice.[83]

Theoretically there was no reason why the board could not be brought to justice. Corporations had been identified as separate legal persons since the late nineteenth century. Their liability to

---

82. Concern within the industry had been first raised after the appointment of Edmund Davies. The *Colliery Guardian* argued that Davies' south Wales background (which he emphasised after his appointment with statements such as 'I want to be of the greatest service to the people to whom I belong') made him partial and unsuitable for the 'cold dispassionate pursuit of facts' that was needed. *Colliery Guardian*, 28 October 1966. There was also private disquiet about the Tribunal Report outside the coal industry. Geoffrey Howe felt that the Tribunal had inflicted an 'injustice' on some of those he represented. Howe, *Conflict of Loyalty*, pp. 41-42.
83. *Hansard*, 5th series, vol. 751, column 1956.

tort actions had been established through vicarious liability for the actions of their employees. However, this principle was not applied wholesale to criminal law. Employers were only deemed responsible for their employee's criminal acts in cases of libel or public nuisance, or in other cases in accordance with the principles of secondary participation. The first case of corporate manslaughter brought in England and Wales involved the south Wales mining company Cory Brothers. During the 1926 miners' strike, the company had erected an electrified fence around its property. An unemployed miner was killed when he stumbled against it and the South Wales Miners' Federation brought private prosecutions for manslaughter against the company and three of its directors. However, the trial judge decided that a company could not be indicted for offences against the person.[84]

In 1944, the law regarding corporate liability developed significantly through three cases that established the principle of identification.[85] This involved companies being deemed responsible in criminal cases normally requiring *mens rea* ('the criminal state of mind, accompanying an act which condemns the perpetrator of the act to criminal punishment; criminal intent' – *OED*). Corporations of course do not have minds but it was established that a corporation could be guilty if a director or manager could be seen as acting, not for the corporation, but as it. Thus individuals could be identified as the corporation. In 1957, it was further clarified that where directors and managers are in effect the mind of a company, their actions could be said to be those of the company. Consequently, companies, through the actions of their senior officials, could be guilty of any criminal offence except those requiring a mandatory custodial sentence.[86]

---

84. 810 1 KB [Glamorgan Assizes] *R v Cory Brothers and Company Limited.* 1927 Feb. 2; Celia Wells, *Negotiating Tragedy: Law and Disasters* (London: Sweet and Maxwell, 1995), pp. 170-71. Cory was also the company that owned the Pentre tip that killed James Williams in 1909; but they were not prosecuted for that.

85. *DPP v Kent & Sussex Contractors Ltd* [1944] KB 146. *R v ICR Haulage Ltd* [1944] 30 Cr App R 31. *Moore v Bresler* [1944] 2 All ER 515.

86. Law Commission, *Criminal Law: Involuntary Manslaughter*, Consultation Paper no. 135 (London: HMSO, 1994), paras. 4.11-4.16.

In 1965, a welder-burner, Glanville Evans, was drowned when a railway bridge which his employers were demolishing collapsed into the river Wye. It was alleged that the workmen had been instructed by the managing director to burn the bridge into sections, starting in the middle, which the prosecuting counsel asserted was 'almost as ludicrous as telling a man sitting on a branch of a tree to saw that branch'. The jury at the inquest committed Evans' employers to court. Consequently, in *R v Northern Strip Mining Construction Ltd* (Glamorgan Assizes, 1965) the company was prosecuted for unlawful killing. The prosecuting counsel was Philip Wien QC; the defence counsel was W.L. Mars-Jones QC. The case against the firm rested upon the instructions having come from the Managing Director rather than the foreman, for whose actions the company was not necessarily liable. The prosecution failed because it was not shown that the instruction to begin demolition in the middle had come from the managing director. The validity of the indictment itself was not challenged.[87]

Eighteen months later and a few miles away, Philip Wien QC was counsel for the NCB at the Aberfan Tribunal, and W.L. Mars-Jones QC was counsel for the National Union of Teachers (representing the surviving Pantglas teachers and the relatives of those killed). Thus their roles were reversed; in effect Wien was counsel for the defence and Mars-Jones was one of the counsel for the prosecution. But there is no evidence that either of them regarded the Northern Strip Mining case as relevant to Aberfan. At Aberfan there were no allegations that the functional equivalent of 'managing director' of the Coal Board had instructed the tipping gang to build up the fatal tip. Lords Ackner and Howe, and Sir Ronald Waterhouse (three Aberfan counsel who were still alive in 1996) 'all share ... the recollection that criminal proceedings were never under consideration in this case'.[88] Nonetheless, the criticisms in the Tribunal Report meant that the Attorney General did consider the bringing of charges against the individuals named blameworthy to varying degrees. On 4 August

---

87. *The Times*, 2, 4, 5 February 1965.
88. Letter from The Rt Hon Lord Howe of Aberavon, CH, QC to IM, 2 December 1996; telephone interview with Lord Ackner, 27 November 1996.

1967, it was reported that he had announced that no proceedings would be taken. The decision met a mixed response in Aberfan.[89]

Aberfan residents had first raised the possibility of bringing manslaughter charges with their solicitors before the Tribunal had even begun sitting.[90] As already noted, their belief that the NCB's culpability was demonstrated at the opening inquest at Aberfan, held on the Monday after the disaster when, amidst shouts of 'murderers', a bereaved parent called for the cause of death to be recorded as '"Buried alive by the National Coal Board." That is what I want to see on the record. That is the feeling of those present. Those are the words we want to go on the certificate.'[91]

Following the publication of the Report the matter was again discussed. The press reported that some villagers were scouring the Report for evidence of negligence and if they found it they would demand legal action.[92] The issue was discussed at a meeting of the Aberfan Parents' and Residents' Association. Although some members of the village wanted to bring charges, Desmond Ackner told his clients that any prosecution against any of the nine individuals named in the Report as partly to blame would be unlikely to succeed. The decision was announced with a statement to the press:

> The Parents' and Residents' Association of Aberfan are unanimously and strongly averse to any prosecution of any Coal Board officials implicated in the Aberfan Disaster. No such prosecution will be brought by them or on their behalf.
>
> They fully accept the findings of the Tribunal. There is no question of their pursuing any vendetta or seeking retribution from those who have been found to be blameworthy.[93]

---

89. *The Times*, 4-5 August 1967.

90. Note, 22 November 1966, file 1, Cyril Moseley Papers, NLW.

91. *Merthyr Express*, 28 October 1966, p. 18. The words 'Buried alive by the National Coal Board' are set as a recitative in Karl Jenkins, *Cantata Memoria – for the children*, as a baritone solo against Welsh songs sung by a choir of 116 children.

92. *The Times*, 4 August 1967.

93. Attendance re Aberfan, 10 August 1967, file 6, Cyril Moseley papers, NLW.

The consideration thus seems to have been of charges against the named NCB officials rather than the Board itself. The case against Northern Strip had involved alleged reckless conduct by the firm's managing director thus directly implicating the company itself. Northern Strip was small; the NCB was enormous. That issue has bedevilled attempts to bring corporate manslaughter charges right down to the present day. Prosecuting organisations for the combined fatal failures of its staff was simply not part of the legal culture of the 1960s. Indeed, health and safety offences in the workplace were not generally regarded as criminal matters (see below). Thus Aberfan was not viewed in the popular mind as a criminal act but a tragic accident. This drew upon and shaped the legal response.

It was thus not surprising that the 1970 Robens Committee on Health and Safety at Work argued that the use of criminal law was generally inappropriate, and even in fatal cases normally contemplated only prosecutions for breach of regulatory statutes. (In any case there were no such breaches at Aberfan – see below.) It did not discuss corporate manslaughter.

After the sinking of the car ferry *Herald of Free Enterprise* in 1987, which killed 193 people, the inquest jury returned a verdict of unlawful killing against the coroner's advice. The ferry company and seven of its employees were prosecuted for reckless manslaughter. However, the trial judge halted the trial and directed acquittals before the prosecution case was completed, arguing that it was impossible to establish recklessness on the part of any one individual and thus the company. It is possible to compare the Aberfan Tribunal Report with the Sheen Report on the ferry tragedy point by point, whence it is fairly clear that the culpability of the Coal Board over Aberfan was comparable with that of Townsend Thoresen over the *Herald of Free Enterprise*.[94] Yet even had any charges been brought against the NCB, they would have run into the same problems that faced the prosecutors of P & O (the owners of Townsend Thoresen). Despite the obvious failures of the company, the law simply did not allow the failures of individuals to be aggregated into criminal responsibility by their employer.

---

94. E.g., because of the false assurances given to Merthyr Borough Council: *Aberfan Report*, p. 56; BD52/12, BD52/199.

Between the criminal and the civil law yawned a great gulf. It has long been established in civil law that an occupier of land has strict liability for any damage caused by the escape of anything from that land. This doctrine was specifically applied to coal tips in a case which Ackner claimed 'any competent law student in his last year' would know (although Sheppard, the Director General of Production for the Coal Board, did not).[95] Strict liability means that the plaintiff need not establish that the defendant was negligent. Thus the Coal Board was civilly liable for the deaths, injuries, and destruction of property caused at Aberfan, and would have been regardless of the culpability of individual employees. What, then, could the Tribunal achieve? Beyond investigating the possibility of criminal negligence, the Tribunal provided reassurance to both the bereaved and public that the disaster had not been taken lightly and that all would be done to identify those responsible and what was needed to avoid a repeat. There may have been no need to show negligence in civil law but there was a need to publicly establish the cause and fault, and perhaps for some people to say sorry. Yet only one witness made any unforced admission of responsibility for any aspect of the disaster. Vivian Thomas, the colliery mechanical engineer, the most junior official in the whole Coal Board hierarchy above the tipping gang, courageously said: 'I had no instructions at all about any tips ... but I was responsible. It is no good shirking it. I was responsible for the tip.'[96]

Once the Tribunal Report was published a single inquest was resumed. It lasted just four minutes. The coroner announced that,

> It is not for me to decide any question of civil liability. As far as criminal liability is concerned, the whole matter has been investigated very

---

95. *Rylands v. Fletcher* [1868] LR 3. HL 330; *Attorney General v. Cory Brothers & Co Ltd*, [1921] 1 AC 521 (Cory was the case of a tip slide, in the Rhondda Valley); *Aberfan Report*, p. 39; cross-examination of W. Sheppard by D. Ackner, *Aberfan Tribunal Transcripts*, Day 51, p. 2824.
96. R. Vivian Thomas, *Aberfan Tribunal Transcripts*, Day 17, p. 931; Howe, 'The Aberfan Disaster', p. 112. See also Howe's eloquent plea in mitigation of his clients, *ibid.*, pp. 112-4 and his defence of a Tribunal rather than other forms of redress for the victims, *ibid.*, p. 114.

thoroughly. The Tribunal assessment is tantamount to a finding of accidental death in each case.[97]

This interpretation is perhaps questionable given the force with which the Report had condemned the NCB. Accidental death was certainly not how many people in Aberfan felt about their losses and the press reported that some parents felt the verdict should have been manslaughter: buried alive by the National Coal Board.[98] But that was not how the legal system worked. Nonetheless, at a meeting of the APRA, although some people felt that the coroner could have expressed himself more sympathetically, there was a general sympathy with the way he had handled proceedings. As the chairman of the meeting said, he had an 'unenviable task'.[99]

Why did the regulatory authorities fail?

One body to escape lightly from the Aberfan Tribunal's strictures was HM Inspectorate of Mines and Quarries. It is hard to see why, when the Tribunal considered whether two entirely innocent bodies – Merthyr Tydfil Borough Council and the NUM – should bear some share of the blame. Its own evidence revealed severe failure and regulatory capture.

Statutory regulation of coal mines in the UK goes back to 1842. In 1954 it was consolidated into that year's Mines and Quarries Act. That Act laid down very detailed powers of inspection underground. These have evolved through the harrowing history of mine disasters, some of which have involved higher death tolls than Aberfan. The inspection procedures incorporated the workforce – union representatives accompanied managers and inspectors. But moles do not understand the habits of birds. Only accidents involving injury or death to colliery employees were reportable under the

---

97. *The Times*, 29 September 1967.
98. *The Times*, 29 September 1967.
99. Attendance re Aberfan 28 September 1967, Cyril Moseley papers, file 6, NLW.

1954 Act. Because of the 'little short of miraculous' survival of the whole tipping gang, who had gone for a cup of tea when the slide started,[100] the Aberfan disaster was not even a reportable accident under the 1954 Act.[101] On the day of the disaster, the Inspectorate tried to dissuade Richard Marsh from visiting Aberfan. The Inspectors accompanying Marsh to the disaster pointed to the Mines and Quarries Act to show that neither the Inspectorate nor the Minister had any legal responsibility for tips or the disaster. Marsh remembered the Inspectorate as 'working strictly to the book' with an ethos not to get involved in things that they were not responsible for.[102]

The Mines Inspectorate annual report for 1966 begins with an expression of sympathy that is careful to point out that the disaster was not reportable under the 1954 Mines and Quarries Act for which they were responsible. That year's annual report for the South Western division of the Inspectorate, which incorporated Aberfan, does not even mention the disaster.[103]

The records of inspections of Merthyr Vale colliery since 1961 were produced to the Tribunal. The Inspectorate visited the colliery frequently between 1961 and 1966, but never once did they look at the tips which towered over the valley. Yet the Chief Inspector for the region covering Merthyr Vale freely accepted that he regarded tip

---

100. *Aberfan Report*, p. 30.
101. If they had died or been hurt in the slide, the disaster would have been reportable and there would have been a case to answer under the 1954 Act. But figures from the Robens Report show that the Mines and Quarries Inspectorate was remarkably unwilling to prosecute. Of the sixteen prosecutions under the 1954 Act in 1970, five had been initiated by the NCB itself, eleven by Procurators Fiscal in Scotland and none at all by the Inspectorate. This total of sixteen prosecutions, in one of the two most dangerous industries in the UK, compares with 2,940 under the Factories Act 1961, 432 under the Offices, Shops, and Railway Premise Act 1963, and 311 under seven other regulatory statutes. Robens Report, Table 5.
102. Lord Marsh interview.
103. H.S. Stephenson, *Report of HM Chief Inspector for Mines and Quarries (under the Mines and Quarries Act 1954) for 1966* (London: HMSO, 1967). C. Leigh, *Reports of HM Inspectors of Mines and Quarries (under the Mines and Quarries Act 1954) for 1966, South Western Division* (London: HMSO, 1967).

stability part of the duties of the Inspectorate so as to protect the men working there.[104] He was invited to describe what a tip inspection should cover. These are his words:

> We would look at the tip itself, we would look for cracks, we would look for swellings, holes, and as long as the symmetry of the tip was satisfactory then we would regard that as being in order.[105]

The Aberfan tips had had almost all the faults he lists since 1944. The Inspector was cross-examined not by the fearsome Ackner but by his junior. The Inquiry transcript shows that he was not hostile. In his response to further questions, the Chief Inspector revealed that he, too, was a mole. He was a former colliery engineer. Neither he nor any of his staff had professional expertise in soil mechanics; nor did they consult anyone with such expertise. Like the industry they were regulating, the Mines' Inspectorate was dominated by mining engineers. What happened to the mineral once it was extracted from the ground was simply not part of their conception of the industry.

This was self-evidently the capture of a regulatory body by, and in the interests of, those whom it regulates. This has commonly been observed with price and quantity regulation. But this example shows that it can occur with safety regulation also. The danger is greatest when regulatee and regulator are both public-sector bodies with a revolving door between them. The Tribunal commented on the 'greater alertness' of the Powell Duffryn company to the 1939 slip than that of the Coal Board from 1963 onwards.[106] Regulation was devised by the miners for the miners, and although surface workers were miners too they were not the ones who ran the industry. Moles may make good rules for moles, but not for birds.

Ministerial briefing notes for the Aberfan debate show that the government was prepared for criticisms of the Mines' Inspectorate. In

---

104. *Aberfan Report*, p. 35.

105. *Aberfan Tribunal, Transcript of Oral Evidence*, Day 52. Evidence of Cyril Leigh, Chief Inspector of Mines and Quarries for Wales, p. 2868.

106. However, before nationalisation the Mines' Inspectorate was sometimes too close to the mining companies. Iain McLean and Martin Johnes, *Aberfan: Government and Disasters* (Cardiff: Welsh Academic Press, 2000), pp. 191-2.

the event of any relevant question the Minister was to maintain that the Mines and Quarries Act made it clear that safety provision was the responsibility of the owners while the Inspectorate's role was to enforce that provision. Where provision had not been made through the failure to recognise danger then responsibility should lie with the mining profession. The briefing notes claim that it was unfair to argue that, with hindsight, the dangers should have been foreseen when no one had ever been killed by a tip.[107] The Minister was to concede that dangers could have been anticipated in south Wales where tips had slid before but, given that, it was strange that no one had ever asked the Inspectorate to assess tips. The brief also pointed out that when the Inspectorate was not carrying out its specific duties, it was looking at other areas of mining where experience had shown there were specific dangers.[108]

Such answers may have partially excused the failures of the Mines' Inspectorate but they hardly excuse the industry and its regulators' failure to look beyond the demands of extraction. This was the same narrow outlook that had left the industry behind the times in terms of marketing and sales. As a nationalised industry with a virtual domestic monopoly, that had initially mattered little. However, natural gas, nuclear power and international competition had begun to challenge that complacency. Aberfan now shook it to its core.

The other regulator of the NCB was the Coal Division of the Ministry of Power. It was never realistic to suppose that a dozen administrative civil servants could effectively regulate an employer of hundreds of thousands of people (60,000 in south Wales alone, in 1966). But it did not have to be as egregiously captive as it was in 1967. The Coal Division most frequently told ministers that Robens was indispensable. The Coal Division argued that a contractor must not be allowed to produce coal more cheaply than the Coal Board, or to clear away the Aberfan tips (this story is discussed in Chapter 5 below). When the Tribunal recommended that the 1954 Act 'should be extended to include provision for safety of the general public',

---

107. Incorrect. A boy had been killed at Pentre in 1909 (see above).
108. POWE 52/212 Aberfan Debate – Draft Brief, 23/10/67, role of HM Inspectorate of Mines & Quarries.

the Coal Division objected, calling this a 'revolutionary innovation'.
(However, the revolutionary idea that the NCB had a duty to the public
safety was incorporated obliquely into the 1969 Act and became a
central feature in the 1974 Health and Safety at Work Act.) We have
found only three acts of symbolic rebellion over Aberfan: the Division
refused to supply arguments in support of Robens' personal conduct,
it argued unavailingly that Morgan should be dismissed, and it
refused Robens' request to appoint Sheppard Deputy Chairman of
the Board. Otherwise, it saw its role purely as protection of the public
corporation it sponsored. The interests of the people of Aberfan and
the wider national interest were not among its concerns.[109]

A corporatist culture

Britain in 1966, at the height of post-war corporatism, had a
producer-dominated political culture. That encouraging competition
in coal might reduce prices was given as a reason against it. So
ingrained was British corporatism that the Tribunal devoted a section
of its report to discussing whether the NUM should be held partly to
blame for the disaster. It answered no; but even raising the question
implies that the union might be held formally responsible for running
the industry.[110] Indeed, even Will Paynter, General Secretary of the

---

109. *Aberfan Report*, p. 132. Recommendation XVIL. Robens indispensable:
POWE 52/94, R. Dearing to C. Thorley, 1 September 1967; POWE 52/215,
draft note for Minister to put to Cabinet, 25 August 1967. Ryan: see above.
'Revolutionary innovation': POWE 52/68. Coal Division memo on Tribunal
findings, 26 July 1967. Refusal to endorse Robens' conduct: BD11/3810,
briefing note for Aberfan debate, Section 2, 'The Chairman's evidence to the
Tribunal'. 'Require [Morgan's] resignation': POWE 52/94, R. Marshall to
A. Blackshaw, 31 July 1967. Refusal to promote Sheppard: POWE 52/94.
Dearing to Thorley, draft briefing note for Minister.
110. Just one corporatist move was frustrated. Wilson wanted to appoint a
miner as a member of the Tribunal. Edmund Davies refused, pointing out
that if a miner was appointed, then a mine manager would also have to be,
and that this would probably frustrate the Tribunal because the manager

NUM, felt that 'union leaders must accept some responsibility for the failure to anticipate and take action to avert this terrible disaster.'[111]

Corporatism may have heightened the influence of unions but it provided no remedy for corporations behaving badly and did little for the needs of consumers. The most shocking revelation from the papers released since 1996 is that the arrogance and obfuscation of the Coal Board continued unmodified after 21 October 1966. Lord Robens noted that at the Tribunal

> what was required of the National Coal Board was a simple plea of 'guilty'. This we were all ready to give, but we were misled by the terms of reference of the tribunal, which were framed to uncover facts rather than to apportion blame.[112]

Nobody else seems to have noticed the Coal Board's readiness to plead guilty, nor does it emerge anywhere that we have found in the National Archives. Although Lord Robens always insisted that he accepted liability on behalf of the Coal Board immediately after the disaster, this message did not reach the insurance department of the Coal Board. As late as April 1967, a Board insurance official wrote: 'We considered earlier whether to admit liability. At that time there had been no general admission of liability and I decided ... that it would be unwise to do so. However, in view of what transpired when the Chairman visited the [Tribunal] hearing last week, my officials ... have decided that the time is now ripe to accept liability'.[113] The Coal Board's internal insurance department was thus refusing to accept liability that, as Ackner reminded the Tribunal, was uncontested and incontestable, and that had lain on coal mine proprietors since 1869. Their attitude explains why Laurie Lee found 'crumpled song-books, sodden and smeared with slime, the words of some bedtime song still

---

would be inclined to side with his negligent colleagues. PREM 13/1280, Prime Minister's office memo, 22 October 1966.
111. Will Paynter, *My Generation* (London: Allen & Unwin, 1972), p. 130.
112. Robens, *Ten Year Stint*, pp. 252-3.
113. COAL 73/2, W.J.P. Webber memo, copied to Lord Robens, 25 April 1967.

visible on the pages surrounded by drawings of sleeping elves' when he visited the wreckage of Pantglas School in 1967 (chapter 1).

Corporatism and the power it gave the NCB saw the needs of Aberfan marginalised in the weeks, months and years that followed the disaster. The Board and government played out their own private game based on their own needs. Neither even said sorry. But that was not how things were done in those days.

3

Uneasy Relationships: The Aberfan Disaster, Merthyr Tydfil County Borough Council and Local Politics

'I was tormented by the fact that the people I was seeking justice from were my people – a Labour Government, a Labour council, a Labour-nationalised Coal Board.'

Bereaved husband and parent[1]

After the disaster, the NCB erected 37 caravans in Aberfan for those who had lost their homes when one of the Board's tips had collapsed. Its South-Western Division then issued a demand to the local council for £72 a year rent for each caravan. The Mayor called this 'scandalous' but A.H. Kellett, the divisional chairman, said it was a 'normal bookkeeping operation between two authorities.' He went on, 'That is as far as I am prepared to take it. It is unfortunate that it is Aberfan in this case.' In the end, Lord Robens intervened and the council were allowed to have the caravans rent-free.[2] Yet the fact that the NCB expected at first to be reimbursed was typical of

---

1. John Collins, quoted in an unaccredited press clipping. ADA, Merthyr collection, D/17.
2. *Daily Express*, 6 January 1967.

both its penny pinching and arrogance in the wake of the disaster and its disregard for both Aberfan and the local authority. It is an extraordinary example of its failure to accept liability that Ackner correctly described as 'uncontested and incontestable'.

The causes of the Aberfan disaster were rooted in not just the shortcomings of individuals within the National Coal Board but also the attitudes, structure and economic power of the Board itself. This chapter examines how this situation shaped the local political context, thus both contributing to the failure to prevent the disaster and governing aspects of its aftermath. It goes on to look at the impact of the disaster on the balance of power in local politics in the Aberfan area. Merthyr Tydfil County Borough Council (MTCBC) not only had to reassess its relationship with the village, but itself suffered heavily in the disaster's aftermath.

'A State within a state'[3]: the NCB in south Wales

In the atmosphere of disbelief and anger that follows disasters, there is often a questioning of and antagonism towards officialdom.[4] The National Coal Board was the obvious target for much of the local anger and the accusations that the disaster should have been avoided. But people looked to the Borough Council too. After all, the local authority had been receiving complaints about the tip and the flooding it was causing for years; if the Council had forced the issue with the NCB then the disaster might have been avoided. At public meetings that followed the disaster, the Borough Council's Director of Education and his colleagues suffered what he described as 'bitter' criticisms and 'expressions of hatred' that were sometimes personalised.[5]

---

3. IM interview with Alan Blackshaw, 1999.

4. David Cohen, *Aftershock: The Psychological and Political Consequences of Disaster* (London: Paladin, 1991), p. 65.

5. SWCC, Interview with John Beale (Director of Education, Merthyr Tydfil County Borough Council), 1986, AUD 521.

After the initial shock of the disaster, public anger in the village became more firmly focused on the NCB but the local authority was still in the dock as the Tribunal considered whether it should bear any responsibility for the tragedy. MTCBC had received complaints about flooding from the mountainside from 1949 and had expressed concern about the stability of the general tip complex from as early as 1944. In 1964 parents living nearby also passed a petition to the Pantglas headmistress complaining of the danger to children from the flooding. She forwarded it to the Council. Yet, despite pressurising the NCB on the matter, there was no resolution of the problems. The Tribunal noted that it could not understand why the Council could not reach 'an amicable settlement of what appears to be a simple drainage problem.'[6]

While the flooding was less serious in its consequences, anxieties (not unconnected) over a tip slide were potentially far graver. The NCB told MTCBC that there was no danger but that it would still investigate the matter. It did nothing and, in 1963-4, a series of letters headed 'Danger from coal slurry being tipped at the rear of the Pantglas Schools' were exchanged between the Borough Engineer's department and Mr D.L. Roberts, the NCB's local Area Mechanical Engineer. The language in the MTCBC letters was strong enough that the Tribunal considered that the Coal Board should have investigated the matter. Roberts visited the tip complex but 'treated the matter so cavalierly as to render his visit useless.'[7] Further concerns were expressed by the Council during the discussion of the NCB's plan for an aerial walkway to allow further tipping on the mountain. Yet, the Tribunal noted, the Board's assurances that all was fine were accepted and Council officials never inspected the tips themselves (a visit by any of the Council's qualified engineers would have revealed the potential dangers), pressed their complaints higher than area level in the NCB or took legal action to deal with a situation that 'they thought dangerous to their burgesses.'[8] Given that the problem

---

6. *Aberfan Report*, pp. 20-23.

7. *Aberfan Report*, p. 99.

8. The Tribunal's findings on the Council can be found in *Aberfan Report*, pp. 107-110. Quote from Attorney's Questions to the Tribunal. *Aberfan Report*, para 246.

was one of safety not planning, the Tribunal's implications that the Council could have used its planning powers (or indeed a summons for nuisance) to restrict tipping at Aberfan are unfair.

The language used in the Council's complaints to the NCB suggests considerable worry over the stability of the tips. However, Mr Bradley, the local authority's deputy engineer, told the Council's counsel that while he entertained fears of a substantial slip, he never imagined that it would lead to loss of life.[9] Yet even a small slip could have endangered lives and property but the Council still did not pursue the matter vigorously. Nonetheless, the Tribunal felt that the Council should not be 'condemned on hindsight' and pointed to what it had done in alleviating it of any blame. It received 'no enlightening help' from the Welsh Office of the Ministry of Housing and Local Government, to whom it had written in 1957 arguing that the tipping area should not be extended. It had secured a promise that no more tailings (fine particles which are the final discard of modern coal filtration; the Council justifiably felt they were a cause of tip instability) would be tipped. It received assurances from 'high-ranking' NCB personnel that there was nothing wrong with the tip. The Council's engineers were felt by the Tribunal to have been perfectly reasonable in their assumption that the NCB had qualified experts inspecting the tips. Tragically, this was not so.[10]

The Council's acceptance of the NCB's reassurances cannot be attributed to it trusting the board's judgements and words alone. Its counsel argued that:

the local authority can make representations to whomsoever it pleases, but in making those representations it is governed by the fundamental character of its being, namely that it is an elected body. In doing so it mirrors the feelings and expressions of the people it represents. If there is no further demand for a certain course of action not prescribed as a legal duty, the local authority takes this course at its peril, and particularly when such a course may – or may not – jeopardise the daily bread of its people.[11]

9. *Tribunal Transcript*, Day 53, p. 2983.
10. Quotes from *Aberfan Report*, para. 109.
11. *Tribunal Transcript*, Day 71, p. 4002.

Thus the Council's defence not only pointed towards what it did do but also argued that there was no popular demand for it to be more pressing in its concerns. As the counsel implied, the whole issue was complicated by the impact any restriction of tipping might have on the future of the Merthyr Vale colliery on which Aberfan was economically dependent. After the euphoria that greeted nationalisation in 1947, the 1950s and 1960s were a more sombre period for the coal industry. A programme of pit closures was gathering pace, which the NCB was felt to be executing unsympathetically.[12] Nor had the return of a Labour Government in 1964 halted the trend. That year there were 72,000 miners employed in the south Wales coalfield. By 1966 the figure was 58,000.[13] Amidst a wider backdrop of depopulation and social and cultural change in valleys communities, the closure of collieries was helping create a belief that a traditional working-class way of life was coming to an end. The growth of manufacturing in south Wales had tempered this unease but the ongoing job losses in the coal industry were starting to reawaken memories of the dark days of the 1930s.[14]

It was in this context that concerns over tip stability at Aberfan took place. The Tribunal spent almost two days considering whether fears over the future of the Merthyr Vale colliery had been a factor in the way local agencies handled the disaster. It concluded that the NCB was not considering closing the colliery but conceded that such fears were not groundless in the event of tipping being restricted. MTCBC's counsel argued that this context did not overrule all other considerations (in other words safety) but it must be considered when assessing what actions the Council took. Indeed, he claimed that the fear of unemployment must have been present in the minds of many in Aberfan.[15] S.O. Davies, the Labour MP for Merthyr Tydfil, went further. He claimed to have been worried about tip stability and the danger to the village but said he had not pushed the issue

---

12. Hywel Francis & David Smith, *The Fed: A History of the South Wales Miners in the Twentieth Century* (London: Lawrence and Wishart, 1980), p. 457.
13. Francis & Smith, *The Fed*, appendix IV.
14. Martin Johnes, *Wales since 1939* (Manchester: Manchester University Press, 2012), ch. 5.
15. *Tribunal Transcript*, Day 71, p. 4003.

because of fears amongst the workers that such a dispute would lead to the closure of the pit. However, the Tribunal rejected his evidence, arguing that he did not understand the grave implication of what he was saying and that he was affected by hindsight. Thus, while it would be wrong to assert that specific worries over the future of the Merthyr Vale colliery prevented action by the Council or other local bodies, the NCB's economic domination of the region did have repercussions on its general relationship with the local area. As the Tribunal argued, fears over the future of the pit may have subconsciously affected the attitudes and, in effect, the judgement of many. Taking the issue of tip safety too far could have had catastrophic consequences for Aberfan.[16]

Whether the fears over the tip and the future of the colliery were conscious or not, the result was a sense of guilt in Aberfan which hindered its recovery.[17] This issue also influenced the campaign to have the remaining tips removed from the mountainside above the village. In 1967, an Aberfan resident told Richard Marsh, the Minister of Power:

> The real reason we want that particular tip removed is that we cannot stand the sight of it. Many of us are aware that the reason no complaint was made about the tip, which we knew had water in it, but which obviously we never thought would do the damage it did, was our belief that if action were taken to renovate it or make it safe for a time, the additional cost would have rendered a pit uneconomic, and would have resulted in its closure.

Marsh has suggested that this sense of guilt strengthened an urge to blame the disaster upon bodies outside the local community.[18]

Merthyr Tydfil had become a county borough in 1908, bringing new responsibilities to its Corporation that touched upon many aspects of local life.[19] In the year of the disaster, Merthyr was the

---

16. *Aberfan Report*, p. 111.
17. MJ interview with Colin Murray Parkes.
18. Quoted in Marsh, *Off the Rails*, p. 117. MJ interview with Lord Marsh.
19. R.S. Evans, 'The Development of Local Government', in *Merthyr Tydfil: A Valley Community* (Merthyr, 1981), pp. 252-253. County boroughs

smallest all-purpose local authority in Wales, and the fifth-smallest in Britain. Since becoming a borough, its population had fallen by nearly 20,000 to just 57,000.[20] Most of the other county boroughs of a similar size were prosperous county towns. The only ones smaller than Merthyr were Canterbury, Burton-on-Trent, Great Yarmouth, and Dewsbury. None of these had anything remotely like Merthyr's social problems, compounded by population decline and the lowest rateable value per capita of any county borough.[21] In 1967, it was claimed that Merthyr's rates were the highest of any county borough in England and Wales.[22] That year, a white paper on local government in England and Wales suggested that Merthyr should cease to be a county borough. It noted that

> The Local Government Commission [for Wales, which reported in 1962] made a convincing case for regarding Merthyr Tydfil as too small and too lacking in resources to continue to carry out in modern conditions the full range of county borough functions and this case is strengthened by the further decline in its population since the Commission's report was published.[23]

(abolished in 1974 but re-created in Wales in 1996 under the title of unitary authorities) are all-purpose local authorities responsible for all local services.

20. 'Merthyr Tydfil Local Government Reorganisation', TNA: BD 11/3791.
21. *Registrar General's Statistical Review of England and Wales for the Year 1966* (London: HMSO 1967), Part I, Table 13. Bruce Wood, *The Process of Local Government Reform, 1966-74* (London: George Allen & Unwin, 1976), p. 117.
22. James Belt, a Residents' Association candidate in the Cyfarthfa Ward in Merthyr, also said that the average county borough rates in England and Wales were 12/9 in the £ while in Merthyr they were 17/6. *Merthyr Express*, 5 May 1967.
23. *Local Government in Wales*, Cmnd. 3340 (Cardiff: HMSO, 1967). The Welsh Office noted that the Council was 'violently angry about the proposal that the town should cease to be a county borough, arguing that their services are excellent. They have made particular reference to the way in which their education department coped with the aftermath of the Aberfan disaster.' Merthyr Tydfil Local Government Reorganisation, TNA: BD 11/3791.

The local authority's counsel at the Aberfan Tribunal argued that the Corporation was of 'modest dimensions but charged with functions as great as those of the cities of Cardiff, or Birmingham, or Liverpool' and that this should not be forgotten when considering the time and attention that it devoted to investigating the concern over the tips above Aberfan. Yet he still contended that it had done all that could be expected and acted with honour and dignity.[24]

Desmond Ackner QC, counsel for the parents' association, explained the Council's failures to push the matter by saying that

> as the tips overshadowed, towered above, and indeed dwarfed the village, so did the National Coal Board the Council. Those whose function and duty it was to look after the welfare of the inhabitants of Aberfan discharged that function admirably in all other respects, but in regard to this matter, in relation to the National Coal Board, they were not big enough for the job.[25]

The Corporation's counsel retorted that the

> National Coal Board from its very nature believed that no one outside its own confines could make an effective contribution, and if someone else other than the Merthyr Corporation, if the Welsh Office had made representations of the same character, they would have been treated likewise.[26]

Thus the question of why concerns about tip safety were not pushed further extended beyond subconscious fears about the future of the colliery into the very nature of the NCB itself. As MTCBC's counsel argued, the NCB was a powerful and arrogant organisation that felt it had a monopoly over all wisdom concerning the skills and precautions required in its industry. The question was not so much whether the Merthyr Corporation was too small but whether the NCB was so big that it was not easily approached or influenced and

---

24. *Tribunal Transcripts*, Day 71, p. 4006; Day 73, 4069.
25. *Tribunal Transcript*, Day 69, p. 3902.
26. *Tribunal Transcript*, Day 71, p. 4005.

could thus treat those local authority officials that did approach it with disdain and contempt.[27]

The causes of the disaster thus lay not just in the mistakes and fallibility of NCB employees but in the very nature and status of the Board itself. Its economic domination of the region meant that no one was keen to push complaints that might endanger the life of a colliery. Its nationalised monopoly meant it could brush aside the concerns of a small local authority, whilst regulation of its practices was minimal in the corporatist atmosphere of the 1960s. Added to this, was the board's large and bureaucratic character, that allowed the undetected breakdowns in communication between key members of staff that led to the tip not being properly inspected or maintained. For Aberfan, a village whose livelihood depended upon the NCB, the consequences of the board's shortcomings proved to be fatal.

Aberfan and local politics

When, after the publication of the Tribunal report, a meeting was held in Aberfan to discuss the possibility of criminal charges, it emerged that some people felt that the Tribunal should have blamed MTCBC as well as the NCB.[28] They found it difficult to accept that the local authority had been warned about potential dangers and not taken every possible precaution. Yet local disillusionment with the Council ran far deeper than the circumstances surrounding the disaster. MTCBC was naturally based in Merthyr itself (five miles to the north of Aberfan) and, to people in the village, the Council seemed remote and high-handed with little understanding or sympathy for its smaller outlying communities.[29] They felt that it had a history of neglecting Aberfan, not least in its failures to solve flooding in the village. In the aftermath of the disaster, a number of groups were formed in Aberfan to consider how the community could help itself cope and rebuild. In their discussions, the local authority was criticised for

---

27. *Tribunal Transcript*, Day 71, p. 4005.
28. NLW, Moseley papers, Attendance re Aberfan, 10 August 1967, file 6.
29. Miller, *Aberfan*, p. 20.

failing to provide safe play areas or adequate council housing, and for neglecting the environment and local infrastructure.[30] During the disaster's aftermath, it also became clear how some people saw local politics as nepotistic and self-serving. One villager told the Aberfan Parents' and Residents' Association solicitors that he did not complain about the tips because he felt that the councillors would not bite the hands that fed them. He regarded them as having 'cushy numbers' and easy jobs at the collieries.[31] While such an extreme view may have been a minority one, there was sometimes a general distrust of the three councillors who represented the ward of Aberfan.[32] Thus while the disaster itself was seen as a tragic manifestation of years of neglect by the local authority, it also exposed some of the latent anger over the way the village, like other mining communities in south Wales, had been treated by local government.[33]

Local disillusionment was compounded by some naive and ill-thought-out actions by MTCBC following the disaster. A duplicated standard letter of sympathy sent to the bereaved from the Mayor hardly conveyed an image of sincere personal empathy, but more serious errors of judgement were to follow.[34] A significant mistake was arranging for the pupils that had attended Pantglas school to be educated at nearby Merthyr Vale, on the other side of the valley. This school stood under a disused tip and had a clear view of the Aberfan cemetery where friends and relatives were buried. Attending the school would also have involved crossing the busy A470 trunk road. These factors naturally upset the parents and they lobbied for alternative arrangements. While the Council's plans would have been reasonable in other situations, they failed to take account of the special circumstances and consequently were seen as unnecessarily bureaucratic. The Council eventually gave way and erected a

---

30. Ken Roberts, *The Reconstruction of 'Community': Aberfan* (Coventry: Warwick Working Papers in Sociology, 1985), p. 11.
31. NLW, Moseley papers, Note dated 16 November 1966, file 1.
32. Austin, *Aberfan*, pp. 172, 180-181.
33. Elsewhere in the Valleys, this disillusionment had already led to Residents' Associations putting forward candidates at local elections. See, for example, *Merthyr Express*, 5 May 1967.
34. Austin, *Aberfan*, p. 178.

temporary classroom in Aberfan but by then the affair had already
further damaged relations with the village.[35]

The Corporation's control over the Disaster Fund also increased
tension between the local authority and the village. Disaster Fund
meetings took place in Merthyr not Aberfan which, as a care worker
in the village later pointed out, 'might have been a thousand miles
away'.[36] Early on, the Fund was thought to be acting very slowly
in everything from paying out money to the bereaved to deciding
what to do with the disaster site. This created significant local
tensions and it took a representation from the NUM before the
fund released any money to help immediate problems. Some of the
fund's hesitations centred upon the legal problems of giving out
donations before a trust deed with clear objectives had been drawn
up. However, such technicalities were hardly of concern to those in
Aberfan in need of the money that had been donated for their benefit.
Even as funds were slowly released, the village's representation on
the provisional committee was limited to just one local councillor
from its ward, although the lobbying of the Parents' and Residents'
Association's solicitor ensured that the villagers' wishes were at
least listened to.[37] The Council appeared to think there was no local
leadership in the village but it was also influenced by the fact that
under charity law recipients could not be trustees.[38] Concern also
arose over the fact that the money was temporarily invested in the
Corporation's mortgage stock. While this was logistically sensible,

---

35. Miller, *Aberfan*, pp. 116-117; Austin, *Aberfan*, p. 179; SWCC, Interview
with Mair Jones (headmistress), 1986, AUD 526; John Beale, 'Aberfan:
Recovery', unpublished paper in ADA, Merthyr collection, I/02, p. 1.
36. SWCC, Interview with Audrey Davey (Aberfan social worker), 1986,
AUD 524.
37. *The First Report of the Management Committee of the Aberfan Disaster
Fund*, 1968, p. 10. For an example of close communication between the
Fund and the solicitors representing the Aberfan residents see ADA,
Dowlais, C/006/26 & C/006/29. As one villager acknowledged, having
prominent members of the Welsh establishment on the committee did open
doors that Aberfan could not have opened on its own. SWCC, Interview with
Cyril Vaughan (former member of Disaster Fund Management Committee &
Parents' & Residents' Association), 1986, AUD 527.
38. Miller, *Aberfan*, p. 111.

with the village's minimal representation on the fund's provisional committee, it further aggravated a worsening relationship.[39] Some of these problems could have been avoided with better communication. The Council did gradually come to recognise its duty to fully inform villagers of what it was doing and consequently the atmosphere of distrust receded. Simple actions such as pinning minutes of Council meetings to notice boards in Aberfan went some way to repairing the relationship but the years after the disaster saw an atmosphere of distrust and suspicion between the village and local authorities.

While many of the tensions were misunderstandings and problems of communication, they were also products of the local political environment. Thanks to its integral links with the mining unions and its work during the depression, when other parties offered little more than despair and inactivity, the Labour Party dominated local and parliamentary politics in south Wales. However, after the triumph of its national successes in 1945-51 and lacking any realistic opposition, Labour in south Wales became complacent and somewhat removed from the communities it was meant to serve, something only too evident at Aberfan. While there were individuals who were popular, the political climate of the region had become stagnant and the support of communities was often assumed rather than worked for. The party's national policies were also beginning to lose their way. Manufacturing was only slowly making up for the pit closures (which in themselves were hardly the expected outcome of nationalisation) and unemployment was rising in a stagnant economy. Yet, at the March 1966 general election, Labour had reached a zenith by winning 32 of the 36 Welsh seats. Passive disillusionment with the party may have been growing but Labour were still entrenched, not only in the politics of the region, but also in its culture. Until a credible, radical alternative emerged, it was unlikely that this position would change.

Plaid Cymru's unexpected victory (helped by the disillusionment of local miners[40]) in the 1966 Carmarthen by-election provided that alternative. Suddenly the party was thrust into the limelight and

---

39. Benedict Nightingale, *Charities* (London: Allen Lowe, 1973), p. 180.
40. Francis & Smith, *The Fed*, p. 453.

seemed to become a serious alternative to the Labour hegemony. In July 1967, residents of Aberfan visited Westminster demanding an inquiry into the administration of the Disaster Fund. With their local representative, S.O. Davies, being a trustee of the fund, they instead asked for the 'MP for Wales', Gwynfor Evans, the new member for Carmarthen. Evans was not there but later refused to take up the cause for fear of being seen as making political capital out of the disaster.[41] The refusal of Plaid Cymru to become involved in the affairs of the disaster fund caused some minor consternation in Aberfan and a small group staged a demonstration in Cardiff claiming that the party had let them down.[42] Evans responded by saying that 'It would be unforgivable if Plaid Cymru did or said anything that would influence in any way the unhealed wound left by the tragedy. If we have disappointed some who wanted us to fight more publicly for a certain policy, the sole reason is our anxiety to do that which is best for all who are involved.'[43]

The well-publicised disputes over the Disaster Fund made any external intervention potentially controversial and emotionally provocative. Yet, given the public support for Aberfan's desire for a more generous distribution of the fund, this may have been a missed opportunity for Plaid Cymru. Nonetheless, the party continued to make electoral advances in south Wales during the late 1960s, almost winning by-elections in the safe Labour seats of Rhondda West and Caerphilly. It was threatening to become the radical new voice, not just of Welsh-speaking Wales, but also of ignored and marginalised industrial south Wales. The growth in Plaid Cymru's support across the south Wales valleys was rooted in the same general disillusionment that Aberfan felt with its Labour local authority. Indeed, the disaster perhaps symbolised all that was malignant about the political culture of south Wales.[44] For a brief period, out of

41. Robert Griffiths, *S.O. Davies: A Socialist Faith* (Llandysul: Gomer, 1983), p. 280.
42. *South Wales Argus*, 11 August 1967; *South Wales Echo*, 12 August 1967.
43. *Western Mail*, 14 August 1967.
44. Man-made disasters are often seen as points of reference that symbolise the political and social conditions of a particular moment.

the stagnation of Labour politics in south Wales and the tragedy of Aberfan, a new political force seemed to be emerging.

In 1968, S.O. Davies resigned from the Management Committee of the Disaster Fund in response to its agreement to pay £150,000 towards the removal of the remaining tips that overlooked Aberfan. Because of government pressure, the committee had little choice but to pay the money (see Chapter 5) and the situation angered Davies enormously, causing him to write a stinging letter to the Prime Minister. He asked Harold Wilson, 'Don't you think that the Aberfan Tips have already taken, far, far too much out of this village ...?'[45] The situation and later outbursts against Wilson further alienated Davies from his constituency party. His position was already in serious jeopardy because of his advanced age, he was by now approaching 90, and sympathy for Welsh nationalism. In 1970, Davies was deselected but, in the general election later that year, he was re-elected to Parliament as an independent Labour candidate; the first such case in Britain since 1945.[46]

Across Wales, Plaid Cymru's share of the vote rose from 4.3 per cent in the 1966 general election to 11.5 per cent in 1970. In some valley constituencies, Plaid's vote grew to over twice this figure. The constituencies in which the Plaid Cymru vote went up by 10 percentage points or more between 1966 and 1970 were, with only one exception, all either mining seats or Welsh-speaking seats.[47] The Party of Wales may have been emerging as an alternative voice for those unhappy with Labour but in Merthyr, with Davies taking the left-wing anti-Labour vote, Plaid Cymru's share actually fell.[48]

---

45. ADA, Dowlais collection, C/007/02.
46. See Griffiths, *S.O. Davies*, pp. 279-290 & Alun Morgan, 'The 1970 Parliamentary Election at Merthyr Tydfil', *Morgannwg*, 12, 1978.
47. The exception is Cardiff West: no PC candidate in 1966, 10.06 per cent PC vote in 1970.
48. Calculated from information in Arnold J. James & John E. Thomas, *Wales at Westminster: A History of the Parliamentary Representation of Wales, 1800-1979* (Llandysul: Gomer, 1981).

Table 3.1

Labour and Plaid Cymru share of the vote (percentage) in the eastern half of the south Wales coalfield (Merthyr and neighbouring constituencies), 1966 and 1970 General Elections[49]

	Aberdare	Bedwellty	Caerphilly	Pontypridd	Rhondda East	Rhondda West	Merthyr
1966	Lab 73.3 PC 8.6	Lab 86.2 PC 0	Lab 74.2 PC 11.1	Lab 74.9 PC 0	Lab 77.4 PC 7.5	Lab 76.1 PC 7.5	Lab 74.5 PC 11.5
1970	Lab 60.0 PC 30.0	Lab 74.6 PC 10.0	Lab 61.8 PC 28.5	Lab 58.5 PC 10.4	Lab 68.6 PC 24.3	Lab 74.8 PC 14.0	Ind. Lab 51.9 Lab 28.7 PC 9.6
% Mining*	21.2	23.5	23.9	10.7	17.1	18.7	12.4

*Percentage of employed engaged in mining or quarrying

NB No Plaid Cymru candidates stood in Bedwellty and Pontypridd in 1966

49 Derived from James & Thomas, *Wales at Westminster*; 1966 sample census; *The Times Guide to the House of Commons* (London: Times Newspapers Ltd, 1970).

Before the 1970 election, Davies had written to Harold Wilson to ask for the Disaster Fund money taken to remove the tips to be repaid, arguing that the Labour Party's chances in Merthyr might be destroyed if this was not done.[50] His stance over Aberfan was only one contributory factor to Davies' re-election, but it reinforced his reputation as an honest and principled politician at a time when the image of many of his profession, in both Parliament and Merthyr Town Hall, was somewhat different. Thus, at least temporarily, in the late 1960s there was a degree of political backlash against the Labour Party in the south Wales coalfield. Whereas in the past, the political stagnation had met with muted disquiet or indifference, voices of objection were now being raised. The link with Aberfan was not direct but it was a factor in exposing Labour's failings and, in the Merthyr constituency, it contributed to an independent rather than Plaid Cymru candidate taking much of the anti-government vote.

Far more significant than any post-disaster swing to Plaid Cymru after the disaster was the way the community took matters into its own hands. It formed residents' groups to put forward its opinions more clearly and effectively, which in turn contributed to the self-respect and confidence of the village. The Aberfan Parents' and Residents' Association, aided by the efforts of its solicitor, campaigned hard and became the village's public voice in a way that MTCBC, and even the ward's councillors, were not. These groups also became more important as the press reported and sometimes exaggerated quarrels in the village, furthering local resentment at the establishment and underpinning a sense that Aberfan had to stand up for itself. Yet the formation of local groups also led to further tension in the village's relationship with the Council. A brief written for the Prime Minister noted that

> This vigour of a kind of ad hoc democracy caused friction for a time with the Corporation (and in particular the Merthyr Vale Ward Members who cover Aberfan) who saw these organisations as usurping the functions of the elected Council members.[51]

50. S.O. Davies to Harold Wilson, 7 May 1970, SWCC: MNA/PP/16/37.
51. Prime Minister's Visit to Aberfan, Notes of people and affairs in the village, TNA: BD11/3814.

Where lobbying failed, elements of the village were prepared to take more radical action to ensure that their grievances were not ignored. Nineteen residents briefly refused to pay their rates because of a dispute over the uneven treatment given to different sections of the village and anger over the delay in cleaning up the disaster site and removing the school's ruins. The Parents' and Residents' Association accused Merthyr Council of 'sickening indifference' to the village. Again, the dispute owed much to the Council's failure to communicate its plans properly while the full clearing of the disaster site was awaiting the Tribunal's decision on who was liable. While this dispute continued, the debris from the disaster remained in a disturbing state. The dispute was quickly resolved but, nonetheless, it did illustrate the new determination in Aberfan to stand up against the traditional agencies of power.[52]

While the Disaster Fund was hesitating over making additional payments to bereaved parents, some parents even appealed for help from the Free Wales Army, a group of pseudo-militarists trying to bring about political independence for Wales through threats of violence. There were claims, although difficult to substantiate, that the FWA had threatened to blow up Merthyr town hall and 'all the councillors inside it' unless the Disaster Fund acted. The records of the Fund do not suggest that the FWA influenced its decision to make further payments to parents but at least one father thought they had and he purchased a gold watch to present to them as a thank you. Direct action was part of the cultural currency of the 1960s and frustration over the Government's delay in deciding whether to remove the remaining tips from above the village led a variety of different militant tactics to be considered, clearly revealing the greater resolve the disaster had brought about. The Tip Removal Committee saw such action as a last resort and was keen to avoid individual parents acting independently, especially after distress was caused by a fake bomb warning in the village. It circulated the community with notice of its plan 'to abandon letter-writing etc, and take some action to show the powers that be that we in Aberfan are not prepared to wait any longer.' It did not want to hurt or target any individual. Instead, the

---

52. Quoted in Nightingale, *Charities*, p. 182; Miller, *Aberfan*, p. 101; *Merthyr Express*, 17, 24 February 1967.

protest, it declared, must be 'against the lack of soul, lack of feeling, the absence of justice, against a reluctance of a governmental system to do the right thing by a community that has suffered so much.'[53] After a fractious meeting with the Secretary of State for Wales, where coal slurry from the tip was dumped on his desk, the decision was finally taken for complete removal (see chapter 5).

The reaction of Aberfan in forming groups to represent its needs and issues was characteristic of community reactions to disasters. In the wake of a significant disaster within a community there is normally a mass mobilisation of people and resources in order to meet immediate priorities such as rescue work. Subsequently, a period of consensus follows with high levels of community participation. This often leads to the questioning of decisions made by traditional authorities and demands for greater consultation.[54] Events in Aberfan followed this model through residents, including those not directly bereaved, trying to assume a degree of control in local affairs for themselves. When the relationship with the local authority appeared to be in disarray, there were plans to secure a greater say through standing against established councillors for election to the Borough Council in 1967. The seats were to be contested on a personal rather than party basis for the first time. Thus Aberfan began to follow a trend already established elsewhere in the valleys, of residents' associations putting up candidates against Labour because of the failure of 'political monopoly by one party'.[55] In a high turnout (68 per cent), the residents' association won 'considerable' support in Aberfan. However, overall in the Merthyr Vale ward, Labour managed to retain the two contested seats, but it could no longer be assured of its position.[56] Later that year, Eddie Thomas, a famous boxing trainer

---

53. Circular from Tip Removal Committee to village, nd (June or July 1968). Glamorgan Archives: Aberfan and Merthyr Vale Tip Removal Committee papers, D1368.
54. Kathleen J. Tierney, 'The Social and Community Contexts of Disaster', in Richard Gist & Bernard Lubin (eds.), *Psychosocial Aspects of Disaster* (New York: Wiley, 1989), pp. 23-4, 32.
55. Councillor from Dowlais Ratepayers' Association quoted in *Merthyr Express*, 3 March 1967.
56. *Merthyr Express*, 19 May 1967.

from Merthyr, planned to stand as a Plaid Cymru candidate against the Mayor, while attacking him personally over the Disaster Fund.[57] The fact that Thomas was from outside Aberfan was an indication of just how widely the disaster had coloured people's perceptions of local politics.

It is a further characteristic of the aftermath of disasters that the recovery period is marked by disillusionment and conflict.[58] The stresses of the situation and the already broken social norms can lead to behaviour that would otherwise be untypical. The cases of internal conflict within Aberfan became infamous yet very greatly exaggerated. Much can be put down to the work of unscrupulous journalists taking comments out of context and misusing them.[59] Nonetheless, a perception of a divided community at Aberfan has survived to an extent and has been instrumental in more recent disasters taking careful steps to prevent any sort of similar public conflict, real or imagined.[60] Such divisions and disillusionment often lead to a gradual reduction in community participation in local politics and, again, Aberfan followed this pattern. No candidates from the Aberfan Ratepayers' Association stood at the next set of local elections. In the by-election following the death of S.O. Davies in 1972, the official Labour Party candidate was elected; normal party politics had clearly resumed.[61] The election of a Conservative government in 1970 had revitalised Labour's blanket

---

57. The personal nature of the attacks attracted much criticism and led to the local Plaid Cymru branch threatening to withdraw its support. Thomas eventually decided not to stand. *Merthyr Express*, 18 June 1967.

58. Tierney, 'Social and Community Contexts of Disaster', p. 31.

59. SWCC, Interview with Rev. Kenneth Hayes, Bryn Carpenter & Doug Pearson. AUD 528.

60. For example, see Roger W. Suddards, *Administration of Appeal Funds* (London: Sweet & Maxwell, 1991), ch. 2.

61. Ted Rowlands secured the seat in 1972 with a majority of 3,710 over Plaid Cymru whose vote had increased by 385 per cent. In the 1970 general election, S.O. Davies had won a majority of 7,467 over the official Labour Party candidate. Normal politics had resumed but the rising tide of Plaid Cymru was still evident. Indeed, in 1976 Plaid Cymru won a majority on the Merthyr Council. Figures calculated from James & Thomas, *Wales at Westminster*, p. 176.

support across south Wales, demonstrating that the rise of Plaid Cymru had been largely a transient reaction to the disillusionment with Wilson's administration rather than the beginning of a genuine political realignment.

Yet, in Aberfan, despite the renewal of the Labour hegemony, community groups remained active in the village to a far greater extent than they ever had been before the disaster. To this day, Aberfan boasts groups from a local nursery to a male voice choir to a village magazine, whose origins lie in the community activity that developed in response to the disaster. There is also a determination in Aberfan not to let bureaucracy and authority allow dangers to go unseen or implement schemes that would be harmful to the community.[62] Consequently the village is much stronger for it.

Disaster Management and Merthyr Tydfil County Borough Council

For all the justifiable complaints thrown at it, the disaster left MTCBC in a difficult position to which it adapted to its credit. It found itself having to cope with many and varied practical tasks in the days, months and even years that followed the tragedy. Its initial involvement was naturally in the rescue operation where Council employees played an important role. Yet even then they were subject to criticism. A Civil Defence Officer, who was decorated for his efforts in the operation, accused Council officials of not having made themselves prominent or even known.[63] The accusations were

---

62. SWCC, Hayes, Carpenter & Pearson interview, AUD 528. This determination reached its peak in the village's successful campaign to overturn plans to run the new A470 through Aberfan. The planned route would have cut the village off from the cemetery. The route finally chosen runs above the cemetery and through the disaster slide site.
63. The Civil Defence Officer was responding to allegations from the Chief Constable that he had been decorated for something he didn't do. ADA, Dowlais, B/007/08.

strongly denied, and although there was some confusion in the rescue operation, the Council appears to have conducted itself admirably.

The disaster dominated the attention of the Council in the following months. Individual senior Council officials, particularly the Town Clerk and the Director of Education, found themselves having to cope with an excessively large workload. Tasks such as compiling evidence for the Tribunal and finding alternative housing and educational facilities were time-consuming, emotional and controversial duties that had to be carried out in difficult circumstances. The Director of Education wrote, 'in those early days of shock and intense grief it was far from easy to think coolly, perceptively and with future horizons in mind.'[64] Within his department, the limited number and experience of the staff made the problem worse. Consequently, the responsibility, 'strain and pressure ... weighed heavy' on them.[65] Even non-urgent work such as dealing with the sacksful of letters that arrived at its offices every day was beyond the Council's means. It was forced to take on volunteers who worked late into the night, acknowledging the donations that arrived.[66] The impact of the small size of the borough upon its Council's resources was being exposed by the disaster. Inevitably, some normal services were forgotten in the early chaos.[67] Council meetings were suspended and other tasks were put aside. One Aberfan pensioner, for instance, complained that her meals-on-wheels had not been delivered.[68] Yet the fact that the whole process of local government in Merthyr did not temporarily collapse was a tribute to the resourcefulness and energy of the Council staff.

As well as having to cope with the extra administrative tasks, some Council members and officers also had to live with the guilt that they might have personally done something to prevent the disaster. Even after the Tribunal Report exonerated the Council, individual officials

---

64. Beale, 'Aberfan: Recovery', p. 1.
65. SWCC, Beale interview, AUD 521.
66. Miller, *Aberfan*, p. 30; Austin, *Aberfan*, p. 180.
67. Such an administrative overload was characteristic of the problems experienced by other local government in post-disaster situations. See Allen H. Barton, *Communities in Disaster: A Sociological Analysis of Collective Stress Situations* (Ward Lock Educational, 1969), pp. 284-94.
68. ADA, Dowlais, B/002/17.

must have wished that they had pressed their concerns harder.[69] Adding to the pressure was the constant attention of the world's media. In particular, Stanley Davies, the Mayor, found himself in the spotlight and subject to levels of pressure that he could never have imagined his period of office would entail. The confusion and cases of misinformation that followed the disaster did not help his position. Incidents such as publicly accepting an offer that had never been made of a new school from the Canadian government were embarrassing for the Mayor and added to his difficulties.[70] Davies' health deteriorated under the pressure and he died suddenly in 1969. As one villager put it, 'The burden of his cares for us in Aberfan really brought about his death.'[71]

During the rescue operation, the various organisations, companies and individuals involved had ignored or bypassed usual procedures to help the victims and their families. The inevitable result was confusion and a bureaucratic nightmare. Voluntary and public departments wanted equipment back, while companies and traders wanted compensation for goods and services supplied. With no obvious alternative body to take responsibility, claims were sent to the Council. Thus it was left with the unenviable task of assessing who was liable for what and for how much. In the confusion and haste of the rescue operation, equipment such as picks and shovels had been lost and goods eaten or used before they could be accounted for. In many cases, there was simply no way of verifying that the value being claimed was justifiable or indeed that the goods had even been supplied at all. Government departments might be understanding over the loss of their shovels but others were not always so.[72] The prolonged arguments over who should foot the bill for 100,000 paper cups illustrated the extremes that arose.[73] One firm appears to have tried to take advantage of the confusion by asking for payment for 100,000 sandbags which were allegedly never supplied

---

69. *Aberfan Report*, pp. 107-10.
70. See Austin, *Aberfan*, pp. 170-71.
71. SWCC, Vaughan interview, AUD 527.
72. See the correspondence between the Council and the Ministry of Health. ADA, Dowlais, B/002/09.
73. ADA, Dowlais, B/001/47.

or ordered. The invoice was passed between different organisations amidst denials of being responsible for ordering the bags. It took an investigation by the Welsh Office to reveal the possibly fraudulent nature of the claim by the suppliers.[74] Such confusion simply placed more pressure on the already beleaguered Council.

The growing number of claims had its own momentum, thus adding to the workload. A fish and chip proprietor from Aberfan noted that he had supplied goods, with no intention of claiming costs, as part of what he took as a common effort. It was only since other shopkeepers were submitting claims that he felt he should do the same.[75] A trust deed for the Disaster Fund was not drawn up until January 1967 and a secretary/treasurer not appointed until May that year. Before then, sorting out much of this bureaucratic nightmare fell on the shoulders of the Council's town clerk and treasurer who respectively acted as honorary secretary and treasurer of the provisional committee of the Disaster Fund. They were tasks that brought great anxieties and little credit.

Dealing with the housing problems that many villagers faced was perhaps the most difficult task the Council faced. Houses had been destroyed, others damaged and many people evacuated as a safety precaution. Organising alternative accommodation and repairing damaged houses was no easy task. It required patience, tact and hard work on the part of the Council. With some evacuated residents wishing to return to their houses immediately, irrespective of any danger, and others expressing completely understandable but almost irrational fears, finding a compromise was not easy.[76] In the end, the Council had no option but to let individuals decide for themselves. The Secretary of State for Wales was asked to appoint independent consultants to assess the damage to houses.[77] This was a task that would have normally been undertaken by the Council's own housing department but, in the circumstances, they felt it was best done by outside experts. With the world's eyes upon Aberfan, should the Council make a mistake or do anything that could be deemed thoughtless or inappropriate then a

---

74. See ADA, Dowlais, C/009/03.
75. ADA, Dowlais, C/009/03.
76. For example, see ADA, Dowlais, B/004.
77. ADA, Dowlais, B/001/26.

swift backlash would be inevitable. The people of Aberfan had already suffered enough at the hands of authority and there was likely to be little sympathy for anyone else who was deemed to be hindering the village further. The residents of Aberfan too were more likely to accept the word of outside experts rather than that of the local establishment who had already let them down.

Many of the logistical and legal problems that the Council faced were entirely new to it. It had neither the experience nor ability to foresee many of the potential problems. In overcoming such hurdles, the Council was helped greatly by the Welsh Office, which fulfilled its role as an important link between local and central government. For example, it tried to persuade the Council and NCB to communicate over the Disaster Fund to ensure the money was handled sensibly.[78] Civil servants also anticipated problems over donors to the fund wanting large sums given to the bereaved families regardless of need. Thus the Welsh Office advised some sort of consultation with the large donors to avoid any such problems.[79] It also stressed the need to make clear publicly that the village was been consulted over the use of the fund and suggested that the Council should encourage the formation of a residents' group with whom visible liaison could take place.[80] Of course, as a government department, the Welsh Office was anxious to avoid any controversy that might cast further bad light on the establishment. However, its advice and active help aided significantly the local authority in dealing with the disaster's aftermath. Much of the good work the Welsh Office did was overshadowed in the controversy that surrounded its obstinate role in the funding of the removal of the remaining Aberfan tips (chapter 5). However, although a great deal of the Welsh Office's work was not visible to the public, Merthyr Tydfil Borough Council fully appreciated it.[81]

---

78. ADA, Dowlais, B/002/06.
79. Similarly, the Council were legally advised to avoid having too many representatives on the Management Committee of the Fund for fear of giving the impression that it was using the Fund to escape its own responsibilities. ADA, Dowlais, C/005/25-26.
80. ADA, Dowlais. C/005/42.
81. For example, see the thanks to the Education Department in Beale, 'Aberfan: Recovery', p. 7.

The fledgling department was proving its, and the case for devolved government's, worth.[82]

Yet, at the same time, the Welsh Office Under-Secretary designated to liaise with Aberfan saw the village as 'emotionally wrought', wrote of moderates and extreme factions in the village and sought local allies to help him deal with the 'Aberfan folk'.[83] When it came to the tip removal, the Under-Secretary thought the village would expect a degree of consultation on technical matters 'beyond what would be reasonable, and they may have to be spoken to firmly.'[84] He believed he had a friendly relationship with the village,[85] but he later said that he would not read all of the second report of the Disaster Fund Management Committee and recommended that the Secretary of State for Wales not read it at all.[86] The Welsh Office undoubtedly helped the local council but its more direct dealings with the village disclosed a civil service that seemed more concerned with finance and minimising the public outcry than seeing to the needs of the village.

The disaster also left the Council with a financial burden as it tried to meet the numerable administrative costs and much of the price of the rescue operation. While the NCB did compensate the Corporation for the loss of the two Aberfan schools, it was slow in paying up. Even in March 1970, the NCB had only paid £50,000 of the Council's £200,000 claim. It did not settle in full until August that year. This must have had serious effects on the cash flow of the smallest county borough in Wales.[87] Similarly, while it had been agreed in principle

---

82. The historian K.O. Morgan, has suggested that, by bringing government closer to the people, the Welsh Assembly will prevent the type of injustices that Aberfan suffered at the hands of government. K.O. Morgan, 'Welsh devolution: the past and the future' in Bridget Taylor & Katarina Thomson, (eds.), *Scotland and Wales: Nations Again?* (Cardiff: University of Wales Press, 1999), pp. 199-219.
83. TNA, Siberry to PSO, Welsh Office, 8 June 1967, BD 11/3802. Also see, for example, Siberry to Treasury, 27 February 1968, BD 11/3804.
84. TNA, Siberry to Daniel, 11 December 1968, BD 11/3806.
85. TNA, Siberry to Erastus Jones, 17 October 1968, BD 11/3814.
86. TNA, Siberry to King, 5 October 1970, BD11/3814.
87. McLean, 'On Moles and the Habits of Birds', pp. 289-290; *Merthyr Express*, 20 August 1970.

that the state should meet the expenses incurred by the Corporation at the Tribunal, securing payment was a lengthy, problematic process that encountered repeated delays and queries. The series of letters between MTCBC and various government departments are a clear indicator of the excessive bureaucracy that plagued the public sector. Even the price of curtains for the Tribunal was queried by the Ministry of Works.[88] Financial remuneration was ultimately forthcoming but the continual delays were yet another headache for Council officials to cope with.

The Council officials were as touched by the disaster as everyone else in the region and they did try and alleviate the suffering in the village in the months, and years, that followed. Hence the Council almost immediately supported the complete removal of the remaining tips overlooking the village and argued that there were strong psychological grounds to demolish rather than rebuild the Pantglas schools.[89] Yet its previous neglect of Aberfan, implication in the disaster's cause and a series of clumsy errors in the aftermath meant that much of the Council's good work and own problems were obscured. Achievements such as securing money for a nursery despite a government moratorium on such spending or the sympathetic and flexible handling of bereaved children returning to school were significant.[90] Such work did much to make up for the Council's earlier mistakes and deserves credit.

Merthyr Tydfil County Borough Council undoubtedly learnt from its mistakes. After the furore over the initial minimal representation of villagers on the committee of the Disaster Fund, it helped devise a very carefully considered plan to elect representatives from Aberfan. The exact election process caused further controversy but this time the Council officials involved made every effort to ensure that it was done fairly and took into consideration the views of all concerned.[91] Similarly, there was a new determination in the Council that the NCB fulfil all its safety obligations in future. After the tragedy, there was

88. ADA, Dowlais, D/001/68-69.
89. ADA, Dowlais, C/005/32 & C/005/51.
90. SWCC, Beale interview, AUD 521.
91. *First Report of the Management Committee of the Aberfan Disaster Fund*, pp. 11, 20. Also see ADA, Dowlais, C/006/13, C/006/16.

concern in the neighbouring village of Merthyr Vale over the safety of a tip there. The Council wasted no time in ensuring that it was fully inspected and declared safe. No further risks were to be taken, no matter how small.[92] The Council was also no longer willing to tolerate misdemeanours of any kind by the Coal Board. Hence the dropping of refuse on the road by lorries travelling from the Merthyr Vale colliery now brought harsh warnings where in the past it would have been ignored.[93]

A number of lessons for disaster management can be derived from Merthyr Council's handling of the Aberfan disaster. Disasters present considerable administrative and logistical problems that must be handled sensitively if the suffering of the victims is not to be exacerbated. Such difficulties can only be surmounted through a flexible approach that is willing to depart from bureaucratic norms. Central to that approach must be a consideration of the interests of the bereaved and survivors. Merthyr Council gradually learnt this lesson but not until after it had angered people in Aberfan and damaged its relationship with the community. Today, the need for a versatile approach that prioritises victims and the bereaved is set out in the disaster management guidelines laid down by the Emergency Planning Department of the Home Office and similar bodies.[94]

Such guidelines are invaluable. Merthyr Council made mistakes because of its inexperience in dealing with any situation remotely comparable with the disaster. Most local authorities today would find itself in a similar position should they have to cope with disaster. Thus the attempts to disseminate the lessons and experiences of earlier disasters are vital if future mistakes are to be avoided. There is also perhaps an argument for the creation of a specialist and experienced, government-funded, disaster response team. Such a unit would advise and help those services and authorities dealing with the aftermath of a disaster. The idea of a lead 'disaster squad' was rejected by the government in 1989 to keep 'prime responsibility'

92. For example, see ADA, Dowlais, B/001/45.
93. ADA, Dowlais, B/001/36.
94. See, for example, Emergency Planning Society, *Responding to Disaster: The Human Aspects*, Guidance Document, 1998.

for handling disasters at the local level.[95] In the absence of any such body, policy guidance and the dissemination of lessons and information takes on added importance and there was indeed much work undertaken to learn from the experiences of the disasters of 1980s. In the absence of any major domestic disaster in the UK during the 1990s and 2000s, how effectively those lessons have been learnt and disseminated remains to be seen.

'My people'

The anger that followed the Aberfan disaster was contributed to by the political context in which the tragedy and its aftermath took place. As one bereaved father remembered 'I was tormented by the fact that the people I was seeking justice from were my people – a Labour Government, a Labour council, a Labour-nationalised Coal Board.'[96] The disaster presented the local political establishment with a colossal challenge. It was to be a challenge that both revealed the strengths and shortcomings of Merthyr Tydfil County Borough Council. The disaster had its origins in the inability of the Council to overcome the arrogance of the NCB arising from the latter's dominant position in the local economy and the former's limited resources. The intense public concern and pressure that followed the disaster changed that relationship but the Council was still left with an immense administrative task in the tragedy's aftermath. It was a tribute to the energy and resourcefulness of its staff that the extreme workload that the disaster created was coped with, despite intensive media attention and the extremely difficult and emotional circumstances. Initially mistakes were made but these were gradually overcome and a new relationship established with the inhabitants of Aberfan.

---

95. See *Hansard*, 6th series, vol. 154, col. 512, written answer by Douglas Hurd.
96. John Collins, quoted in an unaccredited press clipping. ADA, Merthyr collection, D/17.

Aberfan, with the mine in the foreground, the tips on the mountain and Pantglas Junior School on the right. (© South Wales Police Heritage Centre)

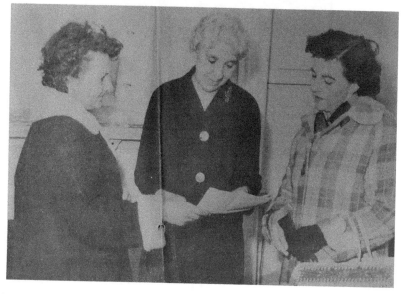

Ann Jennings, the headmistress of Pantglas Junior School receiving a petition from concerned parents in 1964 about the potential danger of the tips above the school. The headmistress took the petition to Merthyr Council but the parents' fears were ignored. (© Media Wales)

19 May 1947: This aerial image shows Aberfan tip no. 4 having already slipped (which the National Coal Board attempted to deny had happened) with run-off pointing directly towards the farm and school that were destroyed in 1966. (© RCAHMW)

14 September 1963: This shows tip no. 7 (the disaster tip) with spoil directly on top of the run-off material shown in the 1947 photo. (© RCAHMW)

FROM: Divisional Chief Engineer.

TO: Area Chief Engineers.
        Area Mechanical Engineers.
        Area Civil Engineers.
        Group Engineer, Somerset & Bristol.

Date: 12th April, 1965.

SUBJECT: Control and Management of Colliery
         Rubbish Tips.

An incident occurred recently within a Colliery of this Division involving the slipping of the rubbish tip resulting in severe financial loss. I should, therefore, if you would arrange with your colleagues, for a detailed examination of every tip within your area, and to take the necessary action for its immediate safety and ultimate good management.

A copy of a report is attached, indicating certain conditions that should be borne in mind during the examination, and I should be obliged if you could let me have a report by Friday, the 30th April, 1965.

I would like to draw your attention specifically to the dangers of including material such as "tailings" in the general rubbish for disposal, and in particular to the serious adverse affect this type of material has on the angle of repose that can be expected.

(signature)

---

repose from as high as 27° to as low as 4/5°. The tip then becomes completely unmanageable.

6. **Precautions to Prevent Sliding.**

6.1. The height of a tip should be limited to avoid overloading the supporting ground.

6.2. Where a slide would cause damage to property, no tip over 20 feet high should be placed on a hillside unless the ground is a compact gravel or of better quality than this.

6.3. The advancing tip should be so aligned, along a sloping surface, that water draining off the ground above it can be collected, if necessary, by a system of drains cut in the ground, and led past and clear of the tip. Along the uphill edge of the advancing tip, no bays or recesses should be formed in which water can collect.

6.4. On the dip side of the tip, deep drains (not less than 18 inches) should be cut leading downhill to prevent water accumulating and to keep the ground dry. A herringbone system is illustrated in Appendix VII as well as the method of packing the drains with flat stones placed on edge.

6.5. Tipping should never be extended over springs of water, where continuous or intermittent, or over bogged and water-logged ground.

6.6. The composition of the tip material must be carefully watched for variation and the disposal of materials, such as "tailings" must be carried out separately, preferably into redundant shafts or similar enclosures where the failure to maintain a good angle of repose is of no consequence.

12 April 1965: The Powell Memorandum.

Following a tip slide at Tŷ Mawr Colliery, Rhondda, in March 1965, the NCB's Divisional Chief Engineer D.L.J. Powell circulated a memorandum warning of the danger of slides, listing specific recommendations, to mine engineers across south Wales. (© Crown Copyright)

Friday 21 October 1966: Following weeks of heavy rain, tip no.7 slid down the mountain towards the farm, the school and the village of Aberfan. (© South Wales Police Heritage Centre)

(Above) 9.25am: 'The tip has come down on the school'. The first news of the landslide reaches Merthyr police station. (© South Wales Police Heritage Centre)

(Below) The official entries from the log book as the emergency services are alerted. (© South Wales Police Heritage Centre)

Within minutes the emergency services arrived at the scene, to be joined by miners from the local colliery, many of whom were fathers of the children at Pantglas School. (© South Wales Police Heritage Centre)

"We didn't know what to expect. I had no idea of the scale of the thing. It was a great shock. There was absolute chaos and somehow I had to organise that chaos", John Parkman, Senior Police Officer. (©South Wales Police Heritage Centre)

(Left) A rescued child is carried from the remains of the school as distraught and bewildered mothers wait for news of their sons and daughters.
(© Media Wales)

(Below) Hundreds of volunteers, having heard of the disaster on news broadcasts, travelled immediately from across Wales to assist in the desperate rescue effort.
(© Media Wales)

(Above) No children were found alive after 11am.
(© South Wales Police Heritage Centre)

(Left) 'Among the rubble', wrote the young journalist Laurie Lee, 'there also lie crumpled song-books, sodden and smeared with slime'.
(© Media Wales)

(Above) After all hope of finding survivors had ebbed away, volunteers continued the heartbreaking task of recovering bodies from the vast expanse of slurry. (© South Wales Police Heritage Centre)

(Right) Houses in nearby streets were devastated, with many residents losing everything. (© Media Wales)

Prime Minister Harold Wilson (centre), Welsh Office Minister George Thomas MP (right), and Secretary of State for Wales Cledwyn Hughes MP (left) visit Aberfan. (© Media Wales)

Lord Robens, Chairman of the NCB, with local Coal Board officials in Aberfan. (© Crown Copyright)

The headlines in the *South Wales Evening Post* (above) and the *Sunday Citizen* (below) tell the harrowing story.

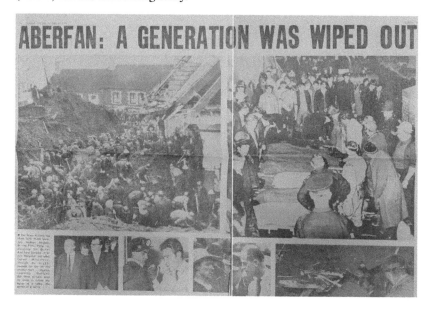

'Don't blame God, blame stupid men'

'We told them the whole blasted lot would come down—and it has, hasn't it?'

Newspaper headlines from (top to bottom) the *Sunday Express*, *The News of the World* and *The People*.

(Right) 'They have killed our children'. *The South Wales Echo* reports on the first day of the Inquest. (© Media Wales)

(Above) A nation in disbelief. An evocative illustration from the *Sunday Citizen*.

(Left) 'We are absolutely without contrition': a scathing editorial in the *South Wales Argus* takes aim at NCB Chairman Lord Robens. (© South Wales Argus)

Press Statement

ABERFAN DISASTER - RELIEF TO FAMILIES

In the spirit of the declaration by the Prime Minister that immediate relief should be given to all who have suffered as a result of this disaster, the National Coal Board, in agreement with the Mayor of Merthyr and in consultation with the Welsh Office, is to pay £50 to every family which has lost a member.

Eight parties of N.U.M. and N.C.B. officials are now visiting homes in the village and payment to the 140 families involved should be completed within a few hours.

National Coal Board
Merthyr Vale

25th October 1966

The initial £50 compensation payment was later increased to £500.

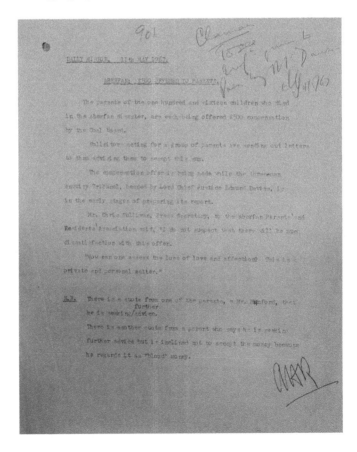

Thursday 27 October 1966. The mass burial of 81 children. The grieving families are joined by Welsh Office Minister George Thomas MP. (© Media Wales)

The victims of the Aberfan disaster with the coal tips still looming large in the background. (© Media Wales)

9.13am, 21 October 1966: a moment that will be forever etched in the memories of many people in Wales, and beyond, recorded by a clock recovered from Pantglas Junior School. (© Media Wales)

The disaster left an indelible mark on the village and the lives of those who lived there. Yet an examination of local politics in the area illustrates how some good has come out of the tragedy. Before the disaster, the interests of Aberfan and other similar communities were marginalised by both local and national government due to the entrenchment of the Labour Party in Welsh politics. A lack of competition had induced a state of complacency. The interests of those communities who had helped create the Labour hegemony were consequently marginalised since there was no urgent need on the part of the party to seek votes or new ideas. Instead, such thinking was left to the national party.

Although not a realistic parliamentary threat, the rise of Plaid Cymru drew upon the resultant dissatisfaction and forced the Labour Party to reassess both its position and policies in Wales. In Aberfan, this dissatisfaction and the anger that emerged out of the disaster was partly aimed at the Merthyr Corporation, a local authority that, under a burden of excessive work and in the stagnant political atmosphere, had also lost touch with its outlying communities. The disaster revealed the fatal danger of the complacency that prevailed in the Council and especially the cumbersome NCB. Consequently, it reawoke the political will of the village and ensured that they were no longer willing to tolerate apathy and mismanagement from above. The more extreme challenges to the local establishment that arose may have been relatively short-lived but their legacy was a number of active community groups and projects in Aberfan that continue to serve the village. Once the local establishment began to recover from the heavy burdens that the disaster placed upon it, it too took a more active interest in the welfare and the safety of those who it served. The new voices from below were now finding ears above that listened. Such empowerment has not been able to overcome wider economic trends. In 1989 the Merthyr Vale colliery shut and Aberfan today suffers from the same hardships that the rest of the south Wales valleys are experiencing. Nor can anything ever make up for the tragedy of 21 October 1966, but the revitalisation of the local political context is a welcome development and its legacy should ensure that Aberfan is never so catastrophically ignored again.

4

The Management of Trauma

'[One bereaved father would at times go] into a room on his own and sit down and just grieve and he was then in agony trying to visualise what his wife and his children went through before they died. ... [T]his is what is happening in dozens of homes in the village.'[1]

Note by APRA solicitor

Post-Traumatic Stress Disorder

The survivors, bereaved and wider community have to face many traumatic problems in the aftermath of a sudden and unexpected man-made disaster. Acute grief, denial and detachment, anger and hypervigilance are all common responses that must be managed before lives can be rebuilt. For some victims, these reactions can be severe and long lasting. Since 1980, this has been classified as Post-Traumatic Stress Disorder (PTSD), a condition that acknowledges that extremely traumatic events can produce chronic responses in normal individuals. The traumatic experience need not be catastrophic but rather any event that is exceptional and threatens the physical wellbeing or integrity of self or others.

The concept of PTSD grew out of work on Vietnam veterans and victims of other man-made disasters such as the Holocaust, the effects of the atom bombs on Japanese cities during World War Two and the

---

1. NLW Cyril Moseley Papers, File 2, 'Note', 22 November 1966.

effects of being taken hostage.[2] The observation of chronic responses to trauma has a longer history, dating back to studies of what was then called 'shell shock' in troops who served in the First World War. However, before the diagnosis of PTSD, prolonged disorders following trauma were often conceptualised as anxiety or depressive neuroses and ascribed to pre-existing psychiatric problems. In such cases, disasters or other causes of extreme stress were considered 'nonspecific triggers that might serve to release, exacerbate, or prolong a predictable diathesis to psychiatric symptoms'.[3] With PTSD, in contrast, the emphasis is placed upon external stressors rather than pre-existing psychological conditions. However, the prevalence and exact nature of PTSD remain controversial.[4] Many of its symptoms overlap considerably with general anxiety and stress disorders thus complicating the validity of its classification as a separate condition. It is also debatable whether the emphasis should be on the actual event itself or the cultural and social significance that is placed upon it. Different people and cultures can regard similar events in different fashions and not everyone who experiences a traumatic event develops PTSD.[5]

Although PTSD was not a recognised condition in 1966, there was, by the late 1950s, a growing awareness in the USA of the potential long-term psychological effects of disasters. Yet much of the evidence for what was termed 'disaster syndrome' was

---

2. Peter E. Hodgkinson & Michael Stewart, *Coping with Catastrophe: A Handbook of Disaster Management* (London: Routledge, 1991), p. 11. For a synthesis of the development of the knowledge of trauma in war veterans see Judith Lewis Herman, *Trauma and Recovery: From Domestic Abuse to Political Terror* (London: Pandora, 1994), pp. 20-8.
3. Rachel Yehuda & Alexander McFarlane, 'Conflict between Current Knowledge about Posttraumatic Stress Disorder and its Original Conceptual Basis', *American Journal of Psychiatry*, 152, 12 (1995).
4. L.N. Robins, 'Steps towards evaluating post-traumatic stress reaction as a psychiatric disorder', *Journal of Applied Social Psychology*, 20 (1990), 1674-1677. It can be argued that diagnostic tools for PTSD are subject to a Western bias and thus not always appropriate in different cultural contexts.
5. Gerald C. Davison & John M. Neale, *Abnormal Psychology* (New York: John Wiley, 7th edn, 1997), p. 147.

anecdotal and its influence in Britain was marginal.[6] There were varied views and opinions about how to deal with the problems but very little conclusive evidence about what techniques worked. American social workers felt their professional skills could have a critical role in helping victims come to terms with their experience. Yet the UK centre of academic evidence-based psychiatry in 1966, Maudsley Hospital, did not accept that social workers had a primary role.[7] Survivors of disasters instead had to rely on local support networks and whatever facilities local authorities made available. However, there was very little outpatient psychiatry in Britain for non-psychotic illness and few people working in related disciplines.[8] Victims were therefore generally reliant on traditional forms of counselling and help such as visits from friends, family and ministers of religion, messages of condolence and, above all, the healing power of time.

Trauma and Aberfan

Aberfan was a disaster with no real precedent in contemporary British history.[9] The loss of so many children in a small community was bound to have severe psychological consequences. Bereavement by disaster is more intense than by expected death and thus more difficult to come to terms with. Grief also tends to be more acute in cases where children are lost and where the disaster is man-made

---

6. For a summary of thinking on the syndrome see Martha Wolfenstein, *Disaster: A Psychological Essay* (Glencoe: The Free Press, 1957).
7. Richard I. Shader & Alice J. Schwartz, 'Management of Reactions to Disaster', *Social Work*, 11, 2, April, 1966, pp. 102-4. Letter from Prof. Richard Mayou to IM, 1 March 1999.
8. Letter from Richard Mayou to IM.
9. The only comparable British disaster was in 1883 when 190 children were killed in a crush in a Sunderland theatre. See Michael Wynn Jones, *Deadline Disaster: A Newspaper History* (Newton Abbot: David & Charles, 1976), pp. 20-21.

rather than natural.[10] It was obvious that the traditional networks of support would struggle to cope adequately, particularly since so many people in the village were affected. There were also forecasts that the disaster would lead to psychological problems on a scale that would be too large for local professional services to cope with.[11] Consequently the local services were inundated with offers of help.[12] Yet even the resources available elsewhere, in terms of trained people, were minimal, and there were no agreed or proven methods.[13] Offers of help may have been forthcoming but, in these circumstances, they may not have been effective.

The depth of the trauma that the disaster had inflicted quickly became apparent. In the first few weeks after the disaster, a psychiatrist noted the following groups of symptoms: disorders of sleep, changes of mood, anxiety symptoms, changes in behaviour, phobic reactions, physical or psychosomatic symptoms.[14] Of the 86 children he assessed, 55 were found to have fairly or moderately severe symptoms, although none were classified as very severe. Of the 83 adults examined, 90 per cent were classified as having moderate to severe symptoms.[15] One child survivor, who would wake in the middle of the night screaming, remembers, 'I would have nightmares, bed-wetting, irritability, unable to concentrate. All

10. Jane Littlewood, *Aspects of Grief: Bereavement in Adulthood* (London: Routledge, 1992), p. 143. The Disasters Working Party, *Disasters: Planning for a Caring Response, Part One: The Main Report* (London: HMSO, 1991), p. 5. Also see Charles B. Wilkinson & Enrique Vera, 'Clinical Responses to Disaster: Assessment, Management and Treatment' in Gist & Lubin (eds.) *Psychosocial Aspects of Disaster*, pp. 240-1. Yehuda & McFarlane, 'Conflict between Current Knowledge about Posttraumatic Stress Disorder and its Original Conceptual Basis'. Shader & Schwartz, 'Management of Reactions to Disaster', p. 102.
11. See letter from David T. Maclay, *British Medical Journal*, 29 October 1966, p. 1075.
12. R. Bevan to Chairman, Welsh Board of Health, 9 November 1966, TNA: MH 96/2179.
13. Letter from Richard Mayou to IM.
14. James M. Cuthill, *The Aberfan Disaster – A Study of the Survivors*, Unpublished paper, p. 5.
15. Ibid, pp. 5, 10.

these are classic symptoms of post-traumatic stress disorder. We now know what it is. In those days it didn't exist.'[16]

Local doctors and social workers acknowledged that Aberfan would need professional psychological and social work support. But there was no guarantee that Aberfan would accept it. The stigma of seeking psychological help was stronger in the 1960s than it is today. Outpatient psychiatric and neurosis treatment was still very much in its infancy and consequently psychiatric services were associated with asylums and severe mental illness. Psychiatric medicine is still popularly associated with vulnerability, failure and a sign of weakness.[17] In a mining community such as Aberfan, that had lived through the desperation of the inter-war depression, the constant dangers of working underground and the pressures of the Second World War, the stigma of being given help for emotional and psychological problems was probably stronger. Indeed, even the surviving children felt it. One child wrote in 1970,

> There was talk amongst the survivors that their parents had letters for each child that survived to see a psychiatrist. I was totally horrified to hear this from my friends. God, what would people think about me seeing a SHRINK? I confronted my parents and told them bluntly there was no way that I was going for these head tests and talks. A few weeks went by and Susan Maybanks had her letter to go, and my boyfriend, David. As far as I knew I did not get one. I questioned them when they came back from their appointment, and I thought it was a very disturbing thing they put them through. Hadn't they been through enough? But I was very adamant that I was not going. My parents tried their best to reason with me, and told me of the importance, but each time I got very upset of even the thought.[18]

This reluctance to see the psychiatrist was despite the fact that he was only assessing the children to help them claim damages. The

---

16. Sue Elliott, Steve Humphries and Bevan Jones, *Surviving Aberfan: The People's Story* (Guildford: Grosvenor House, 2016), p. 106.
17. See Hodgkinson & Stewart, *Coping with Catastrophe*, p. 104.
18. Madgwick, *Aberfan*, p. 45. Madgwick wrote this book as a 12-year-old child in 1970.

general distrust of authority and outsiders that had developed after the disaster complicated the situation further and added to the reluctance to accept the help of mental health professionals.[19] Press reports that psychiatrists were about to descend on the village did not help matters either.[20] After one mother had to be admitted to hospital, there were rumours that anyone visited by the local mental welfare officer would be taken to a mental hospital. This was, after all, what the officer's work normally entailed. The rumours led to the welfare officer being taken off work with bereaved families.[21] It is thus not surprising that the local consultant psychiatrist reported that he found it difficult getting people to realise they needed help.[22]

Psycho-social Care at Aberfan

This was the context in which Merthyr Tydfil County Borough Council took the decision to handle the disaster using its own welfare services. The offers of outside help were 'tactfully declined' and 'fended off'.[23] Local services had set to work very quickly, although their work was deliberately not publicised for fear of making the situation worse.[24] Dr English, the consultant psychiatrist responsible for Aberfan, wrote to the *British Medical Journal* saying that the existing service was adequate. He continued,

---

19. *The Times*, 12 October 1971. Although for those who did receive help, the fact that it was from someone beyond the local community appeared to alleviate some concerns. Interview between MJ and Dr J.M. Cuthill, 20 April 1999.
20. Cuthill interview.
21. Joan Miller, *Aberfan: A Disaster and its Aftermath* (London: Constable, 1974). p. 63.
22. A. Gray to A. Owen, 6 November 1967, TNA: MH 96/2179.
23. R. Bevan to Chairman, Welsh Board of Health, 9 November 1966, TNA: MH 96/2179. *The Times*, 12 October 1971.
24. F. Williams to Lady Traherne, 10 November 1966. R. Bevan to Chairman, Welsh Board of Health, 9 November 1966. TNA: MH 96/2179.

What we wish to avoid is the risk of predisposition to mental illness as a consequence of people outside the area anticipating such among the bereaved families, and allowing their fears to be made known to the residents of Aberfan. ... If, however, there is a marked increase in cases of breakdown directly due to the disaster, the doctors treating the patients must understand the community as it is in normal circumstances, to be aware of the fears and thoughts they share in day-to-day living, and this can best be done by the doctors whom they know well and whose advice they trust.[25]

Thus the decision not to accept external assistance was rooted in a desire to help Aberfan. The continuation of this policy was influenced by outside bodies' proposals to carry out research in association with the assistance they were offering. The people of Aberfan were already suffering from the glare of publicity and had no wish to become guinea pigs. Thus research plans were declined and the existing services struggled on alone.[26]

In line with the then current thinking, some of the relevant officials thought that residents of Aberfan who were seriously disturbed by the disaster had prior family problems or, in the case of children, pre-existing difficulties such as enuresis or temper tantrums.[27] 'Broadly speaking' wrote the local child psychologist, 'the children who were most affected were those with other anxiety creating situations in their backgrounds. Of the first few cases that were referred, several were from families in which there had been a striking number of grief situations in the past, and this seemed to have made them and their parents more vulnerable.'[28] The tendency to view the situation through such a lens must have clouded the view

25. Letter from Dr H.L. English, Morgannwg Hospital, Bridgend, *British Medical Journal*, 19 November 1966, p. 1266.
26. Gaynor N. Lacey, 'Observations on Aberfan', *Journal of Psychosomatic Research*, 16 (1972), p. 258; *The Times*, 12 October 1971; A. Gray to A. Owen, 6 November 1967. TNA: MH 96/2179. Also see Tony Austin, *Aberfan: The Story of a Disaster* (London: Hutchinson, 1967), p. 181.
27. *The Times*, 12 October 1971.
28. Lacey, 'Observations on Aberfan', p. 259.

of the need for a more comprehensive scheme of counselling and psychological support.

Helping Aberfan thus fell largely on the shoulders of the local available services and, in particular, two local psychiatrists and the local general practitioners. The three GPs in the area were under tremendous pressure; indeed, one had lost a child himself in the disaster. Two left within a year of the tragedy. Finding replacements proved problematic and those doctors who were brought in were not Welsh and, in a community distrustful of outsiders, had problems winning the confidence of their patients.[29] There was outside support and advice available to the psychiatrist, general practitioners, and social workers, especially from the Tavistock Institute in London. Its advice was found useful; however the Institute's plans for an outside team to help and research in Aberfan meant that it never seems to have fully won the trust of the local services.[30] The work of the psychiatrists was complicated by their different terms of reference.[31] Dr Cuthill had clients referred to him primarily by the Parents' and Residents' Association's solicitors. He was to assess them for compensation claims but not to treat them. Adult clinical work fell on the shoulders of Dr English (the consultant psychiatrist who was based in Bridgend, a town outside the local area), while the local authority's child psychiatrist was designated to work with the children.

Of the 218 bereaved adults who continued to live in the area, 83 were examined or treated by a psychiatrist.[32] There was a consensus of feeling amongst the psychiatrists involved that there were many more adults probably in need of help.[33] Some did not want it; others were not referred by their GPs. There was speculation that the GPs concerned were unaware that Cuthill was initially assessing for compensation rather than treating clients. Certain GPs were also

---

29. A. Owen to J.W.M. Siberry, 15 November 1967. G. Prys Davies to James Griffiths, 22 November 1971. TNA: MH 96/2179.
30. Parkes interview. See the discussion of the Institute's plans in the Welsh Board of Health records. TNA: MH 96/2719.
31. R. Bevan to A. Owen, 7 December 1971. TNA: MH 96/2179.
32. Cuthill, *The Aberfan Disaster*, p. 11.
33. Cuthill interview. Detailed notes of discussion with Dr Cuthill, 6 December 1968.

said to have an antipathy towards psychiatry.[34] Even the outpatient facilities in the local psychiatric hospital were not fully utilised. Cuthill's fears that the adults he had seen were probably just the tip of the iceberg thus seem well founded.[35]

Children were initially referred to the child psychologist through their schools. The child psychologist, therefore, did not see children who showed no sign of disturbance at school but did so at home. Subsequent research has shown how both schools and parents report fewer signs of psychopathy in children than children themselves. Particularly in cases where the parents are also affected by the trauma, children learn not to unburden their problems on others and thus their suffering can go unnoticed or misunderstood. Given that children as young as eight are thought of as being vulnerable to PTSD or similar traumatic syndromes, the consequences can be significant.[36] A long-standing division between the education and health departments of the local authority hindered communication between those treating adults and children. It took prompting by an external advisor to get the two groups to meet to discuss the services they were offering. They found, not surprisingly, that they were working with clients from the same families. The wellbeing of children and their parents influenced each other but organisational divisions had initially obscured this and any possible solution.[37] Even within the borough council, there was a feeling that the service available to the children was inadequate. Such shortcomings mirrored a wider shortage in child psychiatry

34. Cuthill, *The Aberfan Disaster*, p. 11. G. Prys Davies to J. Griffiths, 22 November 1971; A. Jones to A. Owen, 25 November 1966. TNA: MH 96/2179. Parkes interview.
35. Detailed notes of discussion with Dr Cuthill at the meeting held on 6th December 1968. Aberfan Disaster Fund Management Committee minutes. GA: D/D X295/12/1/3.
36. William Yule, 'The Effect of Disasters on Children', *Bereavement Care*, 9, 2 (1990), pp. 2-3, 4. Knowledge about PTSD in children is still underdeveloped. One child survivor at Aberfan noted her inability to speak to her parents about the disaster, Gaynor Madgwick quoted in *Daily Mail Weekend*, 5 October 1996. A study of 13 surviving children from the *Herald of Free Enterprise* disaster concluded than more than half had suffered from PTSD. *The Times*, 1 September 1988.
37. Murray Parkes interview.

across Britain and the underdeveloped field of children's psychology. The Education Department's fears of being held liable for the disaster do not seem to have helped the co-ordination of services either. The psychiatrist assessing the children for legal purposes did review their condition periodically for eight years and was thus able to offer some treatment or alert others to those in need of help.[38] Nonetheless, a number of children awarded compensation for psychological damage never received medical help for it.[39]

Subsequent research has suggested that early, proactive support can help prevent chronic stress and trauma.[40] Much of the support social workers give today is actually practical rather than counselling: helping with funeral arrangements, compensation claims and the like. This eases the logistical concerns of the bereaved and establishes a relationship with social workers which helps later counselling. Aberfan did get such support early on. An advice centre was quickly set up and staffed by members of the Wales and Monmouthshire Council of Social Service. It did much-needed work in helping people fill in claim forms and deal with the offers of compensation.[41]

The initial daily support on offer from the local authority was hampered by the council's limited resources. It had two mental health officers and five trained social welfare officers, three of whom were classified as home teachers to the blind, while the other two covered a wide range of general tasks from helping the elderly and disabled to dealing with 'problem families'. Initially, the non-psychiatric help given to Aberfan was their responsibility. They did their best but were not trained for such a situation.[42]

Consequently, with the help of the Tavistock Institute, Audrey Davey, a family caseworker, was appointed in November 1966. Initially

---

38. Cuthill interview. G. Prys Davies to J. Griffiths, 22 November 1971. TNA: MH 96/2719.
39. *The Times*, 12 October 1971.
40. The Disasters Working Party, *Disasters: Planning for a Caring Response, Part One: The Main Report* (London: HMSO, 1991), p. 5.
41. The Council of Social Service for Wales and Monmouthshire, Citizen's Advice Bureaux, Department Participation in Aberfan Information Centre, Report January 1967. TNA: MH96/2179.
42. E. Lewis to A. Owen, 9 November 1967. TNA: MH 96/2719.

there were some misgivings, and even opposition, to her appointment within the local authority. Such doubts were based in a feeling that it would only keep the disaster fresh in people's minds.[43] Davey's initial task involved visiting and listening to bereaved families, enabling people to come to terms with their loss. Such work was invaluable; the ability to face up to what has happened is integral to recovery. Some people, but fewer than she expected, turned her away because she was a social worker; given the distrust of officials and experts in the village, trust had to be won rather than assumed.[44] All bereaved families were visited at least twice and those with special needs received more intensive help.[45] Davey gradually won the trust and respect of the community to such an extent that she was invited to be part of a village delegation that lobbied the government for the removal of the tips.

Although she was acting with the advice and support of psychologists, much of her work appears to have been based upon common sense, kindness and empathy. She encouraged people to talk and form support groups that were inclusive rather than exclusive to certain sections such as the bereaved. This undoubtedly had beneficial effects, not only for the individuals concerned, but also for the whole community. As one report on her work concluded, 'Audrey is still the piercing point. She is the link between the personal and the social, and between the people and the helpers.'[46]

However, Davey was overworked and in need of additional help. Lack of time meant she had to focus on the bereaved parents, the most vulnerable group, meaning that others in need of support may

---

43. Miller, *Aberfan*, p. 88. Welsh Board of Health Memo, E. Lewis, 6 January 1967. TNA: MH 96/2179.
44. Miller, *Aberfan*, pp. 92-93. Audrey Davey interview, SWCC: AUD/524. Davey also had to cope with opposition to her appointment from members of the Children's Department in the Merthyr Council. E. Lewis to A. Owen, 9 November 1967. PRO: MH 96/2719. That Davey was Welsh, a consideration in her appointment, seems to have helped her in winning the confidence of Aberfan. Parkes interview.
45. *The Times*, 12 October 1971.
46. Confidential note 're Miss Audrey Davey' sent by Bishop of Llandaff to Sir Cennydd Traherne, 13 March 1968. NLW: Diocese of Llandaff papers, box 6.

not have initially received it.[47] There were thus moves to bring in further outside support. The Tavistock Institute, the Welsh Board of Health and local psychiatrists acknowledged the need for additional caseworkers to help Davey.[48] All felt though that any additional support should be introduced gradually so as not to overwhelm the village. In contrast, some GPs and others in the local authority were against the idea of extra help, and it came to nothing. After two years in Aberfan, Davey still felt that her job was unfinished and the local consultant psychiatrist wrote to the Welsh Board of Health emphasising the need for Davey to continue in her post. However, the local authority refused to pay for her to stay or to employ another social worker, while the Disaster Fund would not finance work which it felt other authorities had an obligation to support. At least one observer, a local solicitor, felt that by allocating money to 'bricks and mortar' rather than attending to the social needs of the village, the fund had not got its priorities right.[49] There was certainly an awareness of the likelihood of long-term psychological problems amongst the children at least, but a lack of money meant no further daily help for Aberfan was forthcoming.[50]

Community Help in Aberfan

Alongside the professional help available, a form of community self-help had been developing. It provided a network of support for the

---

47. Parkes interview. Some of the non-bereaved in Aberfan did feel that they had not been offered enough support or advice on how to cope with their trauma. After Aberfan and other disasters, some survivors did feel isolated and as if their trauma was not seen as important or valid as that of the bereaved. Mention is sometimes made of a 'hierarchy of grief'. For such problems after Hillsborough see Simon Hattenstone & Tom O'Sullivan, 'Those who were left behind', *Guardian Weekend*, 8 May 1999, 23-30.
48. A. Gray to A. Owen, 6 November 1967. TNA: MH 96/2719.
49. G. Prys Davies to J. Griffiths, 22 November 1971. TNA: MH 96/2719.
50. *The Times*, 12 October 1971. English to Bevan, 22 March 1968. TNA: MH 96/2719. Lacey, 'Observations on Aberfan', p. 260.

bereaved that was to prove effective in overcoming many problems. There is naturally a degree of romanticism in the idea of self-supporting, tight-knit, Welsh mining communities.[51] Such notions gloss over the fractures that exist within small communities and that can detract from the value of community networks of support. At Aberfan, the strength of this community support was also hindered to an extent by the fact that few people were not directly affected by the disaster. According to the child psychologist, this reduced the support families, friends and neighbours could give each other.[52] Nonetheless, the strength of community is cited by many in Aberfan as having been integral in the road to recovery.[53]

Local ministers of religion were important too, providing not only spiritual care but also wider emotional support. Consequently, ministers, especially the Rev. Kenneth Hayes, the minister of Zion English Baptist Church, came to the fore as community leaders and earned wide respect. Many of the survivors and bereaved talk about how their faith helped them come to terms with their losses. The faith of some was strengthened by the whole experience, while a few previously non-religious residents became members of chapels and the church.[54] Others had their faith tested or even destroyed by the tragedy.[55] The disaster did not overcome wider secular attitudes but nonetheless proved that religion still had a significant role to play in 1960s Britain.

One minister who played an integral role in helping Aberfan was another 'outsider'. Erastus Jones was a Welsh minister who was invited to Aberfan by the local council of churches to serve the community there in whichever ways he thought appropriate. Initially, Jones and his wife, working from a caravan they named Tŷ

---

51. For an exploration of this idea and the fractures within such communities see Martin Johnes, *Wales since 1939* (Manchester: Manchester University Press, 2012), ch. 5.

52. Lacey, 'Observations on Aberfan', p. 259. Similar circumstances and effect have been noted at Buffalo Creek where there was also a high proportion of victims to non-victims. Kai T. Erikson, *In the Wake of the Flood* (London: George Allen & Unwin, 1979).

53. *The Times*, 12 October 1971.

54. SWCC interviews.

55. See, for example, interviews in *Daily Mail Weekend*, 5 October 1996.

Toronto (Welsh for Toronto House – Jones' work was funded by a gift from the Welsh community of Toronto) slowly built up local contacts and helped the tip removal campaign with practical administrative work. Through such efforts they became accepted in the village.

Jones recognised that rehabilitation required the community to overcome its divisions. The work of Tŷ Toronto led to the formation of an umbrella community association and the holding of conferences to embrace and encourage dialogue between different groups in both Aberfan and the adjoining village of Merthyr Vale. The first conference, entitled 'The Way Ahead', was successful in helping to bring down barriers such as those between different churches, the bereaved and the non-bereaved, those who had lost houses and those who had not. It also embraced outside interested authorities, such as the Disaster Fund and Merthyr Council. An important part of the conference was a paper on how people react after disasters. This showed the people of Aberfan that their reactions were not abnormal but instead to be expected in the traumatic circumstances. Through enabling dialogue and discussion, the hope was that the anger would be channelled into the more creative purpose of community development.[56]

The focus of Tŷ Toronto was communal rather than individual because,

> we thought that a healthy community could best help its individual sufferers through to recovery, since the very numbers of those personally in need were beyond our resources. We thought also that perhaps friends and relatives could do a better job than strangers and professionals, given the encouragement of a purposeful community.[57]

This also helped overcome one of the initial problems that the official help was concentrating on the bereaved, rather than being freely

---

56. Outlining that extreme feelings are normal responses to traumatic situations continues to be a cornerstone of post-disaster counselling today. Such information is now usually conveyed quickly through the distribution of appropriate leaflets to those people affected.
57. This account of the work of Tŷ Toronto and the Way Ahead conference is derived from Erastus Jones, 'Working in Aberfan and the Valleys', *Social and Economic Administration*, 19, 1 (1979). Cf Parkes interview.

available to all. Tŷ Toronto grew ambitiously and culminated in declaring 1974 the 'Year of the Valleys'. It developed a programme that embraced grassroots groups and academics from across south Wales to deepen the valleys' 'self-awareness and to open new doors to a region whose economic, cultural and social cohesion was undergoing such rapid change.'[58] The programme's long-term goals of aiding the valleys' socio-economic regeneration failed but within Aberfan, Tŷ Toronto helped the community rebuild itself.

Also important in helping Aberfan's recovery were the donations and messages of condolences the village received. The Disaster Fund received nearly 88,000 donations, most of them accompanied by a letter or card.[59] In the words of one bereaved mother, 'People all over the world felt for us. We knew that with their letters and the contributions that they sent to us. ... They helped us to build a better Aberfan.'[60] For all the problems the fund later caused, it and the simple gestures of writing a note of condolence, meant a great deal to the people of Aberfan and showed them that they had the world's sympathy. Contemporary disaster theory makes it clear that social workers can often initially do little more than listen to victims. In doing this they help the victim acknowledge that the trauma is indeed awful and cannot be prevented. In witnessing it the social worker is telling the victim that they are not alone.[61] The sympathy and donations that the world sent to Aberfan had much the same effect. It verified their pain and thus was a small step in helping their recovery.

Obstacles to recovery in Aberfan

The recovery of Aberfan was hindered by a number of factors which made the village infamous. In 1968 a psychiatrist noted a greater

---

58. Paul H. Ballard & Erastus Jones (eds.), *The Valleys Call: A Self-Examination by People of the South Wales Valleys during the 'Year of the Valleys', 1974* (Ferndale: Ron Jones Publications, 1974), p. 15.
59. *First Report of the Aberfan Disaster Fund Management Committee*, p. 4.
60. Elaine Richards interview, SWCC: AUD 519.
61. Hodgkinson & Stewart, *Coping with Catastrophe*, pp. 116-7.

degree of suffering in the village than he would have anticipated from the disaster alone. He attributed the prolonged problems to post-disaster affairs in the village.[62] In the wake of the disaster, people in Aberfan understandably felt uneasy living in the shadow of the remaining tips. During the campaign for their removal, Kenneth Hayes wrote to the Prime Minister:

> Every time it rains people are afraid to go to bed, ... and all of us subconsciously are awaiting the alarm to sound. ... The mental wellbeing of the community today, and the safety of the unborn generations depends on the removal of tips.[63]

The arguments, delays and haggling over the cost caused considerable anger in Aberfan for the two years before the government agreed to remove the tips (see chapter 5). Such an atmosphere was hardly conducive to recovery.

Stimuli that resemble or symbolise the original traumatic event are thought to exacerbate the symptoms of PTSD.[64] Indeed, avoidance of stimuli associated with the trauma is one of the symptoms of PTSD. After the 1988 terrorist attack which brought down a passenger plane on to the small Scottish town of Lockerbie, the local community had to live with visible impact of the disaster for many weeks as wreckage and bodies were slowly recovered. This continued exposure to the disaster contributed to a high rate of PTSD.[65] The continued presence of the tips at Aberfan seems to have had a similar effect, exacerbated, perhaps, by feelings of guilt that they were created by the village's own economic raison d'être. It is also a common feature of disasters that the victims fear a repeat of the tragedy; thus the people of Aberfan were reacting rationally in demanding the removal of the

---

62. Detailed notes of discussion with Dr Cuthill at the meeting held on 6th December 1968, Aberfan Disaster Fund Management Committee minutes, GA: D/D X295/12/1/3.
63. Rev. K. Hayes to H. Wilson, 29 January 1968, PRO BD 11/3791 PM's papers after Aberfan Disaster.
64. R.E. Kendell & A.K. Zealley (eds.), *Companion to Psychiatric Studies* (Edinburgh: Churchill Livingstone, 1993, 5th edn), p. 518.
65. Kendell & Zealley (eds.), *Companion to Psychiatric Studies*, p. 519.

tips, despite the official assurances that they were safe.[66] The child psychologist responsible for the village felt that recovery only really began to take place when the aggression towards forms of authority began to subside. Specifically, she saw the continued presence of the tips as aggravating the fears people had of situations such as sleep, the dark and extreme weather.[67] A local GP also noted that worry and controversy over the tips was affecting people's health.[68]

The family caseworker made a strong appeal to the Welsh Office for complete removal. The meeting's minutes recorded her arguments:

> The villagers had done admirably in rehabilitating themselves with very little help. A Government gesture was needed to restore confidence and only complete removal of the tips would do this. Many people in the village were on sedatives but they did not take them when it was raining because they were afraid to go to sleep. Children did not close their bedroom doors in case they should be trapped.[69]

Five months later, a minister working in the village wrote to the Secretary of State for Wales:

> It is the considered judgement of all of us that symptoms and conditions are being perpetuated because the tips are still there. Does this need spelling out? No amount of 'expert' opinion can remove the fear of another slide. The disaster is not allowed to recede unto history while the killer is in the present. Resentment and hatred are continually renewed, and these emotions produce ill-health. Changing the shape of the symbols and covering it up will not change its significance.[70]

---

66. Miller, *Aberfan*, p. 89.
67. Lacey, 'Observations on Aberfan', p. 258.
68. Arthur Jones quoted in Doel & Dunkerton, *Is it Still Raining in Aberfan?*, p. 49.
69. Meeting with Aberfan Deputation at Welsh Office, London, 7 February 1968, TNA: BD 11/3804.
70. Erastus Jones to George Thomas, 23 July 1968, GA: Aberfan and Merthyr Vale Tip Removal Committee minutes D1368.

The injustice of the delays and resultant anger and hurt was all the worse since it was unnecessary and political.

Those helping Aberfan felt strongly that the insensitive, and sometimes unscrupulous, attention of the press hindered the village's recovery.[71] The facts reported were usually correct but the interpretations could be less reliable. Unused to dealing with the media, villagers found their comments being taken out of context and twisted. Debate in the village on what to do was portrayed as argument and the words or actions of a minority depicted as the norm.[72] At least one freelance reporter went further by supplying newspapers with untrue stories and encouraging villagers to spread false rumours.[73] Controversies over the use of the Disaster Fund and arguments between individual residents made sensational stories for a hungry press but did not give a complete picture of village affairs. There was a feeling that the press was uninterested in happy stories about the village and only published those that told of conflict.[74] Concerns were raised in the information division of the Welsh Office that the stories would reflect badly upon Wales unless action was taken.[75] Yet there was little a government department could do without being criticised for attacking the freedom of the press, something that had already happened at Aberfan. Thus the Welsh Office told Merthyr Tydfil County Borough Council that it could not intervene in shielding Aberfan from media attention on the first anniversary of the disaster.[76]

---

71. Davey interview, SWCC: AUD/524. Lacey, 'Observations on Aberfan', pp. 257-8. The insensitive, and sometimes inaccurate, attention of the media has been a problem for many victims of violent crimes and disasters, most notably after the Hillsborough disaster. For a survey of the impact of the media upon survivors of violent crime and disaster see Ann Shearer, *Survivors and the Media* (London: Broadcasting Standards Council, 1991).

72. Kenneth Hayes interview, SWCC: AUD/528.

73. P.L. Marshall to B.H. Evans, 1 September 1967, TNA: BD 11/3809. The false stories were not published.

74. Audrey Davey interview, SWCC: AUD/524.

75. P. L. Marshall to B. H. Evans, 1 September 1967, TNA: BD 11/3809.

76. Siberry to Town Clerk, 9 October 1967, TNA: BD 11/3809.

Guilt and anger are normal sequels to a disaster. Disasters create situations where emotions run high and many of the previous social barriers are broken down. Anger is also a symptom of PTSD and a reasonable response when people are being treated inappropriately by authority. Thus disasters create situations where pre-existing and new tensions often boil over. The press's failure to recognise these circumstances meant that Aberfan was often portrayed as 'some kind of delinquent community'.[77] The village was thus caught in a vicious circle. The normal angry response of victims to a disaster was added to by problems with the local authority, Disaster Fund and NCB. This resulted in the community being misunderstood and misrepresented which in turn ensured that its demands and needs were not heard.

People's attitudes and beliefs are important in determining how they recover from traumatic experiences.[78] In Aberfan, traditional working-class notions of masculinity appear to have hampered the recovery process. Miners, in particular, are associated with notions of strength and emotional resilience. Davey was worried about the fact that fathers could not talk about their feelings, while one survivor felt that it was harder for him to come to terms with the events because he was a man.[79] The surviving daughter of one bereaved man remembers her father breaking down: 'I think for a long time he became sort of lost and very emotional.'[80] In 1968, a psychiatrist wrote that while some bereaved mothers were getting back to normal, there was some evidence that the health of the fathers was tending to deteriorate. An external advisor had earlier noted that

---

77. Miller, *Aberfan*, p. 93.
78. Hodgkinson & Stewart, *Coping with Catastrophe*, p. 21.
79. Audrey Davey interview. SWCC: AUD/524. Gerald Kirwan quoted in *Daily Mail Weekend*, 5 October 1996, p. 12. There was a similar reluctance amongst male survivors of Hillsborough and older males in Lockerbie to seek help. Tim Newburn, *Making a Difference? Social Work after Hillsborough* (London: National Institute for Social Work, 1993), p. 50. Margaret Mitchell, 'The Role of the General Practitioner in the Aftermath of the Lockerbie Disaster' in Newburn (ed.), *Working with Disaster*, p. 90.
80. Sue Elliott, Steve Humphries and Bevan Jones, *Surviving Aberfan: The People's Story* (Guildford: Grosvenor House, 2016), p. 103.

the men, and, in particular, the bereaved men, were not in a frame of mind to accept the designated help. He suggested providing help that was not associated with psychiatry, religion or any of the other 'helping professions'.[81] A bereaved fathers' group had only lasted two meetings, in contrast to the successful mothers' group. Instead, much male grief was denied rather and shared and faced.[82]

Aberfan and recovery

In 1967, the Medical Officer for Merthyr said he was satisfied that everything was being done that was possible for Aberfan. Colin Murray Parkes, the consultant from the Tavistock Institute in London who was voluntarily supporting the work, said in 1971 that he agreed and accepted that his plan for a team of outside help had been inappropriate.[83] Despite the initial problems, the care on offer did gradually improve and those involved in helping the village felt that in the second year after the disaster there were significant improvements in morale and wellbeing.[84] Yet, at the time, there was perhaps not a full awareness of the long-term consequences of personal tragedies. In some contemporary literature, disasters were even seen as having therapeutic effects including 'frequent cases of remission of pre-existing neurotic and psychosomatic symptoms'.[85] Research into the long-term impact of disasters in the USA and Australia during the 1970s and 80s showed that the long-term psychological consequences can be severe.[86] Survivors of Second World War concentration camps were found to suffer forty to fifty

81. H. L. English to A. Bevan, 22 March 1968; C. M. Parkes to L. Abse, 24 October 1967. TNA: MH 96/2719.
82. Miller, *Aberfan*, pp. 90, 94. Murray Parkes interview.
83. *The Times*, 12 October 1971.
84. Murray Parkes interview.
85. Charles E. Fritz, 'Disasters', in *International Encyclopaedia of the Social Sciences*, vol. 4 (New York: Macmillan & Free Press, 1968), p. 206.
86. Disasters Working Party, *Disasters: Planning for a Caring Response, Part One: The Main Report* (London: HMSO, 1989), p. 5. Also see Beverley Raphael,

years of continuous PTSD symptoms.[87] No two disasters are alike, so drawing valid comparisons is difficult. Nonetheless, subsequent research does suggest that long-term effects would be likely at Aberfan.

In 1972, a dam of coal slurry burst, flooding Buffalo Creek Hollow; in a West Virginia community of some 5,000, 125 people were killed, 1,121 injured and 4,000 made homeless. Fourteen years later, 193 survivors were examined. Sixty per cent suffered from PTSD initially, while 28 per cent had the condition fourteen years later, including a number who had not been originally diagnosed.[88] One of the explanations given for this continuing high rate of PTSD was that it was 2-3 years before the disruption to life in the community settled down. There were continuing lawsuits, much of the housing had been destroyed, the community had been broken up and people rehoused in temporary trailer parks that did not reflect pre-existing social groupings. Thus people were separated from the support of their friends and neighbours. Another cause of the long-lasting trauma was that the disaster became a central reference point in the lives of the community's inhabitants.[89]

Aberfan experienced a similar prolonged rupture and constant reminders, which was thought to be holding back its recovery.[90] But unlike Buffalo Creek, the structure of the community at Aberfan was preserved

---

When Disaster Strikes: A Handbook for the Caring Professions (London: Unwin Hymen, 1990 edn), ch. 8.

87. Kendell & Zealley (eds.), *Companion to Psychiatric Studies*, p. 519.

88. Rosenhan & Seligman, *Abnormal Psychology*, p. 241. Bonnie L. Green, Jacob D. Lindy, Mary C. Grace, Goldine C. Gleser, Anthony C. Leonard, Mindy Korol & Carolyn Winget, 'Buffalo Creek Survivors in the Second Decade: Stability of Stress Symptoms', *American Journal of Orthopsychiatry*, 60, 1 (1990), 43-54.

89. Bonnie L. Green, Mary C. Grace, Jacob D. Lindy, Goldine C. Gleser, Anthony C. Leonard & Teresa L. Kramer, 'Buffalo Creek Survivors in the Second Decade: Comparison with Unexposed and Nonlitigant Groups', *Journal of Applied Psychology*, 20, 13 (1990), p. 1046. Also see Erikson, *In the Wake of the Flood*.

90. Detailed notes of discussion with Dr Cuthill at the meeting held on 6th December 1968, Aberfan Disaster Fund Management Committee minutes, GA: D/D X295/12/1/3.

and strengthened through communal activities. Parkes, an external advisor, felt that the community support and development programmes prevented Aberfan from suffering the scale of psychological damage experienced at Buffalo Creek.[91] Today group therapy is regarded as a useful therapeutic exercise for mild to moderately affected victims, while professional help is acknowledged as being secondary to the support of friends, family and community.[92] Such help allows traumas and fears to be listened to and confronted in an understanding and supportive environment. There is a lack of actual controlled evidence on the benefits of various grief and PTSD treatments, but there is a consensus that different forms of social support are important.[93] Communal expressions of grief, such as the annual Aberfan memorial services, can also help cement that social support. At Aberfan, the community groups allowed adults to talk through their experiences and emotions and channel their anger into something creative, while the caring work of individuals like Davey and the clergy helped the bereaved come to terms with their losses.[94]

Studies of the Three Mile Island accident at a nuclear power station in Pennsylvania in 1979 concluded that while social support networks reinforced the ability of individuals to cope, and minimised the unpleasantness of post-disaster stresses, they did not grant the ability to terminate such problems.[95] This appears true of Aberfan where significant psychological problems remained in both the short and long term. In 1968, Davey estimated that there were still thirty-plus families that needed constant care and attention.[96] Later

---

91. C. M. Parkes, 'Planning for the Aftermath', *Journal of the Royal Society of Medicine*, 84 (January 1991), p. 22 & preface & conclusion in Erikson, *In the Wake of the Flood*.
92. Disasters Working Party, *Disasters: Planning for a Caring Response*, p. 3.
93. Davison & Neale, *Abnormal Psychology*, pp. 151-152.
94. The channelling of anger was something identified by Parkes in his plans for community development aided by a team of outside experts. C. M. Parkes to Leo Abse, 24 October 1967, TNA: MH 96/2719. Cf Murray Parkes interview.
95. Hodgkinson & Stewart, *Coping with Catastrophe*, p. 58.
96. Bishop of Llandaff to Sir Cennydd Traherne, 'Re Miss Audrey Davey – Confidential note', 13 March 1968, NLW: Diocese of Llandaff papers, box 6.

that year, a bereaved mother died of an overdose of barbiturates. In recording an open verdict, the coroner noted,

> I have no hesitation or doubt in saying that the Aberfan disaster contributed very materially to this woman's death. You can see the picture of her lying in bed ill, and the only solace and comfort to her in her illness was the photograph of the child she was clutching.[97]

This was an example of the tragic extremes that the disaster's aftermath brought. A village GP noted that after the disaster, Aberfan suffered from excessive drinking, stress, disturbed sleep and psychological problems. For people with existing health problems their conditions got worse, while there was a series of breakdowns in the village for about the next six years.[98] In 1971, a follow-up of those who had claimed compensation classified the recovery of 80 per cent of the adults as 'pretty poor', although 66 per cent of the children were rated good or excellent.[99] The local consultant psychiatrist noted that year that he was worried that morbidity regarding the disaster was higher in the village than had hitherto been revealed.[100] A local GP believed that at least twenty mothers and fathers died prematurely since the disaster, while many others suffered health problems linked to the mental anguish. He felt he was still seeing the effects of the disaster in 1991 and claimed that Aberfan had more prescriptions issued and a higher incidence of illness than other parts of Mid Glamorgan.[101] In 1999 a clinical study of a group of 41 child survivors of the disaster was undertaken. It found that 19 had had PTSD at some point since the disaster and 12 still met the diagnostic criteria for the condition. The study noted:

> A few of the survivors talked about the fear evoked at the sound of a lorry passing their house, or of an aircraft flying overhead. Intense

---

97. *Merthyr Express*, 10 October 1968.
98. Arthur Jones, Aberfan GP in Doel & Dunkerton, *Is it Still Raining in Aberfan?*, pp. 49-50.
99. *The Times*, 12 October 1971.
100. G. Prys Davies to J. Griffiths, 22 November 1971, TNA: MH 96/2179.
101. Arthur Jones in *Campaign Merthyr/Cynon Valley*, 8 November 1991 p. 1.

memories of the disaster are aroused by the slightest noise or smell. A number of the survivors now have children at the age they were at the time of the disaster. This seems to arouse new feelings, as they are now able to see the disaster from their parents' perspective. Many are reluctant to let their children leave the house when the weather is bad, as they are reminded of the appalling weather preceding the disaster.[102]

Even where PTSD was not diagnosed, individuals might still have suffered significantly in coming to terms with what happened. Individuals varied according to their personal circumstances but recovery was a slow and gradual process and the long-term psychological impact of the Aberfan disaster was significant. Fifty years on, the memories, pain and anger are still there.

Nor is the trauma limited to people inside the village. Those taking part in the rescue and welfare operations that follow disasters can also suffer psychological injuries. For example, some police officers who dealt with the dead and injured at Hillsborough were diagnosed with and compensated for PTSD.[103] Today it is generally recommended that workers be debriefed and offered counselling themselves after being involved with a disaster, its survivors and the bereaved.[104]

At Aberfan, approximately 2,500 people were involved in the rescue operation. Many witnessed and took part in the horrific scenes of the recovery of bodies. Many were digging for the children of friends, family, even their own. Others were less intimately involved, having driven from across the country to help, but sometimes equally vulnerable. The burden on the education authority meant that some teachers had to endure the traumatic experience of entering the junior school on the Monday to try and recover teaching materials.[105] A police officer, who worked at the mortuary, wrote that he and his

---

102. Louise Morgan, Jane Scourfield, David Williams, Anne Jasper and Glyn Lewis, 'The Aberfan disaster: 33-year follow-up of survivors', *British Journal of Psychiatry*, 182 (2003), 532-6.
103. Simon Allen, 'Rescuers and Employees – Primary Victims of Nervous Shock', *New Law Journal*, 7 February 1997, 158-159.
104. Hodgkinson & Stewart, *Coping with Catastrophe*, ch. 7.
105. Interview between MJ and Hugh Watkins, 8 April 1999.

colleagues suffered no after-effects beyond a few stomach upsets and a general tiredness brought on by the long hours.[106] Nonetheless, the experience for others had a lasting traumatic effect for which, under today's laws, compensation could have been recoverable from the Coal Board. The press told of grown men crying as they dug. Relatives have told us of rescuers suffering from flashbacks on their deathbeds thirty years later and depression culminating in suicide. A rescuer who returned to Aberfan on 21 October 2016, for the first time in fifty years, told a similar tale.[107] The suffering of Aberfan was multifaceted.

It is now standard practice for victims of disasters suffering from PTSD to claim compensation. Claims for psychological damage were not unknown before the classification of PTSD and were referred to as nervous shock. By 1901 courts were willing to award damages for nervous shock where the plaintiff had been in fear of his or her safety.[108] However, medically proving trauma or nervous shock in the majority of cases was extremely difficult before the classification of PTSD. Some children and adults did receive compensation from the Coal Board for psychological damage in an uncontested, out of court settlement. However, given the paucity of knowledge about the long-term effects and the distrust of psychiatrists, the numbers who claimed were small. Had PTSD been classified in 1966, then there is no doubt that more parents and children at Aberfan could have been awarded substantial sums by the Coal Board.

In 1990, a woman, who had been an eleven-year-old pupil in the adjoining senior school at the time of the disaster, issued a writ against the NCB for psychiatric injury. In around 1978, after having seen a television programme about the disaster, she began to suffer psychiatrically. The plaintiff maintained that, in her treatment, no connection was made between her condition and her experiences as a child. However, the judge rejected this assertion and decided that the plaintiff had been in a position to then bring an action. Because she did not issue the writ until 1990 – partly because her symptoms had

106. Charles Nunn, 'The Disaster of Aberfan', *Police Review*, 16 October 1987, p. 2071.
107. To IM, as they were standing together waiting to be interviewed.
108. Shyamala Rajan-Vince, 'Nervous Shock!', LAWTEL, document no. 0981210. www.lawtel.co.uk.

not been continuous – the court ruled that she could not proceed with her claim. Its reasoning was that the delay would cause significant problems for both sides in adducing and testing the evidence.[109] Thus because it is difficult in court to prove past difficulties, the residents of Aberfan appear to have lost out financially because psychiatric diagnosis and treatment was not as developed in 1966 as it is today.

Conclusion

From their research on Buffalo Creek, Gleser, Green and Winget listed six factors which contribute to the psychopathological impact of disasters.[110] All six are highly applicable to the Aberfan disaster and its aftermath. Using this theoretical framework, the effects of the disaster on the people of Aberfan are likely to have been severe.

(1) The extent to which the disaster poses a serious and unexpected life threat to individuals, their friends and family, resulting in existential fears, feelings of powerlessness and vulnerability, and threat of sudden loss.

The Aberfan disaster was sudden, unexpected and a very real life threat to those in the vicinity of the tips.

(2) The degree of bereavement suffered by the victims as a result of the disaster.

Again, the sheer scale of the loss of life and the age of so many of the victims made the degree of bereavement severe.

(3) Prolongation of physical suffering, life threat, and the lack of normal necessities over an extended period of time, coupled with the impossibility of changing or ameliorating the situation.

---

109. Crocker v British Coal Corporation, *The Times*, 5 July 1995. [1996] JPIL Issue 1/96. LAWTEL, Document no. C0002592. www.lawtel.co.uk.
110. Gleser, Green & Winget, *Prolonged Psychosocial Effects of Disaster*, pp.148-149.

The remaining tips were perceived as a threat and the fear of another collapse was very real in Aberfan. The prolonged refusal of the government and the NCB to agree to complete removal of the tip complex not only extended this period of threat, it also engendered a feeling of helplessness regarding the situation. Even the wreckage of Pantglas School and the destroyed houses had not been cleared away by October 1967.

(4) The extent to which the disaster victims must face displacement or changes in their former environment and new modes of living after the disaster.

For some inhabitants, there was significant displacement as they were evacuated from the disaster area. However, for everyone in the village the disaster brought significant changes to their lives and environment. Not least was the constant media attention and the presence of sightseers which left the villagers unable to rebuild their lives in peace.

(5) The proportion of a community or group affected by the disaster. Thus, victims who are part of a community that is relatively untouched by the disaster will recover better than victims in isolated groups or communities where almost all the individuals are affected by the disaster.

Aberfan and Merthyr Vale comprise a small, distinct community, which, by British standards, is quite isolated. Pantglas School was the community school, to which every village family sent their children. The loss of 144 lives in a community of 4,000 meant that everyone was bereaved, either through family or friends. The impact of this was bound to be profound but at the same time it did at least ensure that the grief was put in the open and not hidden and denied.[111]

(6) The cause of the disaster, that is, whether it was natural or man-made. Disasters that are man-made are likely to result in a widespread

_____

111. Murray Parkes interview. In this sense, Aberfan was very different to most other disasters.

feeling of having been betrayed by those who were trusted. Such loss of trust can lead to conflicts, recriminations and alienation that lessen the sense of community.

Not only was Aberfan a man-made disaster but it was perpetrated by the dominant local employer, the NCB, an organisation that people had struggled hard to bring into existence. The failures of the long-desired nationalised Coal Board and the local authority meant a widespread feeling of betrayal and anger. The fact that bereaved fathers worked for the NCB in the colliery that created the tip waste must have exacerbated such feelings.

Only a small proportion of people affected by disaster ever develop full PTSD but a wider acute trauma and grief is often common and at Aberfan all the conditions were there to expect significant and long-term problems. The resources to help manage this were swamped, as they are at every disaster.[112] Colin Murray Parkes wrote in October 1967 that it would be 'utterly wrong' to imply that the local authority had 'failed to provide adequate care'. He went on, 'I think on the contrary that they have done a tremendous lot for the community, and it is only as time passes that it has become possible for us to see where additional help is needed.'[113] As a senior civil servant noted in 1971, mistakes were made but no one had any expertise in the area and it was pointless and perhaps unkind to criticise them.[114] Aberfan was a new experience for the local social and medical services. More advice and support could have been sought elsewhere but other experts too lacked the experience to know how to handle the situation. Parkes admitted that his idea to send in a trained research team to help had been unsuitable. The people of Aberfan had suffered enough without being descended upon by teams of outside experts. Yet without the research component that Parkes' plan would have entailed, lessons were not learnt for the handling of future disasters. Instead, Aberfan initiated little change in the way that the psychological effects of disasters were handled. Its lessons were never widely publicised.

---

112. Murray Parkes interview.
113. C. M. Parkes to Leo Abse, 24 October 1967, TNA: MH 96/2179.
114. R. Bevan to A. Owen, 7 December 1971, TNA: MH 96/2179.

5

Regulating and Raiding Gifts of Generosity: The Aberfan Disaster Fund

'[B]efore any payment is made each case should be reviewed to ascertain whether the parents had been close to their children and were thus likely to be suffering mentally.'[1]

From the minutes of the Aberfan Disaster Fund Committee Management Meeting, 8 September 1967

Since the nineteenth century, relief funds have been a common response to disasters. Yet they are fraught with potential problems that can further distress those whom they are designed to help. The administration of funds is restricted by the legal and social norms of the day. This is not always conducive to a harmonious and smooth distribution.

The problems that courted relief funds in the nineteenth and early twentieth centuries can be illustrated by reference to the Senghennydd disaster of 1913 in which 439 miners were killed – the worst single loss of life in a mine accident in UK history. Senghennydd is in the Aber valley some 15 miles south-east of Aberfan. A public appeal was quickly launched which raised over £126,000 (equivalent to

---

1. W.E.A. Lewis, Charity Commissioner, *Minutes of Aberfan Disaster Fund Management Committee*, 8 September 1967, GA: D/D X 295/12/1/1.

about £13 million in 2016). It received donations from royalty, colliery owners and the general public. Yet despite this generosity, payments from the fund were carefully limited and distributed in small but regular sums in order to ensure recipients were not lifted beyond their previous station in life. This practice was also determined by fears that working-class widows would not be able to manage large lump sums. Widows thus received weekly payments of between 3 and 10 shillings each with a further five shillings for each dependent child.[2] Charity law limited payments to relieving need but contemporary interpretations of need nonetheless remained narrow, even in such tragic circumstances. The result of distributing funds in such small instalments was that the funds had long active lives. The Senghennydd fund was not wound up until 1952, 39 years after the disaster. Funds set up to help those bereaved in the *Titanic* disaster were still operating in the 1990s.

Paying out sums in small instalments also allowed a measure of scrutiny of the beneficiaries. Two weeks after the Senghennydd disaster, a meeting of Caerphilly District Council heard:

> Mr Mark Harding said he had seen the grocery bill of a person who had received a grant of 10s., and this bill included a quarter of a pound of tobacco, two pounds of bacon at 1s. 3d., butter at 10d. a pot. He did not think these were necessary things.[3]

Like many state and local welfare payments of the day,[4] payments were also subject to a character test. Some beneficiaries of the fund later had their payments stopped for such 'immoral' behaviour

---

2. John Benson, 'Charity's Pitfalls: The Senghennydd Disaster', *History Today*, 43, November 1993. Catherine Welsby, 'Warning her as to her future behaviour': The Lives of the Widows of the Senghenydd Mining Disaster of 1913', *Llafur*, 6, 4, (1995), 93-109.
3. Quoted in Benson, 'Charity Pitfalls', p. 7.
4. For example, eligibility for aid under the Poor Law was dependent upon the approach of the local Board of Guardians, the more extreme of whom would exclude those of 'immoral' character. This attitude was also reflected in the 1908 Old Age Pensions Act which excluded known drunks and others of disreputable behaviour.

as giving birth to an illegitimate child.[5] Disaster funds may have represented the public sympathy for the bereaved but there was both a social and legal reluctance to see people enriched by their tragic losses, particularly if they were thought to be behaving beyond the realms of respectability.

Overseeing the running of charitable disaster funds was the Charity Commission. The Charity Commission has regulated charities in England and Wales since 1853. Its role before the Second World War was very much a distant one with little practical intervention in the operation of charities. In 1960, the Charity Commission had its duties revised and laid down in the Charities Act of that year. 'By the act, the powers of the commission were strengthened, with the general purpose of promoting the effective use of charitable monies.'[6] In 1974, the first year for which the *Civil Service Yearbook* prints the mission statements of Government departments and agencies, the entry for the Charity Commission states, 'The general functions of the Charity Commissioners include maintaining a register of charities in England and Wales, protecting the endowment of charities by controlling disposals of permanent endowment, advising trustees, and providing the services of an Official Custodian of Charities.'[7] By 1999, this had evolved to: 'The Charity Commission is here to give the public confidence in the integrity of charities', and by 2016 to 'We register and regulate charities in England and Wales, to ensure that the public can support charities with confidence.'[8]

The 1974 statement does not clarify in whose interest the Charity Commission operates and the second two are limited in scope. Three identifiable groups require protection: donors, beneficiaries, and the general public. All need to be assured that money raised charitably

---

5. See Welsby, 'Warning her', pp. 104-5.
6. Charity Commission statement 1974. Quoted from the *History of the Organisation of Central Government Departments 1964-92* database at http://www.nuff.ox.ac.uk/politics/whitehall/
7. Charity Commission statement, 1973-4.
8. 1999: Quoted from the mission statement on the front page of the Charity Commission's website, February 1999: http://www.charity-commission.gov.uk/. 2016, ditto, at https://www.gov.uk/government/organisations/charity-commission/about (accessed 3 November 2016).

is spent as donors want it to be on the appropriate beneficiaries. There is a public interest in preventing fraud and in ensuring that charitable tax advantages go only to organisations that deserve it. It is thus the role of the Charity Commission to protect the interests of these groups within the constraints of the law.

This chapter examines the regulation of the Aberfan Disaster Fund by the Charity Commission in the years 1966-69 and the raid upon it by the government to pay for the removal of the remaining Aberfan tips. We show that the Commission protected neither donors nor beneficiaries. It was caught between upholding an outdated and inflexible law that had its origins in the Statute of Charitable Uses 1601, and fulfilling the varied expectations of donors, beneficiaries and the fund's management committee. The process and outcome were unsatisfactory, and even upsetting, to all concerned. Nor were the actions of the government much better. It forced the Disaster Fund into an impossible choice between paying to clear up the Coal Board's responsibility or refusing and risking continued harm to people in Aberfan.[9] The chapter also considers the wider legal and financial climate that limited the sums paid by the NCB to those affected by the disaster. Just as the corporatist culture of the 1960s had protected the NCB from some of the political fallout, so too did it stop the government imposing on the board the costs that it should have faced.

The origins of the Aberfan Disaster Fund

The Mayor of Merthyr, Stanley Davies, issued an appeal on the evening of the disaster for money to help relieve and rehabilitate the village. He was later to recollect that immediately after the disaster he had no

---

9. Many of the problems the Fund encountered were well publicised at the time. Michael Chesterman, *Charities, Trusts and Social Welfare* (London: Weidenfeld and Nicolson, 1979), pp. 339-346, discusses the situation as it then appeared, although he did not have access to the records or to local interviews. However, the archives of the Charity Commission, other government departments and the Disaster Fund itself, as well as interviews with actors involved in the events, all add depth.

specific ideas as to how the money was to be used, beyond that it was 'to help the people of Aberfan generally, including the children and anybody else who needed help'.[10] The horror of the Aberfan disaster had had a profound impact across the world and the Mayor's fund quickly raised a total of £1.75 million (worth about £29.4 million at 2015 prices). The Aberfan Disaster Fund raised more, in real terms, than any other disaster fund in British history: more than twice the real size of the Senghennydd fund. Only the fund raised after the death of Diana, Princes of Wales, has exceeded the Aberfan fund in size.

The inflexibility of charity law, and the Charity Commission's enforcement of it, placed barriers in the way of the fund, causing tension and concern in Aberfan. At the same time, the Commission did not object to the controversial transfer of £150,000 from the Disaster Fund to the NCB as a contribution to the cost of removing the remaining tips above Aberfan. The evidence suggests that they may have told the Government that the donation was permissible.

As soon as money from the public started to flood into the Aberfan fund, all the lawyers involved realised that it was important to avoid the problems that had arisen after some other disasters, including the 1951 Gillingham bus crash[11] and the 1952 Lynmouth floods[12]. If the Disaster Fund were constituted as a charity, then it would be difficult or impossible for the village to be represented on the management committee of the fund. Every inhabitant of Aberfan was a potential beneficiary, and therefore *prima facie* ineligible to be a trustee. Also, charity law would restrict the objects that the fund could be spent on, specifically excluding straightforward cash handouts except as required to relieve 'need'. This raised the possibility of a substantial surplus. For the fund to remain charitable in law, the trust deed would have to specify that any surplus would be used for the public benefit. The Gillingham trustees had been forced to try to trace donors and

---

10. *Minutes of Aberfan Disaster Fund Management Committee* (hereafter *ADF mins*), 2 February 1968, GA: D/D X 295/12/1/2.

11. Gillingham bus crash, Kent on 4 December 1951 involving members of the Royal Marine Volunteer Cadet Corps: *Griffiths v Chatham and District Traction Engine Company Limited and others*, TNA: TS 32/720.

12. http://www.exmoor-nationalpark.gov.uk/learning/Lyn-Enquiry/the-lynmouth-flood-disaster-of-1952, (accessed 1 November 2016).

give them back their money, because, after having spent all that was possible on the primary objects of the fund, the secondary terms of the appeal were not deemed exclusively charitable.[13] Since the initial Aberfan appeal had been made without clear objectives, there was no single and specific intention amongst donors, while the sheer number of Aberfan gifts made a later consultation impossible. (About 50,000 letters accompanying donations survive,[14] and there were approximately 88,000 donations altogether.) Yet it was obvious that many of the donors saw their gifts as charitable. The Charity Commission had warned in its 1965 Annual Report that disaster funds were not automatically charitable. But if the Aberfan Disaster Fund were not to be a charity, it would be subject to taxation. As Chesterman has pointed out, Aberfan illustrated that 'charitable status does not automatically follow even where the element of altruism is entirely "pure" and spontaneous...[T]he law had to distort the intentions of many of the donors to make them fit the mould of legal charity'.[15]

It took some time for the Trust Deed to be drafted, and all the while the money was pouring in. In November 1966, the Charity Commissioners discussed Aberfan for the first time. They were concerned that no objects had been stated when the Mayor of Merthyr made his appeal, and that it was essential to find out the trusts on which the fund was now held.[16] That month, an Assistant Commissioner met with the Mayor of Merthyr and the fund's provisional committee to advise on the terms of a draft deed which had been drawn up by an eminent QC.[17]

The Deed as finally drafted gives the purpose of the charity:

---

13. *Re Gillingham Bus Disaster Fund* [1957] 3 WLR 1069. A bus had crashed into a line of marching cadets, killing 24 of them. The bus company's insurer met most of the claims, leaving a large charitable fund with a small number of direct beneficiaries. The last of the money was not disposed of until 1993, 42 years after the cadets were killed.
14. For conditions of access to these, see our website at http://www.nuffield.ox.ac.uk/politics/aberfan/Condol.htm
15. Chesterman, *Charities*, p. 344.
16. Charity Commission meeting of 8 November 1966, TNA: CHAR 9/2.
17. *Report of the Charity Commissioners for England and Wales for the Year 1966* (London: HMSO, 1967), paras 10-11, p. 6.

The Fund as to both capital and income shall be applicable at the discretion of the Management Committee:

(1) For the relief of all persons who have suffered as a result of the said disaster and are thereby in need; and
(2) Subject as aforesaid for any charitable purpose for the benefit of persons who were inhabitants of Aberfan and its immediate neighbourhood (hereinafter called 'the area of benefit') on 21 October 1966 or who now are or hereafter become inhabitants of the area of benefit and in particular (but without prejudice to the generality of the last foregoing trust) for any charitable purpose for the benefit of children who were on 21 October 1966 or who now are or hereafter may become resident in the area of benefit.

Following a (probably planted) parliamentary question,[18] the Commission corresponded with the Treasury on how to ensure that disaster funds were properly set up and run. The Treasury had drafted a brief circular to be sent to other government departments drawing attention to the powers and experience of the Charity Commission.[19] For the next eighteen months, the Commission took a close and sometimes threatening interest in whether gifts to individuals or work at the Aberfan cemetery were consistent with the charitable purpose of the Trust. However, their surviving records reveal no discussion of whether a donation to remove the remaining tips above Aberfan was consistent with its charitable purposes.[20]

The Fund and the Charity Commission

On 7 July 1967, the Commission heard that the Fund was proposing to spend around £40,000 on providing a memorial at the Aberfan

18. PQ by Alexander Lyon (Lab, York) and replies by the Prime Minister, 25 October 1966. *Hansard*, Commons, 5th series, vol 734, 825-6.
19. Charity Commission meeting of 27 January 1967, TNA: CHAR 9/2.
20. Surprisingly, in view of the salience of Aberfan, the Charity Commission case file on Aberfan has not survived.

cemetery to take the form of a series of arches and pillars. They were alarmed that it had apparently not occurred to the trustees that the provision of a memorial of this sort might not be charitable or within the terms of the fund. This fund, they said, was very much in the public eye and the proposal to erect a monument might be a target for criticism. It was therefore important to make sure that, in accordance with the Trust Deed and the law, the money was used for charitable purposes which were also for the benefit of inhabitants of Aberfan.

The Commissioners discussed the problem at length. They reasoned that it was doubtful whether the provision of a memorial was in itself a charitable purpose. However, maintaining or beautifying a burial ground would be a charitable purpose, even when the cemetery was owned by the local authority, as the Aberfan cemetery is. If therefore the proposed colonnade improved or beautified the cemetery, its provision would be charitable; the fact that it also served as a memorial would be incidental. The cemetery was close to and could be seen from Aberfan so that improving or beautifying the cemetery would be for the benefit of the inhabitants.[21]

By this (it might be thought) tortuous reasoning, the Commission brought itself to approve the memorial, which was duly built and still stands. The question of payments to survivors was more intractable. The first report of the Disaster Fund's Management Committee noted that 'bereaved parents were desirous of receiving major cash benefits without delay and simply as a class, irrespective of other conditions.' The bereaved parents felt that the money had been donated to relieve their situation and thus should be distributed accordingly.[22] However any payments to the bereaved as a class, regardless of need, would have gone against the terms of the Trust Deed and charity law. Suggestions by the Management Committee that, in making payments, it distinguish between families on the grounds of need met with 'resistance en bloc'. The families were united in their grief and became more so upon any proposition that individuals be treated differently. Meanwhile, the deliberations were causing considerable

---

21. Charity Commission meeting of 7 July 1967, TNA: CHAR 9/2.
22. *The First Report of the Management Committee of the Aberfan Disaster Fund*, 1968, p. 27.

anxiety in Aberfan. Thus the committee concluded that it could well be 'disastrous' to follow the obvious interpretation of charity law and distribute funds according to need.[23]

The words 'in need' had added resonance in the south Wales coalfield. The 1930s had witnessed whole communities – men, women, and children – taking to the streets in protest against the means test which strictly governed unemployment benefit according to families' financial resources.[24] A deep-rooted tradition in south Wales and other working-class areas regarded means-tested payments as humiliating and degrading. This helps to explain why the rhetoric of the post-war welfare state was built on the principle of universality not need. Any suggestion of having to go cap in hand asking for money would find scant support anywhere in the south Wales valleys. As one bereaved mother remembered, going to the Fund to ask for money was almost like begging. This was not how they envisaged the fund. The Aberfan Parents' and Residents' Association had expressed concern about the words 'in need' being in the Trust Deed when it was being drawn up. However, their solicitors told them that this was necessary if the fund was to be charitable.[25]

In July 1967, the Management Committee met the Charity Commission to discuss the situation. At first the Commissioners expressed the view that any major cash grant to the bereaved, irrespective of need, would be contrary to the terms of the Trust Deed. Upon discussion, they recognised what they called the 'unprecedented emotional state' of Aberfan and advised that the fund could pay £500 to each set of bereaved parents because of the 'devastating effect of the disaster upon all the people concerned and the intense and mounting state of emotion which had resulted from it'.[26]

---

23. *First Report of the Management Committee of the Aberfan Disaster Fund*, p. 28.
24. Francis & Smith, *The Fed*, ch. 8.
25. Interview, MJ and Mr & Mrs T. (bereaved parents, names withheld), 1 February 1999.
26. *First Report of the Management Committee of the Aberfan Disaster Fund*, p. 29. £500 was the same figure as the NCB was prepared to award per child killed.

A lawyer member of the Management Committee sought the advice of the Attorney General on the upper limit for payments from the Fund. Elwyn Jones, the Attorney General, reportedly said 'the law was the law'. However, the parents and the Management Committee were not prepared to accept this and both wanted a higher payment.[27] The parents understandably sought a significant payment in recognition of their bereavement. This was not to be compensation for the loss of their children – no financial sum could provide that – but rather an acknowledgement that money had been donated to the fund in sympathy for the deaths of their children.[28]

Alun Talfan Davies QC, vice-chairman of the Management Committee, drafted a memorandum outlining the reasons for making a payment of £5,000 rather than £500. The Committee argued that the sum was to relieve mental stress and strain rather than compensate the parents for their losses. £5,000 would allow parents wishing to move away from Aberfan to do so, while giving a new start to those who wished to stay.[29] In September 1967, W.E.A. Lewis OBE, one of the Commissioners, and an Assistant Commissioner attended a meeting of the Disaster Fund Management committee where the memorandum was discussed. There was a 'great deal of argument' and the commissioners were told that grants of £5,000 would be made whether they liked it or not.[30] The Commission conceded that the payments were permissible but gave apparently conflicting advice on the methods that should be followed. They said that all the bereaved should be treated alike (which was what the Management Committee wanted to do) in that all should receive the same sum, but also that

---

27. Telephone interview, MJ and Fund trustee (name withheld), 7 December 1998, recalling an interview between the trustee and Elwyn Jones AG, 1967; *First Report of the Management Committee of the Aberfan Disaster Fund*, pp. 26-30.
28. Interview, MJ and Mr & Mrs T.
29. *ADF mins*, 8 September 1967, appendix B, GA: D/D X 295/12/1/1. *First Report of the Management Committee of the Aberfan Disaster Fund*, p. 29.
30. Noted in minutes of Charity Commission meeting of 7 February 1968, GA: CHAR 9/2. Interview, MJ and Fund trustee.

before any payment was made each case should be reviewed to ascertain whether the parents had been close to their children and were thus likely to be suffering mentally.[31]

This would imply that parents who were found, on examination, not to have been close to their children would not be allowed to benefit. Perhaps fortunately, this advice was not taken. At this meeting, the Aberfan representatives resigned from the committee in order to avoid being both trustees and beneficiaries with the intention that they or other local people should be re-elected after the fund had paid out individual grants. The remaining trustees then agreed the bereaved parents who had lost children 'and are thereby in distress' should receive £5,000 per family. The policy of making flat-rate grants to each family avoided any finding that some bereaved parents were not thereby in distress.

Initially, all families with at least one surviving child who had been a pupil of either of the Aberfan schools at the time of the disaster had received £200 from the fund if they had not also been bereaved. In November 1967, the Management Committee then met a deputation of parents whose children had not been physically injured. They reported that their children were afraid of the dark and loud noises, and that many of them would not sleep alone. Even if they seemed normal at school, their parents had noticed many differences from their previous behaviour at home. The Committee discussed whether these children and their parents were eligible for further payments from the fund. One trustee said that he felt that all children who were mentally injured should make compensation claims from the Coal Board.[32]

With animosity in the village to varied levels of payment, the Committee considered making a further payment to all the physically uninjured children, regardless of evidence of mental suffering, and the Charity Commission were again consulted. The Secretary/Treasurer presented the case for payments to the uninjured children

---

31. W.E.A. Lewis, Charity Commissioner, *ADF mins*, 8 September 1967, GA: D/D X 295/12/1/1.
32. *ADF mins*, 9 November 1967, GA: D/D X 295/12/1/1. *First Report of the Management Committee of the Aberfan Disaster Fund*, pp. 35-36.

and their parents as a class but Commissioner Lewis stated that such payments would be 'quite illegal' and if made the Commission would have to intervene. This was reported at the next meeting of the Management Committee to the dismay of the chairman, Stanley Davies, who had founded the fund. He stated that it had been his intention for the money to help the people of Aberfan generally and that he did not like the obstacles being put in the way. He did not want a repeat of the Senghennydd and Lynmouth funds and in many ways he now wished that the Fund had not been made into a charity and felt that the people of Aberfan would not accept the Commission's decision.[33] Another trustee remembered dealings with the Commission as a battle, recalling the Commissioners as 'interested in legal matters, not justice... acting like lords'.[34]

A meeting of the other Commissioners agreed that the grants proposed would not be charitable. 'The grants made to the parents who had been bereaved were very close to the borderline'. If the Management Committee ignored this ruling, the Commission considered whether it would refer the matter to the Attorney General with a view to making the members of the Management Committee refund the amount misapplied, to remove the present committee members from office or to order the charity's bankers not to pay the cheques. They were reasonably certain that if the Management Committee decided to make such grants that someone on the committee would inform the commissioners immediately.[35]

Confrontation was averted, however. At the next meeting of the Commissioners, Lewis reported that the Management Committee had not pressed very hard for authority to make grants to the parents of uninjured children, that the deputation had listened 'very reasonably' to what he had to say and had asked him to confirm it in writing.[36]

The Committee did receive legal advice that payments to the physically uninjured children were probably lawful because they

---

33. *ADF mins*, 2 February 1968, GA: D/D X 295/12/1/2.
34. Interview, MJ and Fund trustee.
35. Charity Commission meeting of 7 February 1968, GA: CHAR 9/2.
36. Charity Commission meeting of 6 March 1968, GA: CHAR 9/2; cf *ADF mins*, 1 March 1968, GA: D/D X 295/12/1/2.

would ease psychological suffering.[37] However, given the stance of the Charity Commission, the fund's first report noted,

> It is, of course, apparent that the thread of justification for the issue of grants in the case of these surviving children who had not been physically injured, is much finer but the Management Committee is anxious and intends to consider ways and means of affording them such benefit as would be proper in the circumstances.[38]

While considering such means, £100,000 was to be set aside by the Management Committee to meet the present and future needs of children who were physically and psychologically injured. Solicitors for residents in Aberfan had enlisted a local psychiatrist to examine those child survivors who seemed to be distressed. The psychiatrist reported in alarming terms to the Management Committee in December 1968. Of the 81 children he had seen, two-thirds were found to be moderately to severely affected.[39] The intended payments from this reserve fund were shaped by the parameters of charity law. Rather than making a general payment to all the physically uninjured children, those assessed were to receive financial assistance based upon the extent of their psychological injuries.[40] However, after 'considerable thought', rather than making people apply to this reserve fund, one-off grants were made to physically and known psychologically injured children, based upon medical reports on their injuries.[41]

Significantly, the consultant psychiatrist had not seen all the surviving children and it is possible that others too suffered from the symptoms he described. One of those he did see, Gaynor Madgwick, has described her experience:

---

37. *ADF mins*, 29 May 1968, GA: D/D X 295/12/1/2.
38. *First Report of the Management Committee of the Aberfan Disaster Fund*, p. 36.
39. Detailed notes of discussion with Dr Cuthill at the meeting held on 6th December 1968, *ADF mins*. GA: D/D X295/12/1/3.
40. *First Report of the Management Committee of the Aberfan Disaster Fund*, pp. 34-5.
41. C. Geoffrey Morgan, *Second Report of the Management Committee of the Aberfan Disaster Fund*, 1970, p. 10.

There was talk amongst the survivors that their parents had letters of invitation for each child that survived to see a psychiatrist. I was totally horrified. ... Two weeks went by and my parents said they were taking me on a shopping trip to Pontypridd. I put my best clothes on and we were off on our journey. Halfway there my mother told me we were going to see the psychiatrist. This was the only way that she could get me to go. I was horrified, crying and shouting 'I am not going.' I felt that everyone around me thought I was mental.[42]

As shown in chapter 4, in the late 1960s little was known about the set of conditions now labelled Post-Traumatic Stress Disorder. Because of this lack of awareness of the possible full extent of the trauma, not all the children saw a psychiatrist, either for treatment or assessment for compensation. Were Aberfan to happen now, a comprehensive examination of all the physically uninjured children would be likely for medical and compensatory reasons. Many perhaps would be able to make substantial claims for PTSD or related conditions. Fifty years after the disaster, one of the surviving children said:

I can see myself being buried in the nightmares ... I have hot sweats. Sometimes I wake up and I'm reeling. I just shoot out of bed and I don't know where I am. You know, the nightmares are really vivid. And I have them quite regular.[43]

The trauma that was never properly compensated is ongoing.

The donation for removing the tips

The Commission's activism on grants to the memorial or to survivors contrasts starkly with its silence on a proposed donation from the Disaster Fund towards the cost of removing the remaining tips that

---

42. Gaynor Madgwick, *Aberfan: A Story of Survival, Love and Community in One of Britain's Worst Disasters* (Talybont: Y Lolfa 2016), pp. 95-6.
43. Sue Elliott, Steve Humphries and Bevan Jones, *Surviving Aberfan: The People's Story* (Guildford: Grosvenor House, 2016), p. 170.

still towered over Aberfan, a contribution that was the end of a long, drawn-out affair that again revealed the antipathy of both the NCB and the government to the welfare of the community.

Soon after the disaster, people in Aberfan had begun calling for the removal of the remaining tips, but the NCB argued that this was not economically feasible (unless somebody else paid), and that the structures posed no danger to the village. It commissioned a report which priced six different ways of removing the tips at between £1.014 million and £3.4 million.[44] The Tribunal Report accepted the NCB case that complete removal was neither necessary nor economically feasible, giving an estimated cost of £3 million. It is not known whether the Tribunal saw the lower estimates.[45] From then until August 1968, Lord Robens led a doughty fight to minimise the Coal Board's liability to pay for tip removal. One exasperated Welsh Office civil servant wrote to his Secretary of State that Robens' technique consisted of 'vaguely favouring a bigger scheme and allowing this view to be known publicly. But ... adamant that the extra cost should be borne by the Exchequer.'[46] However, this approach faced three problems. The Chief Secretary to the Treasury refused to pay;[47] evidence that the job could be done more cheaply had to be suppressed or countered; some villagers rejected anything short of complete removal, reportedly saying 'The Coal Board put them there; the Coal Board can take them away.'

A local firm, Ryan Industrial Fuels, specialised in tip clearance and salvage of reusable coal. Before the disaster, they had already inspected the disaster tip with a view to tendering for coal removal from it. After the disaster, they maintained that they could remove the tips more cheaply than the Coal Board claimed it would cost. Finally, in April 1968, they submitted an estimate to the Aberfan Tip Removal Committee, which was forwarded to the Welsh Office. This was for £660,000 if they were permitted to recover coal from

---

44. 'Proposed alternative methods of removing the whole of the tip complex', June 1967, TNA: BD52/1/8.
45. *Aberfan Report*, pp. 121-2.
46. G. Diamond to C. Hughes, 8 April 1968, TNA: BD 52/113.
47. TNA: BD 52/115 and 114, passim.

the complex, and about £1.25 million otherwise.[48] Something similar must already have been on the table in October 1967, because the most eye-opening part of the ministerial briefing is the advice given to the Minister on how he should counter any claims in the Commons that the price of tip removal was being exaggerated. As no such claims were made, this part of the briefing note was never used.

> The chosen scheme [viz. an NCB landscaping scheme which did not involve removing the tips] could quickly transform the appearance of the area and total expenditure would amount to £3/4 million to £1 million. (This is deliberately ambiguous. NCB has spent £1/2 million so far and is continuing at £20,000 per week, say another £200,000, + £250,000 to the landscaping, making £1 million in all. Complete removal would cost £3 million.)

The note went on to say that the Minister should say that the question of tip removal was for the Welsh Office, not for him, and that the Tribunal Report had recommended against complete removal. On Ryan's offer, it continued that the Minister should oppose coal recovery on the grounds that

> The sale of the coal is a problem:
> (i)   it displaces deep mined coal when the mines cannot be closed fast enough and their stockpiles are swollen;
> (ii) if non-NCB tips are concerned the contractor can sell the coal cheaply to the detriment of the NCB.

The Minister was advised to say that Ryan had left other tips in 'a shambles', and that the NCB would confirm this.[49] When the Ryan tender arrived in April 1968, a Welsh Office official wrote to the Treasury that 'it is quite unrealistic to think in terms of Ryan doing

---

48. Letter from Aberfan Tip Removal Committee to J. Siberry, enclosing estimate from Ryan Industrial Fuels, 30 April 1968, TNA: BD 52/113. Memo by B. Houghton of meeting between Chief Secretary to Treasury and Secretary of State for Wales, July 1968, TNA: BD52/114.
49. Brief for Aberfan Debate, TNA: BD 52/154.

the job when the NCB have their own contractors with men and equipment on the spot.'[50]

Initially, the NCB tried to push through a scheme where the remaining tips were reduced in height and landscaped. It suggested that complete removal would mean lorries disrupting the village as they carted the waste away.[51] Cledwyn Hughes, Secretary of State for Wales, accepted the case for the tips to be reduced rather than removed on the grounds that they were safe and that full removal would be costly, time consuming and possibly dangerous.[52] Yet his successor George Thomas told a deputation from Aberfan that cost was not the issue: 'One could not balance money against what had happened at Aberfan.' Landscaping was safer, quicker and caused less nuisance.[53] In private, money was always the issue. The NCB maintained it could not afford to pay in full, the Welsh Office was concerned money may be taken from its budget, while there were wider Government concerns that it might commit itself to dealing with mine refuse elsewhere.[54] A Welsh Office under-secretary admitted that, despite the decision not to emphasise cost as an issue, 'it is the root of the matter and it seldom pays to cloud the main issue.'[55]

That under-secretary had been detailed by the Welsh Office to maintain liaison between the village and the Department. He reported frequently, almost in the manner of a colonial governor, expressing hopes that 'moderate' villagers, who were not calling for total removal of the tips, would prevail over 'militants', who were.[56]

50. J. Siberry to G. Diamond, 2 April 1968, TNA: BD 11/3804.
51. See miscellaneous documents in Aberfan and Merthyr Vale Tip Removal Committee minutes, GA: D1368/1.
52. Statement by the Secretary of State for Wales: The Tips at Aberfan, 2 January 1968, Aberfan and Merthyr Vale Tip Removal Committee minutes, GA: D1368.
53. Meeting with Aberfan Deputation at Welsh Office, London, 7 February 1968, TNA: BD 11/3804.
54. 26 July 1968 Minutes of Meeting 157(68), TNA: BD 11/3807.
55. J. Siberry to G. Diamond, 28 May 1968. BD 11/3804.
56. Reports by J. Siberry, TNA: BD 52/113 and 114. On 10 February 1969, for instance, he reported, 'So the hurdle of the unpredictable emotions and reactions of Aberfan seems to be behind us.' TNA: BD 11/3807.

Those who feared the disruption threatened by the NCB's initial claim that complete removal of the tips might necessitate lorries travelling through the village had their worries alleviated by the local authority who came up with a scheme where the tip waste would be levelled completely and spread across the mountainside rather than be removed by road. The majority opinion in the village quickly came to support this over the Coal Board's plan to make the tips smaller. The Secretary of the Tip Removal Committee wrote to the Minister of Power in December 1967 appealing for support for the council's scheme for complete removal:

> The experts may say as often and as loud as they like that the tips do not constitute a danger – as far as this committee is concerned, it sounds like the 'mixture as before'. We, who have to live in the shadow of this evil reminder of tragedy, feel that we should not have to beg, cap in hand, for its removal.
>
> Chesterton said that 'only local things are.' This thing is more than real to us, and its removal would prove an act of faith to those who died, and a tremendous boost to the morale of Aberfan, a psychological shot in the arm to the village in its efforts to rehabilitate itself.
>
> We appeal to you, Sir, to use your authority to grant that which we desire so much – so that Aberfan may be made a safer and more amenable place in which to live and bring up our future children.[57]

As mentioned in the previous chapter, Kenneth Hayes, chairman of the Aberfan Parents' and Residents' Association, wrote to the Prime Minister in January 1968:

> Every time it rains people are afraid to go to bed, ... and all of us subconsciously are awaiting the alarm to sound. ... The mental wellbeing of the community today, and the safety of the unborn generations depends on the removal of tips.[58]

---

57. T.S. Price to Richard Marsh, 11 December 1967. Aberfan and Merthyr Vale Tip Removal Committee minutes, GA: D1368.
58. K. Hayes to H. Wilson, January 1968, quoted in I. McLean, 'The Revd Kenneth Hayes' [obituary], *Independent*, 31 January 1998.

The resolve was then stiffened by two storms in July 1968, which brought slurry from the tips down into the disaster area creating significant alarm and fear of another catastrophe. In the wake of this, the Tip Removal Committee immediately telegrammed the Secretary of State for Wales demanding that he get the tips removed.[59]

Any argument that the NCB was not wholly liable for removing the tips was fatally undercut by the 1965 NCB 'Powell Memorandum', quoted approvingly by the Tribunal, which showed that if it had been implemented, there would have been no disaster. It was circulated in April 1965 to all NCB area mechanical and civil engineers in south Wales. It adapted and expanded a 1939 memorandum from the Powell Duffryn coal company entitled 'The Sliding of Colliery Rubbish Tips'. The 1939 memorandum arose from the Cilfynydd slide, in which an estimated 180,000 tons slid from a tip after heavy rain, blocking the main road, railway, and canal. The Cilfynydd slide was well remembered by older NCB officials, including Clifford Jones (in 1965 Divisional Mechanical Engineer for South Wales) and his immediate superior, Daniel Powell (Chief Engineer for South Wales). Mr Jones had been in charge of removing the Cilfynydd slide from the main A470 road, which took five or six days; and had been handed a copy of the memorandum by his father, who was a more senior Powell Duffryn engineer in 1939.[60] After another tip slide at Tŷ Mawr in 1965, engineers in south Wales rediscovered the memorandum. Mr Powell reissued it, adding a few paragraphs of his own. The most material paragraphs are the following:

6.2   Where a slide would cause damage to property, no tip over 20 feet high should be placed on a hillside unless the ground is a compact gravel or of better quality than this.

6.3   The advancing tip should be so aligned, along a sloping surface, that water draining off the ground above it can be collected, if necessary, by a system of drains cut in the ground, and led past and clear of the tip. ...

---

59. T.S. Price to George Thomas, 1 Jul 1968, Aberfan and Merthyr Vale Tip Removal Committee papers, GA: D1368.
60. *Aberfan Report*, paras 81 and 227.

6.4 On the dip side of the tip, deep drains (not less than 18 inches) should be cut leading downhill to prevent water accumulating and to keep the ground dry. ...

6.5 Tipping should never be extended over springs of water, whether continuous or intermittent, or over bogged and water-logged ground.[61]

These requirements were in the 1939 document and were repeated verbatim in the 1965 reissue. The disaster tip had broken them all. Tips 4 and 5, which remained after the disaster, broke requirements 6.2, 6.3, and 6.4 by a generous margin. They were around 100 feet high. They were on boulder clay and fissured Pennant sandstone, a (much) poorer quality of ground for its purpose than compacted gravel. Tip 4 had previously slid in 1944, so that not only were they not drained as required by the Powell Memorandum, but the 1944 slip had offered a naturally lubricated surface for the disaster slide[62] and would do the same for any future slide. Tip 4 had been drained when it started to bulge, but Tip 5 had promptly been started right on top of the drain by the man (Geoffrey Morgan) who had authorised the drain. Both tips bulged out of conical shape.[63] The failure of either Mr Roberts or Mr Exley to implement the instruction to inspect the Merthyr Vale tips to see if they complied with the Powell Memorandum was the proximate cause of the disaster.

It is true that the technical experts retained by both sides at the disaster inquiry concurred that tips 4 and 5 were now safe, and that removing them would be an impracticably vast job.[64] But they still broke the guidelines of the Powell Memorandum, the NCB's costings were exaggerated and, in light of what had happened before the disaster, people in Aberfan were simply not prepared to accept these new assurances of safety. Villagers used the Powell Memorandum as a lever to put pressure on the government, but to no avail.[65] Cledwyn

---

61. *Aberfan Tribunal Report*, Appendix D. Original copies of the Memorandum are in the Tribunal papers, TNA: BD 52.
62. *Aberfan Tribunal Report*, para 90.
63. *Aberfan Tribunal Report*, paras 83-95.
64. *Aberfan Tribunal Report*, paras 279-80.
65. Siberry to Daniel, 11 December 1967, TNA: BD52/113.

Hughes, Secretary of State for Wales, dismissed, rather summarily, the relevance of the Powell Memorandum, pointing to how the Tribunal had not thought full removal necessary and the safety work already done by the NCB.[66] A letter to George Thomas, Hughes' successor as Welsh Secretary of State, from Aberfan's Tip Removal Committee made clear the anger caused by the refusals of the NCB and the Welsh Office to sanction full removal. It ended with the threat that unless a suitable reply was received, discussions would take place over 'what forms of militant action' to employ.[67] The committee also asked the local MP to pressurise the Welsh Office before Aberfan really 'blows up'.[68]

Further delays saw the threats of militant action become reality. After an unsuccessful meeting between Thomas and representatives of Aberfan, quantities of tip slurry were dumped inside the Welsh Office and the tyres on the Minister's car slashed. Thomas left the meeting in tears.[69] He wrote to Harold Wilson, describing it as 'one of the most harrowing and difficult meetings I have ever had.' Elsewhere he told Wilson that 'I believe they have worked themselves into an irrational state of mind on this issue but we have to contend with the intensity of their feelings, whether these are logical or not, and we also have to bear in mind the general reaction of the press and other commentators and also local opinion in the surrounding area.'[70] Thomas' memoirs record that he told Wilson on the telephone 'I am sorry, Prime Minister, but I can't do it. I just can't tell these people that the tip has to stay. They are afraid. Their protest has not been manufactured, it's a genuine fear from people who have been

---

66. The Tips at Aberfan: Statement by the Secretary of State for Wales, 23 January 1968. Aberfan and Merthyr Vale Tip Removal Committee Papers, GA: D1368.
67. Letter from T.S. Price to George Thomas, 18 June 1968, SWCC: MNA/PP/16/37.
68. T.S. Price to S.O. Davies, 18 June 1968. Aberfan and Merthyr Vale Tip Removal Committee Papers, GA: D1368.
69. Interview with bereaved parent present at the meeting, *Western Mail*, 1 August 1997. MJ interview with Colin Murray Parkes, 28 April 1999.
70. G. Thomas to the Prime Minister, 23 July 1968, TNA: BD 52/114. Draft minute from G. Thomas to H. Wilson, 23 July 1968, TNA: COAL 73/5 & BD 11/3804.

through a terrible experience.'[71] Wilson stated that 'We met the next day; the tip had to go.' One might imagine that would have settled it. But Lord Robens still refused to budge: 'The Coal Board raised difficulties, and I asked the Minister to remind them of a few facts.' George Thomas was also prepared to 'remind Robens of the outcome of the inquiry and make it clear to him that he thinks the NCB have an obligation to the people of Aberfan.' He prepared to cancel a trip to Brunei, anticipating that even this threat would not persuade Robens to pay.[72] In the end, a deal was finally worked out between Thomas, Wilson and the Chancellor of the Exchequer where the Treasury, NCB and 'local interests' would pay £250,000 each, with the government and Coal Board paying more if coal recovery was ruled out leading total costs to exceed £750,000. This new working estimate was less than a third of the board's original highest estimate. George Thomas' public announcement of the arrangement stated that government expenditure of this sort 'has got to be found at the cost of some other Government project such as hospitals, housing, roads etc. It is therefore only reasonable to expect that local interests should make some contribution as well.'[73]

There was never any doubt that 'local interests' meant the Disaster Fund. Forcing it to pay part of the cost of removing the tip complex was controversial at the time, and it has not become any less controversial. The question first arose at a meeting between Robens and the two ministers concerned (Marsh and Hughes, the Secretary of State for Wales) in March 1967: 'Although in some respects there was something to be said for drawing on the Disaster Fund it was felt that, at this stage, such a suggestion would be far too explosive.'[74]

---

71. George Thomas, *Mr Speaker: The Memoirs of the Viscount Tonypandy* (London: Century Publishing, 1985), p. 101.

72. Harold Wilson, *The Labour Government 1964-70: A Personal Record* (Harmondsworth: Penguin, 1974), pp. 694-5. D. Andrews to H. Wilson, 26 July 1968, TNA: PREM 13/1281.

73. Statement by Secretary of State for Wales, 26 July 1968. Aberfan and Merthyr Vale Tip Removal Committee Papers, GA: D1368. Thomas, *Mr Speaker*, p. 101.

74. Minutes of meeting on 6 March 1967, TNA: COAL 73/2. Less than a week after the disaster, an editorial in the *South Wales Echo* had actually

However, by July 1968, with Robens still refusing to budge, ministers had to return to the Fund. George Thomas initially rejected the idea arguing that the general public would see the Government as 'shabby' and the 'village would be enraged'.[75] However, a side step was devised: 'It was right that some of the money should be found locally, but the Government need not suggest that it should be taken from the Appeal Fund.'[76] This was disingenuous; everybody knew that there was no other public body in the valley with any money, and that no private body would see any reason to remove the Coal Board's waste from the Coal Board's property.

The Government's decision was announced at a meeting between Thomas and a deputation from the village and the Disaster Fund in July 1968. The initial news that the tips were to go was received joyously. Talfan Davies said that the Management Committee would be sympathetic if their help was necessary. He claimed that it would fulfil one of the fund's main purposes, the rehabilitation of Aberfan.[77] Yet once the euphoria was over the implication of the phrase 'local interests' began to sink home. Stanley Davies, the fund's founder and chairman, stated that he was against it making any contribution. S.O. Davies, the local MP and member of the Fund's Management committee, called the decision 'the meanest thing I have seen in 34 years in Parliament.' He wrote to the Prime Minister calling it 'disgraceful and contemptible ... sheer blackmail.' An editorial in the only national newspaper in Wales called the decision 'outrageous ... It is enough that the villagers have suffered so much and lived for so long in fear without making them pay for the removal of the tips as well.'[78]

---

suggested using the Fund for 'beautifying by afforestation' the tips above the village. *South Wales Echo*, 26 October 1966.

75. Confidential note by Secretary of State, n.d. but July 1968, TNA: BD 11/3804.

76. Minute of Misc. 157(68), first meeting, 26 July 1968, BD 11/3807.

77. *Western Mail*, 27 July 1968.

78. *Second Report of the Management Committee of the Aberfan Disaster Fund* (Merthyr Tydfil, 1970), p. 4; Joan Miller, *Aberfan: a Disaster and its Aftermath* (London, 1974), pp. 60-2. S.O. Davies to Harold Wilson, 30 July 1968. ADA, Dowlais collection C/007/02. *Western Mail*, 27, 29 July, 6 August 1968.

People in Aberfan were angry at the government's decision too but they also wanted the tips gone. A meeting of the Tip Removal Committee was divided. Feelings were strong but the minutes recorded that there were as many different reactions as there were in the village as a whole; the 'community has been faced with an intolerable choice between paying for tip removal and paying for reconstruction', the minutes concluded.[79] After the meeting, a minister deputising for the committee secretary wrote to the Prime Minister saying that the community felt it was being asked to choose between 'clearing the past' and having the resources for 'building the future ... Add to the pressure of this choice a deep sense of injustice, still very much intertwined with emotions of grief and personal loss and some illness, and you have more anguish upon anguish in Aberfan.' He appealed to Wilson to save the community from 'this impossible choice'.[80]

Quite rightly, the question arose of what donors to the fund would think. After all, they were the ones who had raised the money. Some had already made their views known. Lord Balfour of Inchyre wrote to *The Times* that he and his wife had donated 'for the relief and comfort of the bereaved and distressed. We certainly never contemplated our gift money being used towards the cost of doing work which must be the clear responsibility of Her Majesty's Government, or the National Coal Board or local authorities.'[81] The opinion of donors more widely was sought after an appeal by the secretary of the Parents' and Residents' Association. Only about 100 replies were received. They were divided evenly for and against the donation, as were letters received by George Thomas himself.[82] A Welsh Office briefing note warned officials that, in the original letters accompanying donations, only £33 10s had been earmarked for tip removal and that 'local people would make much' of this fact.[83]

---

79. Meeting, 30 July 1968. Aberfan and Merthyr Vale Tip Removal Committee papers, GA: D1368.
80. Erastus Jones, to Harold Wilson, 31 July 1968, Aberfan and Merthyr Vale Tip Removal Committee papers, GA: D1368.
81. *The Times*, 5 August 1968.
82. *ADF mins*, 8 August 1968, GRO D/D X 295/12/1/2.
83. Background note for Siberry, 25 July 1968, TNA: BD 11/3804.

The final decision to contribute was taken by the fund's Management Committee on 8 August 1968 after a meeting with George Thomas. The swaying factors appear to have been a promise that the fund's contribution would not have to be made for another two years, allowing further interest to accrue, and the realisation that there appeared to be no alternative if the tips were to be removed. George Thomas had told the Committee

> If, however, the local interests do not feel strongly enough to wish to make a contribution themselves then the case for spending a big sum of taxpayers' money over and above what is needed for purposes of amenity and safety is greatly weakened.[84]

S.O. Davies was the only member of the Committee who voted against the fund contributing. He promptly resigned.[85] The Committee was then faced with the task of explaining its decision to the Aberfan Parents' and Residents' Association. This was done at a meeting on 13 August 1968. Fifty members of the association attended to hear the committee's explanation and only one person voted against supporting the decision.[86] This is not to say that it was widely supported, merely that there appeared to be no alternative.

Stanley Davies, the fund chairman, maintained strongly that the Management Committee had not been blackmailed into contributing. He said that George Thomas had told them what the Government and NCB could afford to contribute and that they had to face that 'bald fact'.[87] Blackmail may not be the right noun but it is difficult to see what alternative the fund had. It had taken nearly two years to get the Government to agree to the full removal that people wanted so desperately. With the Government's insistence that there was no more public money available, no one in the fund or Aberfan wanted to risk the tips staying because of a failure to raise the remaining capital needed.

---

84. *ADF mins*, 8 August 1968, GRO D/D X 295/12/1/2.
85. *Western Mail*, 9 August 1968.
86. *Western Mail*, 14 August 1968.
87. *Merthyr Express*, 15 August 1968.

The fund's Management Committee does not appear to have sought the Charity Commission's consent to make this payment.[88] The matter was not recorded in the minutes of any meeting of the Charity Commissioners up to the end of 1969. It is odd that a donation which was bitterly controversial in Aberfan was not discussed, whereas two donations that were not controversial in Aberfan took up a lot of the Commissioners' energy. A Welsh Office memorandum however notes that the Charity Commission had confirmed that such a contribution would be in accordance with the trust Deed.[89]

In the broadest interpretation of the fund's objects, removing the tips could be seen as for the benefit of Aberfan. At the meeting with George Thomas, Tasker Watkins QC, who was a trustee of the fund, noted the need for careful wording for the Committee's decision. He suggested the following statement:

> The Committee having very carefully considered not only the statement of the Secretary of State for Wales but many other aspects of the problem and having had in mind very much the relief which will come to the people of Aberfan by the removal of the tips, have decided to make a contribution but the size of this contribution cannot be determined until the Committee has had time to consider its various commitments.[90]

There is no bar on a charity providing a service that would otherwise be supplied at the expense of the state and taxpayer.[91]

However, the Coal Board owned the tips, and the tips' condition violated the principles laid down in the Powell Memorandum. The Coal Board also had a strict civil liability to compensate anybody

---

88. Interview, MJ and Fund trustee. B. Nightingale, *Charities* (London: Allen Lane, 1973), p. 184, claims that the Charity Commission felt that the donation would help rehabilitate Aberfan and was thus in accordance with the trust deed. We have been unable to get any confirmation of this claim.
89. Welsh Office, Background note for J Siberry [Assistant Secretary dealing with Aberfan], 25 July 1968, TNA: BD 11/3804.
90. *ADF mins*, 8 August 1968, GRO D/D X 295/12/1/2.
91. H. Picarda, *The Law and Practice Relating to Charities* (London: Butterworth, 1977), p. 91.

injured, or any property damaged, by a sliding tip.[92] Given this liability, the NCB's previous failure to observe its own recommendations on tip safety, and the death and destruction already caused, it is surprising that the Coal Board did not remove the tips on its own initiative. This was especially so since, even with assurances that the remaining tips were safe, material had continued to wash down into the village from the spoil heaps after the disaster, causing some minor panic. Aberfan residents did not believe anything the Coal Board said. These facts are powerful evidence against the lawfulness (to say nothing of propriety) of forcing the Disaster Fund to contribute to the removal of tips 4 and 5.

Local anger at the donation was then compounded by the length of time it took for the tip removal work to be completed, even after the fund's contribution had been agreed. Both the fund and the Tip Removal Committee grew frustrated at the delays and lack of information from the NCB on what was happening. Appeals again had to be made to the Welsh Office about the NCB's lack of communication with the community. This also meant that doubts about the size and nature of the contribution could fester. A meeting between the Tip Removal Committee and the Fund in June 1969 agreed that no contribution should be made until the overall cost had reached £750,000 but the two bodies also agreed that the controversy over who paid should not be re-opened and that the tips must go, even if the Fund had to pay £250,000. In the end, the Fund refused to pay more than £150,000 and some of the landscaping of the cleared land was simplified to reduce overall costs.[93] In 1971 it emerged that the still ongoing removal operation was going to cost more than had originally been thought. The Welsh Office rejected the idea of seeking a further contribution from the Fund: 'Any such suggestion would stir up much trouble and unpleasantness. To start a conflagration in Aberfan one has only to kick a stone accidentally.'[94]

---

92. *Rylands v Fletcher* [1868] LR 3, HL 330; *Att Gen v Cory Bros & Co Ltd* (1921) 1 AC 521.
93. Various documents, Aberfan and Merthyr Vale Tip Removal Committee, GA: D1368/3.
94. J. Siberry to Mr Barker, 11 March 1971. BD 11/3807.

The contribution was not forgotten. S.O. Davies continued to lobby on the issue. His successor to the seat, Ted Rowlands, lobbied successive Labour leaders on the issue. Aberfan residents asked Conservative governments three times for the money to be repaid. Despite the Fund's careful investments, hit by inflation, it had problems in managing the disaster's memorials. In 1987, it was forced to hand over control of the Aberfan community centre to the local authority because of financial difficulties.[95] Such problems made the case for a refund all the stronger. In July 1997, Ron Davies, the new Secretary of State for Wales, announced that the Government would repay the money contributed to the removal of the tips by the Disaster Fund, adding that the Fund should never have been asked to contribute in the first place. While the decision was welcomed for helping to guarantee the future maintenance of the cemetery and remembrance garden, there was also a degree of resentment. £150,000 was to be refunded, the exact figure paid, rather than the £1,534,410 that the contribution would have been worth in 1997.[96] Full restoration, allowing for inflation and the interest forgone, was made by the Welsh Assembly Government under Rhodri Morgan in 2007.[97]

Making the polluter pay

The Disaster Fund was not the only source of financial recompense available to those in Aberfan. It was then part of normal legal practice to award damages for loss of expectation of life. In cases where a child had been killed this was complicated by the fact that there were no earnings to measure and take into account in setting the sum. There had been some contestation and debate over the influence of inflation but in the mid 1960s £500 was accepted as a normal payment for a child's loss of expectation of life and this was what the NCB offered

---

95. Telephone interview, MJ and Aberfan Memorial Fund secretary, 29 January 1999.
96. *Western Mail*, 1 August 1997; *South Wales Echo*, 31 July, 1 August 1997.
97. '£1.5m for Aberfan memorial garden' http://news.bbc.co.uk/1/hi/wales/6316717.stm (accessed 3 November 2016).

bereaved parents in Aberfan.[98] The Board's insurance staff, who did not accept liability for the disaster on behalf of the NCB until April 1967, called the award 'a good offer' and urged Lord Robens, their chairman, to resist demands to pay more – 'It is only the hard core [of bereaved parents] who are trying to capitalise.'[99]

One bereaved mother wrote to Lord Robens:

> It's my opinion and that of many others in this deeply sad community that this effort by the NCB puts shame on us all and also those who made the law valid ... The lifelong grief and loneliness being shared by so many here is a condition we realise no amount of money can erase ... my own child [name withheld] who was 9 1/2 years when she was killed, was a healthy intelligent child who should have had a life expectancy of at least 60 years. Dividing £500 by 60 gives her last years a value of less than £8 per year. Some of the children were extremely capable and intelligent and, without doubt would have done credit to both community and country. All of them should be alive today. They are not. They died violently and most cruelly through no fault of their own and because of the neglect of others. ... This matter hurts us here deeply – adds to the feeling that our children – whatever they meant to us, and whatever values they may have been as citizens, are now dead, and being so, value little to this country, and also value little to those who caused them to die. They are now it seems and within the letter of the law, to be written off, as cheaply as possible, and the matter closed. ... Is there no room for social conscience in law and business?[100]

To anybody who is not a lawyer, this statement seems a matter of common sense, as well as strong emotional appeal. Robens did not reply.

---

98. For a full account of the reasoning behind this figure and the legal debate see the first edition of this book, Chapter 7.
99. TNA: COAL 73/2: W.J.P. Webber to Lord Robens, 25 April 1967 (accepting liability), D. Haslam to same, 31 May 1967 ('good offer'); D.H. Kelly to same, 8 June 1967 ('hard core'); Secret Minute of the Board, 16 June 1967 (agreeing not to go above £500 per victim).
100. Names of author and her daughter withheld. TNA: COAL 73/2.

There is, of course, no correct sum that can ever compensate for the loss of the life of a child. Money can simply not do that, whether it is paid by the killer or the sympathetic public. Nor was compensation for loss of expectation of life, in the eyes of the law at least, a payment for any financial loss by parents whose child was killed. Instead, payments upon the death of a child represented a symbolic acceptance of guilt by the negligent party and a recognition of this by the State enforcing the payment. For that reason, these payments, now known as bereavement damages, should not be seen as 'blood money' but some recompense for the bereaved to illustrate that their loss has not gone unacknowledged. Compensation is as much about justice as finance.

Payments from any source also have practical uses. One bereaved parent told the press that the payment of £5,000 from the Disaster Fund would be used to provide for her remaining daughters, paying off her mortgage and maybe a holiday. She summed up 'I am very pleased but what good is money?'[101] Allowing a bereaved family to get away and ease the financial burdens of life was surely a just cause but the idea of people benefitting financially from their loss still made some observers uncomfortable. This explains why the size of the Disaster Fund attracted significant comment in the media and amongst a few there was a sense of distaste at reports of arguments over how the fund should be managed and spent. Newspapers claimed that it could take decades to spend to fund.[102] Some called the fund the second Aberfan disaster.

Although it does not seem to have ever been recorded in writing, it is probable that fears that the money was creating discord and argument influenced the decision to ask the fund to spend some of its resources on removing the Coal Board's tips. But there was also an awareness in government that the NCB was not a private institution whose finances were divorced from the public purse. During the tip removal campaign, the senior Welsh Office official dealing with Aberfan wrote, 'The cost of all the consequences ... to an NCB in deficit, must fall in the end on the Exchequer.'[103] All decision makers

---

101. *The Times*, 9 September 1967.
102. For example, *The Times*, 20 February 1967.
103. J. Siberry to G. Daniel, 6 November 1967, TNA: BD 52/113.

in government agreed. No one felt that it was worthwhile to persuade the Coal Board to pay more in the face of Lord Robens' obdurate resistance. As Marsh pointed out, forcing the NCB to pay would only give Robens an excuse to come and ask for bigger grants in the future.[104]

This is part of a much larger story. The coal industry had been making heavy losses for a number of years. Even Merthyr Vale colliery, although it made an operating profit in 1966 (and was one of the last deep mines in south Wales to close, in 1990), was losing money after finance charges.[105] If the Aberfan compensation claims had been debited to Merthyr Vale, and still more if the cost of removing the tips had been, it would have shown a heavy operating loss. This could have had consequences for jobs that were so obvious that they simmered below the surface of the inquiry, breaking out acrimoniously once or twice (see chapter 3).

Nobody, in 1966, proposed that the polluter should pay. The idea that polluters should pay for externalities that they imposed on society was commonplace in economics, but unheard of in practical politics. Anti-pollution law such as the Rivers (Prevention of Pollution) Act 1951 and the Clean Air Act 1956 relied on regulation and the threat of prosecution, not on charges or permits. Therefore politicians, of both parties, simply accepted that it was pointless to saddle the NCB with costs that would merely increase its deficit. In consequence, nobody faced the true cost of coal. As the *Financial Times* put it soon after the Tribunal Report was published,

[O]ne disadvantage of having industries run by the State that has been spotlighted by the Aberfan disaster is that, when Government stands in the role of owner of an industry, it will be apt to be less mindful of the need to care for the wider interests of the public in relation to that industry than it would be if it were dealing with private enterprise. It will be less inclined, for example, to ensure that due regard is paid to such considerations as the safety of the public

---

104. Lord Marsh interview.
105. Unlabelled file of financial figures, collected from Engineer's Department, Merthyr Town Hall. In Merthyr Tydfil Central Library. Aberfan Disaster Collection.

and the avoidance of loss of amenities than would be the case if it were not so deeply concerned with the profitability of the industry.[106]

This failure extended to the Tribunal itself. Ackner said in his closing speech had the Coal Board been a private corporation facing claims for negligence, its counsel would have advised it that it had no defence.[107] However, as the cost of its 76-day defence was met by the taxpayer, it was not deterred. Similarly, even after the Tribunal had removed any doubt about the NCB's liability for the disaster, it was the Disaster Fund that was left to pay not just the levels of compensation that people felt were fair but even to remove the tips that belonged to the board and were causing so much anguish. There were other examples too of where the fund stepped in to pay for what the NCB would not. The trustees of Bethania chapel, which was used as the mortuary after the disaster, pleaded with George Thomas to get the NCB to pay for it to be demolished and rebuilt, on the grounds that its members could no longer bear to worship there. Thomas passed the plea on to Lord Robens, who rejected it.[108] In the end, it was rebuilt, but with the Disaster Fund committing up to £20,000 to the cost and the NCB just £5,000.[109]

Donors and their protection

When the Mayor of Merthyr set up the Aberfan Disaster Fund, he did not articulate any specific use for the money. Nor was the precise final use of the money central to millions of people's decisions to give. The Fund was generated by media coverage and a sense that something extraordinary and tragic had happened; there was a sense of a national and shared tragedy, a sense of loss and grief

---

106. *Financial Times*, 14 August 1967.
107. *Aberfan Tribunal, Transcript of Oral Evidence*, Day 70, p. 3940.
108. Thomas to Robens, 15.05.68; reply, 5 June 1968. TNA: COAL 73/4 Pt 1.
109. *The Second Report of the Aberfan Disaster Fund*, p. 12.

that extended far beyond the bereaved and survivors.[110] Just as after other disasters, giving to the fund enabled the public to express symbolically its sympathy with those who have suffered.[111] Disaster funds are also rooted in an absence of alternative ways to express sympathy and empathy. A letter to the Aberfan Disaster Fund noted 'I know that no amount of money can buy these children's lives, but what else can one do?'[112] Decisions to give were also, of course, about the giver as well as the disaster. The donation letters sent by parents and people with connections with Wales and mining communities suggest a particularly strong sense of sympathy from those who felt some direct personal empathy or connection with Aberfan. Some commentators can thus be rather cynical about disaster funds. The journalist John Humphrys, who reported from Aberfan, has written 'as with giving money to Aberfan and Dunblane, decisions are taken primarily to satisfy our fickle moral vanity rather than to do the right thing.'[113] But whether the source is vanity or empathy, donations are rarely given to relieve any specific need in the community affected.

Some observers have regarded this giving without any clear need as irrational.[114] In Surrey, a police committee even banned street collections for Aberfan, saying 'It was our unanimous feeling that there has been such an exaggerated wave of sympathy. We thought we would be cluttered up with street collections from every sort of body here, there and everywhere.'[115] But it is not for a police committee or any commentator to say that one or another use of someone else's money is rational or irrational. People have their preferences, and that is all one can say. The lady who gave the money

---

110. Kathleen M. Wright, Robert J. Ursano, Paul T. Bartone, Larry H. Ingraham, 'The Shared Experience of Catastrophe: An Expanded Classification of the Disaster Community', *American Journal of Orthopsychiatry*, 60, 1 (1990), 35-42.
111. C.M. Parkes & D. Black, 'Disasters', in C. M. Parkes & A Markus (eds.), *Coping with Loss: Helping Patients and their Families* (London: BMJ Books, 1998).
112. Quoted in Nightingale, *Charities*, p. 178.
113. John Humphrys, *Devil's Advocate* (London: Hutchinson, 1999), p. 63.
114. Nightingale, *Charities*, p. 179.
115. *The Times*, 4 November 1966.

she had been saving for her winter coat to the Disaster Fund (Chapter 1) was expressing a preference and a wish – 'Please use this small amount in any way you wish.' It was a wish the Charity Commission failed to protect. The trustees did not wish donors' money to be put to removing Tips 4 and 5. Only £33 10s of donations had been offered for that purpose.

Regardless of why people give money to the victims of disasters, they might expect some protection from regulators, especially in a situation where a public board was refusing to cover all its liabilities and the government was unwilling to push the matter because, ultimately, the cost would come back to it. In its annual report for 1967, the Charity Comission drew attention to its general function under the Charities Act 1960 of

> Promoting the effective use of charitable resources by encouraging the development of better methods of administration, by giving charity trustees information or advice in any matter affecting the charity and by investigating and checking abuses.

In the same document, the Commission draws attention to some services that seem relevant to the circumstances of the Aberfan Disaster Fund: for example: 'charity trustees who ... feel uneasy about the way in which it has been the practice to administer their charity should not hesitate to come to the Charity Commissioners for advice'.[116] But when the law was ill-equipped to deal with the kind of problems that the Aberfan fund faced, and the government was creating impossible situations, then the advice of the Commission could not provide a distribution of money that was to the satisfaction of all concerned. Consequently, the regulation of the Charity Commission failed and it was left unclear in whose interest it was operating.

The fashion for mission statements had not yet arisen. They might, for once, have been some use in this case. The Commission did not make it clear how it balanced its duties to the general public, to

---

116. *The Charity Commissioners: how they can help charity trustees* paras 1, 3; cf also para 10. In *Report of the Charity Commissioners for England and Wales for the Year 1967* (London: HMSO, 1968), pp. 33-37.

charity donors, to charity beneficiaries, and to charity trustees. The result was that at Aberfan, the interests of the local people, and of those donors who objected to their gifts going towards the removal of the tips, were not protected. In 1968, 1969, and 1970 a number of members of the public wrote to MPs or Ministers to object to this use of the fund. The form letter drafted by the Welsh Office to reply to these complaints does not address the complaint about alleged abuse of charitable purpose at all.[117]

The Charity Commission was faced with the difficult task of upholding a narrow law that failed to meet the expectations of the different parties involved. The Commissioners did make attempts to find ways around the law, as their actions over the memorial and payments to the bereaved demonstrated. However, the reasoning was tortuous and perhaps even insulting to the people of Aberfan. Thus the injustices of the law were compounded by the Commission. Had their advice always been strictly followed then the situation would have been worse. The Commissioners may have only been doing their job, but the whole affair raises questions about in whose interests they should have been working. Regulation of the Aberfan Disaster Fund did not clearly work in the interest of Aberfan.

But the fund itself, for all its problems, did help the people of Aberfan. It built a memorial at the cemetery and an important new community centre and distributed money directly to bereaved parents and mentally and physically injured children, helping them rebuild their lives. It provided for the material needs of families affected, including giving them holidays and helping them with the costs of replacing homes they had lost. It shouldered the majority of the cost of rebuilding the chapel used as a mortuary that the congregation could no longer bear to use. It established scholarships for future generations. It built a memorial garden on the site of Pantglas school. Despite the proportion taken by the government, the Aberfan Disaster Fund has not been wasted.

---

117. See, e.g., draft reply to letter from L.R. Beard to the Prime Minister, 13 March 1970, TNA: BD 11/3791.

6

Aberfan: Then and Now

Aberfan was a long time ago. Tipping on wet slopes in south Wales stopped after the disaster. Merthyr Vale Colliery closed in 1990. The successor to Pantglas School, now called Ynysowen Primary, occupies a striking new building on the site of the colliery. Deep mining in south Wales ended with the closure of Tower Colliery in Hirwaun, in 2008. The Taff valley, like the other former mining valleys of south Wales, is green again, and the river is clean. The main A470 road from Cardiff to Merthyr and the north runs through the middle of the Aberfan tip complex, but there is almost nothing to show that it was ever there. The only coal still being mined in Wales comes from small drift mines and from opencast sites, including the large Ffos-y-Fran site in Merthyr, on the opposite side of the river to Aberfan. Total coal production in the UK has dropped from 180 million tonnes in 1966 (171m deep mined) to 9 million tonnes in 2015 (3m deep mined); employment in the industry over the same period has dropped from 422,000 to 2,000.[1]

Most of what really happened at Aberfan, before and after the disaster, came into the public domain with the opening of the relevant archives in 1997. The first edition of this book, published in 2000, summarised this research, and has underpinned the work of others, including the producers of TV documentaries in 2006 and 2016. For

---

1. Depart for Business, Energy, and Industrial Strategy, Historical Coal Data: Coal Production, 1853 to 2015, at https://www.gov.uk/government/uploads/system/uploads/.../Coal_since_1853.xls (accessed: 14 November 2016).

this new edition, we have made some small though significant new discoveries, but they do not change our central narrative.

But to anybody who was in south Wales on 21 October 2016, as both of us were, Aberfan felt like the day before yesterday. Several documentaries and a large-scale musical composition[2] brought the horror of the disaster to a new generation. People who remembered what happened flocked to be present at the one minute's silence held throughout Wales at 9.15 a.m. on 21 October. The son of one of the rescuers brought along a stopped alarm clock, which his father had kept as a reminder. It had been in his family because, at the end of the Tribunal where it had been used as evidence of the time the slurry hit Moy Road, there were no owners to whom to return it. It will be deposited in the National History Museum of Wales at St Fagans, stopped at just before 9.15. Some people spoke about their memories for the first time in fifty years; some revisited Aberfan itself for the first time in fifty years.

That anniversary re-affirmed how important Aberfan had become in the Welsh collective memory. Even in 1966, media coverage had depicted Aberfan as a Welsh rather than local disaster, partly just because it needed to describe where the village was. But newsreels and other reports added to this by employing Welsh narrators, choral music and references to the nation's tragic history of mining accidents. Amongst the tens of thousands of letters of sympathy sent to Aberfan were many from people with Welsh relatives, backgrounds or even just holiday memories who wrote of the warmth of the nation and its people. The belief that the disaster is part of Wales' distinct national history continued in subsequent decades. Even the Welsh national football squad visited the memorial garden in October 2016, a recognition of both their own and the disaster's cultural significance to the Welsh nation.

Such gestures are more than simply the product of Welsh national identity. In a small and mobile nation, it is not difficult to find people whose relatives lived in Aberfan or were among the hundreds who went there to assist in the rescue operation. Similarly, there are thousands upon thousands of Welsh people with personal or family

---

2. (Sir) Karl Jenkins, *Cantata Memoria – for the children*, first performed at Wales Millennium Centre, Cardiff, on 8 October 2016.

connections to the coal industry, and for them the disaster is not simply something that happened in another time and another place. It is part of their own family history.

The disaster also sums up the schizophrenic relationship Welsh society has with its coal mining heritage. At one level, there is an immense popular pride in the work miners undertook and the sacrifices they endured. There is also a recognition that it was coal that made modern Wales. Without it, communities such as Aberfan would not have existed at all. But the disaster was just one example of the huge environmental and human cost that coal extracted, and which represented the other side of coal's significance for the Welsh people. Mining polluted the landscape and communities across the coalfield suffered pit disasters; in 1913 the explosion at Senghenydd killed as many 439 men and boys. By the 1960s, safety underground had improved, but in that decade alone 429 miners were killed in accidents in south Wales. Aberfan was, of course, different to nearly all other mining accidents in Wales but the tragedy it evoked was all too familiar.

The disaster led to a gradual but significant programme of clearing land given over to the colliery waste heaps and the tragedy was one of the impetuses for the greening of the mining valleys. But coal has not yet been consigned to the past. Nothing has replaced the scale of jobs that it created and Aberfan looms close in Welsh memories because the economic impact of the failure to replace coal is everywhere in the south Wales valleys. Just as Aberfan was let down by the government in the 1960s, it, and mining communities across Wales, continue to feel let down by the authorities.

The purpose of this final chapter is therefore to record what else has changed and what has not since 1966. It is easy to chronicle some of the things that have changed (or not) since Aberfan, such as new laws. It is harder to measure others, such as changes in social attitudes. This chapter starts with legal changes, moves on to institutional changes, and finishes with social changes. That is not necessarily in descending order of importance, but is in descending order of measurability.

Strict liability

To be paradoxical, our first important change is a non-change. The legal liability of the NCB for what happened at Aberfan rested upon the precedent generated by *Rylands v. Fletcher* [1868] UKHL 1, another case concerning colliery waste and one that continues to be important. In 1860, Thomas Fletcher paid contractors to build a reservoir on his land. As they were constructing the reservoir, the contractors discovered a series of old coal shafts and passages under the land. The old shafts were filled loosely with soil and debris. They joined up with John Rylands' adjoining mine. Rather than blocking these shafts up, the contractors left them. On 11 December 1860, shortly after being filled up, Fletcher's reservoir broke through the loose waste and flooded Rylands' mine.[3] Rylands sued. At issue was not that there had been negligence, but who had been negligent, and what should be Rylands' remedy. As the case progressed, courts at every level found for Fletcher, on the grounds that the negligence was his contractor's not his. However, the House of Lords reversed this and found against Fletcher. In so doing, they established a doctrine of *strict liability*: Fletcher was liable for the damage his reservoir had caused, even though the damage was not his fault. He had not been shown to be negligent. But he had introduced a non-natural feature to his land. That was sufficient to make him liable for the damage to Rylands' mine.

Why is this so important? For multiple reasons. First, in 1966, the National Coal Board was by a long way the UK landowner most likely to have 'strict liability', otherwise known as 'absolute liability', for damage to its neighbours. It was one of the largest landowners in the country, and certainly the largest to have introduced non-natural features to its land. It is the introduction of non-natural features that establishes strict liability under *Rylands*. Considering only south Wales, the NCB and its predecessors were thus liable for a death at Pentre, as well as severe damage at Cilfynydd and Tŷ Mawr, before Aberfan.

---

3. Francis H. Bohlen (1911). 'The Rule in Rylands v. Fletcher. Part I'. *University of Pennsylvania Law Review and American Law Register.* 59 (5), pp 298-326. A.W.B. Simpson, 'Legal liability for bursting reservoirs: the historical context of *Rylands v. Fletcher*', *Journal of Legal Studies* 13, 2 (1984), 209-264.

The *Rylands* doctrine had specifically been applied to tips in *A.G. v. Cory*, a 1921 case about a tip in south Wales that caused damage to a neighbouring landowner.[4] One might have thought that at all levels of the NCB, those responsible for tips would be acutely conscious of the costs they might face. Instead, as Ackner remarked in his cross-examination of Sheppard, the man responsible for production on behalf of the entire NCB, 'any competent law student in his last year' would have known the strict liability rule in *Rylands* and its application to colliery tips in *Cory*, but Sheppard said he did not.[5] Why not?

Ignorance at the top percolated to the bottom, like Mr Fletcher's water. In chapters 1 and 2, we chronicled the appalling attitude of the insurance staff of the NCB to Aberfan claims. It was because of their failure to pay up immediately that the ruins of the school and the children's books were still lying there for Laurie Lee to see when he visited in 1967. It was because of the Coal Board's refusal to remove the remaining tips that the school site was not cleared, nor compensation paid to Merthyr Borough Council, until 1970. Comment on the insurance staff's moral attitudes is superfluous. But on their legal liability, why did the department whose job it was to respond to claims not realise that, under *Rylands*, they should have paid out on each and every Aberfan claim the moment it reached them? Or, worse, if they realised, why did they stonewall?

Secondly, *Rylands* is directly relevant to the question of who should pay for removing the remaining tips, from which slurry continued to wash down into Aberfan village until they disappeared. The fact that the NCB had a strict liability to compensate anyone who suffered loss makes all the stronger our case that the Charity Commission had no right to stand by while the Disaster Fund was raided.

Thirdly, strict liability had paradoxical consequences. Because its liability for damages existed independently of blame, and because the question of criminal or regulatory prosecution was not pursued, the NCB escaped remarkably lightly, at least in terms of financial if not of reputational consequences. Aberfan fell into a hole between the uncontested (but tardily acknowledged) civil liability and the untested criminal liability of the NCB. In some jurisdictions, notably Scotland,

4. *Attorney General v. Cory Brothers & Co Ltd*, [1921] 1 AC 521.
5. Transcript, Day 51, cross-examination of Sheppard by Ackner, p. 3824.

Rylands is not what the lawyers call 'good law' (i.e., a precedent that the courts still follow). But it remains good law in England and Wales. It was good law throughout the years that the NCB failed to pay up. Neither it nor any successor has paid up in relation to the full extent of long-term psychological trauma.

Bereavement damages

Bereaved parents were compensated £500 by the NCB for their children's loss of expectation of life. The law on such damages was a mess in 1966, and it has not become less so. Some lawyers have always argued that damages for bereavement should not be paid at all, on the grounds that there is no living victim, and no payment that will bring back the deceased. The common-law rules that were in force in 1966 have been superseded by a statutory scale. The amount payable for negligently causing death has fluctuated, not being correctly indexed, but has never been large (Table 6.1). Table 6.1 starts in 1941, which was the date of the leading common-law case before the statutory scheme was introduced.

Table 6.1
Damages for loss of expectation of life/bereavement, 1941-2016

Year	Amount in current prices, £	Value (1941 = 100)
1941	200	100
1967	500	91.11
1968	500	86.24
1983	3500	120.13
1991	7500	165.03
1997	7500	134.29
2016	12980	183.88

Sources for Table 6.1: historical RPI (Retail Price Index) tables constructed by Professor David Hendry (by kind permission); *Annual Abstract of Statistics*, various issues; and http://www.moneysorter.co.uk/calculator_inflation2.html#calculator, accessed 14.11.2016.

Whether these sums are appropriate is a value judgement. What we can say, though, is that a perversity in the law has not disappeared: namely, that it is far cheaper for a negligent corporation to kill someone than to cause them serious injury.

For those who have lost someone in a disaster, seeking financial compensation can be uncomfortable. As Celia Wells had argued, personal injury claims always involve a mixture of motives and it is unfair to single out disaster victims without defining how such motivations should be judged.[6] Disaster victims themselves are often offended by the doubting of their motives. The charity Disaster Action repeatedly stresses that their interest is in justice and a recognition of their loss rather than financial gain.[7] Wells also stresses that a comparison between death and injury is poor. The relatives of someone injured will benefit, directly or indirectly, through the awards made to the individual him or herself, while the different order of death to injury is recognised by legal systems in many ways. Wells argues that £7,500 (the tariff at the time of her paper) to a very limited class of relatives could hardly be considered an unduly generous sum.[8] For instance, in the USA in 1997, the parents of a six-year-old boy who died after falling out of a badly designed van were awarded $262 million (£162 million).[9] This makes the £12,980 that the parents of a child killed in the UK in 2016 could expect to receive in bereavement damages pale into insignificance. Thus, just as at Aberfan, it is possible that disaster victims today would continue to feel insulted by the sums offered.

6. Celia Wells, *Negotiating Tragedy*, (London: Sweet & Maxwell 1995), p. 127.
7. For example, see *Disaster Action Newsletter*, Spring/Summer 1997, Issue 4.
8. Wells, *Negotiating Tragedy*, p. 127.
9. R. Colbey, 'New look at disaster pay-outs', *Guardian*, 11 October 1997. The sum was divided into $12.5m for actual damages and $250m for punitive damages. Gary Slapper, 'Corporate Crime and Punishment', *The Criminal Lawyer*, March/April 1998, p. 7.

Regulatory statutes: charities, inquiries, and coroners

Several relevant regulatory statutes have been enacted since Aberfan. The *Mines and Quarries (Tips) Act 1969 c.10* was enacted directly in reaction to the discovery that the Aberfan disaster was not a notifiable accident under the regulations in force in 1966, because no mine workers were killed or injured. Most of this Act is still in force, including the bizarre-looking s.31 which begins 'Ecclesiastical property. 1) No notice under section 14 may be served in respect of a disused tip if the land on which the tip is situated is ecclesiastical property.' After fifty years, the dangers addressed by this Act have presumably been dealt with, whether or not disused tips were on ecclesiastical property.

Numerous Charities Acts have been passed since Aberfan, the principal ones being in 1992 and 2006 before the current consolidated *Charities Act 2011 c.25*, which repeals the 1992 and 2006 Acts. The sheer number of Charity Acts suggests that Parliament is struggling to find the right regulatory framework. In addition, the Charities Act 2011 has extended the 'heads' (categories) of charity so that they include: prevention or relief of poverty, s3(1)(a); promotion of the efficiency of the armed forces of the Crown or of the efficiency of the police, fire and rescue services or the ambulance services, s3(1)(l); relief of those in need by reason of youth, age, ill-health, disability, financial hardship or other disadvantage, s3(1)(j); and a new residual head covering existing charitable purposes or analogous charitable purposes. The Charity Commission commentary published on 16 September 2013 identifies examples within this residual head as including 'social relief, resettlement and rehabilitation of persons under a disability or deprivation (including disaster funds)'. The Act also stipulates that all charities must both have a proper charitable object and be able to show that they operate for the public benefit. These broader definitions would have avoided the need for the tortuous and insulting reasoning undertaken by the Charity Commission to allow the Aberfan Disaster Fund to spend money on the memorial and the bereaved.

As a regulator, the Charity Commission admits that its resources have been cut in recent years. It is widely believed that one factor in this was the forceful inquiries launched by the commission in past years as to whether private schools were providing sufficient public benefit to qualify as charities. Politicians who were not happy with this line of enquiry have accordingly redirected the Commission to look at current political concerns, including the prevention of terrorism and the prevention of harassment by charity collectors ('chuggers') on the street. For better or worse, the Commission would probably not now be in a position to intervene as extensively as it did with the Aberfan Disaster Fund. Absent in current policy documents is any stress on protecting the interests of donors. And, although there are current documents on safeguarding vulnerable beneficiaries, these are couched in the context of alleged (usually sexual) mistreatment of children and vulnerable adults. Thus the Commission's blameworthy actions and inactions at Aberfan do not seem to have been fully resolved by regulatory or statutory change. However, the Commission itself has acknowledged its mistakes at Aberfan and there is perhaps today a culture of thinking more sensitively about victims in general thanks to a 24-hour media, the facility of social media to voice public outrage and the fact that unexpected death is less common in a world better attuned to safety issues in and outside the workplace. It is thus difficult to imagine the Charity Commission not showing a greater sympathy than it did at Aberfan or the media allowing it to do so.

The 1921 Act under which the Aberfan tribunal was held has been superseded by the *Inquiries Act 2005 c.12*. There was nothing much wrong with the Aberfan tribunal arrangements, especially once the Wilson government arranged for legal aid to enable the Aberfan Parents' and Residents' association to hire Desmond Ackner and his team. Pre-enactment worries about the 2005 Act concerned the risk that it would weaken the powers available to tribunals under the act it replaced.[10] It does not seem to have done so, according to a

---

10. E.g., 'Memorandum by Iain McLean, Professor of Politics, Oxford University: On not scrapping the Tribunals of Inquiry (Evidence) Act 1921' in House of Commons, Public Administration Select Committee, *Government by Inquiry: written evidence* HC 51-II, 2005, pp. Ev 44 – Ev 45.

post-legislative scrutiny by a Lords select committee. The 2005 Act retains the 1921 Act's power to compel witnesses to attend.

Any disaster inquiry today might also be affected by the *Coroners and Justice Act 2009 c.25*. This gives a coroner the power to request that an inquest be turned into an inquiry, which is of broader scope and has powers that an inquest does not.[11] This would prevent the oddity that emerged at Aberfan of having a separate inquiry and inquests.

Whereas Edmund Davies and his colleagues did a very good job, the coroner covering Aberfan did a very poor one, although under very difficult circumstances. In the first inquest, he disallowed a parent's cry of *'Buried alive by the National Coal Board'*. Recall, from the local press account in Chapter 1:

> The coroner tried to restore order and said: 'I know your grief is such that you may not be realising what you are saying.' The father repeated: 'I want it recorded – "Buried alive by the National Coal Board." That is what I want to see on the record. That is the feeling of those present. Those are the words we want to go on the certificate.'[12]

A coroner would now have had the option, under the 2009 Act, of turning the inquest into an inquiry under the 2005 Inquiries act. Such an inquiry would of course have found, as the actual tribunal did, that the victims had been buried alive by the National Coal Board.

An issue that remains unresolved is the very limited access to legal aid at coroners' inquests. As a recent Commons Library paper records:

---

11. House of Lords Select Committee on the Inquiries Act 2005, *The Inquiries Act 2005: post-legislative scrutiny*, HL 143, 2013-14, http://www.publications. parliament.uk/pa/ld201314/ldselect/ldinquiries/143/143.pdf; *Government Response to the Report of the House of Lords Select Committee on the Inquiries Act 2005* June 2014, Cm 8903, at http://www.parliament.uk/documents/lords-committees/Inquiries-Act-2005/Cm8903_Government%20response%20 to%20HL%20Committee%20on%20the%20Inquiries%20Act%20 2005_260614_TSO_Print.pdf (both accessed 21 November 2016).

12. *Merthyr Express*, 28 October 1966, p. 18.

The costs of legal advice and preparation in the run-up to an inquest can be met by Legal Help, the advice and assistance arm of legal aid. The costs of representation at the inquest will only be met in cases deemed to be exceptional.

Under the Legal Aid, Sentencing and Punishment of Offenders Act 2012 there are two grounds for the granting of public funding to cover representation at an inquest:

- Where representation is necessary for an effective investigation into the death, as required by Article 2 of the European Convention on Human Rights
- Where the Director of Legal Aid Casework has made a wider public interest determination that the provision of advocacy for the bereaved family at the inquest is likely to produce significant benefits for a wider class of people.[13]

As in 1966, then, bereaved relatives at another Aberfan would depend on the discretion of a government official to be sure of legal representation.

Corporate manslaughter and corporate responsibility

The *Health and Safety at Work etc. Act 1974 c.37*, the product of the departmental committee chaired by Robens, is the most important regulatory statute enacted since 1966. The most important word in its short title is that 'etc'. Following the discovery that Aberfan was not a notifiable accident, the 1974 Act widens the liability of employers – from their employees to everybody.

After the Clapham rail disaster of 1988, when 35 people were killed as a result of faulty signal wiring, British Rail immediately accepted blame. Its chairman, Sir Robert Reid, personally attended court to plead guilty to offences under the 1974 Act when the Railways Board was fined £250,000. Not all employers have been as prompt as Sir Robert

---

13. House of Commons Library *Briefing Paper 04358, June 2016: Legal Aid for representation at an inquest*. At http://researchbriefings.files.parliament.uk/documents/SN04358/SN04358.pdf (accessed 21 November 2016).

Reid. Also, the privatisation and fragmentation of the rail industry since 1988 reopens the possibility of blame-shifting after a rail disaster. But the Clapham case has set a precedent. For serious corporate malfeasance that leads to death and injury, prosecution under the 1974 act seems a more effective route than a corporate manslaughter charge.

The *Corporate Manslaughter and Corporate Homicide Act 2007* (c.19) put into statute something that campaigners had been long demanding.[14] Although corporate manslaughter was charged in the 1965 *Northern Strip Mining* case discussed in chapter 2, the prosecution failed on the grounds that it had failed to prove that the managing director of the company had a guilty mind (*mens rea*). It was considered again after the *Herald of Free enterprise* disaster at Zeebrugge in 1987 (death toll 193), when a coroner's inquest jury returned a finding of unlawful killing (Chapter 2). This more or less forced the hands of the Director of Public Prosecutions to prosecute the owning company for corporate manslaughter. The prosecution again failed because of the impossibility of proving a *mens rea* at the top of a company. When a company's safety culture is appalling, as at Aberfan and Zeebrugge, there is unlikely to be a note from the chief executive saying 'please institute an appalling safety culture'.

Celia Wells has recently reviewed the prosecutions that have taken place since the enactment of the Corporate Manslaughter and Corporate Homicide Act (Table 6.2).

One thing leaps out immediately from Table 6.2. These cases are almost all like *Northern Strip*, and none is remotely like Aberfan or Zeebrugge. They are all small companies, where prosecutors had a reasonable prospect of proving that a director or 'controlling mind' of the company had been so negligent or reckless that they could be claimed to have *mens rea*. Wells reports that between 2009 and 2012 the Crown Prosecution Service opened files on 141 possible cases of corporate manslaughter.[15] But only a small number have proceeded to trial with the results (to 2013) shown in Table 6.2.

---

14. For an examination of the evolution of ideas of corporate manslaughter see Chapter 8 of the first edition of this book.

15. Celia Wells, 'Corporate criminal liability: a ten-year review', *Criminal Law Review*, 12 (2014), 849-878, p. 860. This updates her *Corporations and Criminal Responsibility* (Oxford: Oxford University Press, 2001).

Despite the decades of campaigning that led to the 2007 Act, therefore, the results seem meagre. Does that mean that guilty corporations are controlled as badly as at Aberfan or at Zeebrugge? No, because the prosecutions have gone down another route, namely that of regulatory offences under the Health & Safety at Work Act 1974 (HSWA). Under the HSWA, as with other regulatory statutes, the test of guilt is not the almost impossible standard of *mens rea*, but the common notion of 'vicarious liability'. In an everyday example cited by Wells,[16] 'since the late nineteenth century ... [a] company could be summonsed and fined if, for example, one of its employees sold alcohol to an underage person.' The same approach is taken with HSWA. The company is responsible through its directors, even if the negligent and reckless acts were at a low level. The multiple failures of management revealed at Aberfan would undoubtedly have led to a prosecution and heavy fines if they had occurred at any time since the HWSA was used in this way to prosecute British Rail after Clapham in 1988.

The powers and scope of the Health and Safety Executive, the regulator appointed under the 1974 Act, are wider than was envisaged by Lord Robens and his committee. The most important extension, as already noted, is conveyed by the little word 'etc' in the title of the 1974 Act. Employers have duties not only to their employees but also to anyone who visits their premises or is injured or killed in an accident that does not occur on their premises but for which they were liable. Secondly, the HSE incorporated all the separate industry regulators that existed in 1974, including the Mines and Quarries Inspectorate. There has been a minor outsourcing in recent years, so that safety on the railways is now managed by the Office of Rail Regulation (already renamed Office of Rail and Road) and that in nuclear installations by the Office for Nuclear Regulation. Thirdly, the courts may now levy unlimited fines, and may disbar company directors from serving as directors of any company. Both the HSE and the ORR maintain a public list of prosecutions, prohibitions and improvement notices.

---

16. Wells, 'Corporate criminal liability'.

Table 6.2
Completed prosecutions under the Corporate Manslaughter and Homicide Act 2007, to 2012

Date of fatality	CMCH Act	Outcome	Penalty	Common-law manslaughter	Outcome	HSWA charges
2008	Cotswold Geotech Holdings Ltd	Trial-convicted	£385,000 fine – 10 years to pay	Withdrawn		Yes
2008	Lion Steel	Guilty plea	£480,000 fine – 4 years to pay	Three directors charged	Two dismissed, & charges dropped in exchange for CMCH guilty plea	Yes but dropped in plea agreement
2010	JMW Farms	Guilty plea	£187,500 fine			Not known
2010	PS & JE Ward Ltd	Acquitted				Yes, fined £50,000, 3 years to pay
2010	Cavendish Masonry Ltd	Convicted	Not known			Not Known
2010	Princes Sporting Club Ltd	Guilty plea	Fine of £35,000 and publicity			Dropped in exchange for CMCH guilty plea

Table 6.2 (continued)

Date of fatality	CMCH Act	Outcome	Penalty	Common-law manslaughter	Outcome	HSWA charges
2011	MNS Mining	Acquitted		Manager	Acquitted	Not known
2012	J Murray and sons	Guilty plea	£100,000 fine to be paid in 5 annual instalments	Director/Owner	Prosecution dropped in exchange for CMCH guilty plea	
2012	Mobile Sweepers (Reading) Ltd	Guilty plea	Fine of £8,000 and publicity	Left on file		Director fined £183,000 and disqualified for 5 years

Source: Adapted from C. Wells, 'Corporate criminal liability: a ten-year review', *Criminal Law Review*, 12 (2014), 849-878.

Abbreviations:
CMCH: Corporate Manslaughter and Homicide Act 2007
HSWA: Health & Safety at Work Act 1974

Institutional changes

The legal changes just discussed are both cause and consequence of massive institutional change since 1966. Again and again throughout this book, we have had cause to stress just how dominant was the National Coal Board in the politics of Aberfan. Its presence intimidated so many other actors, including Merthyr Council, the Ministry of Power, the Welsh Office, and indeed the entire Wilson government. Some actions which seem obviously right – prosecution for corporate manslaughter; the resignation or dismissal of Robens and Sheppard; paying insurance claims promptly; paying for the removal of the tips – were not pushed, or not even contemplated. As a small but telling detail, the NCB was so much part of the state that its internal archives comprise the COAL class in the National Archives at Kew. At least this meant there was no obfuscation and full access to their behaviour when the archives were opened in 1997.

The NCB is no more, after the controversial privatisations of the Conservative governments of Margaret Thatcher and John Major (1979 to 1997). The UK coal industry is almost entirely gone. But many of the other industries privatised at that period – including electricity, gas, telecoms, and railways – play at least as large a part in the UK economy as they did in 1966. Their privatisation has had mixed consequences. For instance, in some industries, such as rail, privatisation has led to fragmentation, which could cause massive passing of the buck in the event of a disaster. In others, such as gas, the opposite problem may exist, namely that the successor of the former nationalised company has too much dominance of the industry. Privatisation is neither inherently bad nor inherently good, from the point of view of safety management. But the NCB has not only disappeared; the resurrection of anything like it is inconceivable.

The regulatory changes discussed in the previous section have brought institutional changes in their train. The HSWA Act (and for that matter the Corporate Manslaughter Act) place a duty on directors of companies to promote workplace safety, knowing that they may be held to account if they fail to. Companies and charities alike must maintain a risk register, making them aware not only of the regulatory risk that an HSE prosecution would entail, but the reputational risk as well. Here is where apparently small details such as the regulators' registers of fines and disqualifications may have its effect. As the vice-chairman of a heritage railway, one of us (IM) carefully reads all the reports of the Rail Accident Investigation Branch (successor in that industry to the Railway Inspectorate as safety regulator). In the spirit of "There but for the grace of God go I", any director or manager knows the consequences of neglecting safety. The contrast with Aberfan attitudes at all levels in the Coal Board is striking. Only one person even accepted that he was responsible, and that was Vivian Thomas, Colliery Mechanical Engineer at Merthyr Vale Colliery, right at the bottom of the chain of command that ended with Sheppard and Robens.

Public and private regulation may interlock. Any adverse finding by a regulator, from a reprimand in a report to a successful prosecution, will make it more difficult and more expensive to obtain insurance at the next renewal. And insurance companies have their own, self-interested reason for insisting on a safety culture: a safe company gives rise to fewer claims than a dangerous company. In this context, too, the fact that the NCB self-insured in 1966 turned out to be disastrous.

Social changes

The biggest, but least tangible, change since 1966 is in public attitudes to risk, disaster, and corporate liability. Chapter 2 discussed the bogus resignation offer by Lord Robens in August 1967; his only partially frustrated promotion of W. V. Sheppard to the main NCB Board; and the failure of Harold Wilson's government to force them out. One aspect of this lies with public opinion. Gallup polled the UK public in 1967 on the question of Robens' resignation. The fact that most people thought he should stay undoubtedly influenced not only his behaviour but also the government's. Had public opinion been the other way, the faction in the government which, according to Richard Crossman, wanted to sack him would probably have been larger.

As we have recorded, many attitudes to Aberfan in the early years were conditioned by thinking of it as a tragic accident (which it was, but an accident waiting to happen) or an act of God (which it was not; God did not put the tips there). The first thirty years after Aberfan were marked by a number of multi-fatality disasters, such as the fires at Bradford City (May 1985; 56 deaths) and Kings Cross (November 1987; 31 deaths); the sinking of the *Herald of Free Enterprise*; and, most important of all in its long-term consequences, the Hillsborough disaster (April 1989; 96 deaths). These disasters all affected safety regulation and the public response to corporate failure, although especially in the case of Hillsborough justice has been a long time coming.

In 2016 an inquest jury returned a verdict of unlawful killing on the 96 football fans killed at the Hillsborough football ground in 1989. It concluded that the senior police officer in charge that day was 'responsible for manslaughter by gross negligence' due to a breach of his duty of care. This was the second inquest into the deaths. The first had taken place against a backdrop of police attempts to deflect blame on to the Liverpool fans and had recorded an accidental death verdict. Evidence of the extent of the police's primary responsibility for the disaster and their attempts to avoid it emerged gradually in subsequent years but a private prosecution failed and successive governments did not intervene to ensure blame was placed in the right place.

As at Aberfan, the efforts to pass the buck made the suffering of victims worse. As at Aberfan, the official inquiry noted this refusal to accept responsibility soon afterwards, with Lord Justice Taylor writing that it was 'a matter of regret that South Yorkshire Police were not prepared to concede that they were in any way at fault for what had occurred'. As at Aberfan, the government did little about this. Unlike at Aberfan, the police had altered evidence about what had happened and their culpability. It took a 27-year struggle by the families, supported by an academic named Phil Scraton, for the truth and the documents that proved it, to emerge.[17]

---

17. For an account of the injustices at Hillsborough see Phil Scraton, *Hillsborough: The Truth* (Edinburgh: Mainstream, 2016). Hillsborough was the last in a long history of British football crowd disasters, none of which

The long-term government intransigence on Hillsborough was, as at Aberfan, an example of what can happen when one part of the state kills people and another part of the state is responsible for ensuring justice: the victims simply get lost in games of high politics played out behind closed doors. Some of that game will be documented but, with state papers closed for 30 (and now 20) years, it can be decades before what happened is properly known. By then, it can be too late for some of those affected to see justice. Nor can government always be trusted to release the documents or order an inquiry into what happened even when evidence mounts of wrongdoing. Nobody was killed in 1984 by police violence at Orgreave during the miners' strike but the continued refusal of the government to allow a full public investigation into what happened is a reminder that justice does not always emerge.

In the twenty years in which we have been working on Aberfan, beginning with the release of the documents in 1997, the number and death toll of multi-fatality man-made disasters in the UK has declined. But we have found public revulsion at the behaviour of the Coal Board and its leaders to be growing, not fading, with the passage of time. The fortieth anniversary of the disaster was a bigger public event than the thirtieth; the fiftieth was a bigger public event than either.

People talk glibly about 'closure'. Closure has not yet come to the people of Aberfan. Nor is it likely to, as long as any survivors of the disaster are still alive. We hope that, for the second time, the publication of our findings will keep memories green and help people to understand why it happened and how to stop anything like it ever happening again.

---

had drawn adequate responses from the Government or football itself. See Martin Johnes, 'Heads in the sand: football, politics and crowd disasters in twentieth-century Britain', in Paul Darby, Martin Johnes & Gavin Mellor (eds.), *Soccer and Disaster: International Perspectives* (London: Routledge, 2001), 10-27. Professor Scraton publicly declined the offer of an OBE in 2017.

Bibliography

I. Archival sources

Aberfan Disaster Archive
Merthyr Collection (Merthyr Tydfil Central Library)
Dowlais Collection (Dowlais Library)
For a catalogue of these archives, see our website at https://www.nuffield.ox.ac.uk/politics/aberfan/home.htm

Merthyr Tydfil Central Library
Merthyr Tydfil County Borough Council, minutes and accounts
Transcripts of the Aberfan Inquiry hearings

Glamorgan Archives
British Coal Records, South Wales Area Files, D/D NCB 67/4
Llewellyn and Hann papers, Powell Duffryn solicitors at the Tribunal of Inquiry, D/D LH
Police records on Aberfan disaster, D/D Con 289/4
Aberfan Disaster Fund, Management committee and sub-committee papers, 1967-73 DX 295/12
Glamorgan County Council Civil Defence papers on the Aberfan disaster, GCC/CD
Aberfan and Merthyr Vale Tip Removal Committee papers, D1368

National Archives
Board of Trade Establishment Division papers, BT 13/50
Board of Trade Marine Department papers, MT 9/920/E24382
Board of Trade Consultation Marine papers, MT 15
Cabinet office papers, CAB 128, CAB 164
Charity Commission papers, CHAR 9, CHAR 10
Foreign Office papers, FO 115/1710, FO 369/522
Ministry of Power papers, POWE 52
NCB papers, COAL 29, COAL 73
Prime Minister's Private Office papers, PREM 13
Treasury Solicitor papers, TS 58
Tribunal of Inquiry papers, BD 52
Welsh Board of Health papers, MH 96/2179
Welsh Office papers, BD 11, BD 28, BD 50, BD 61

South Wales Coalfield Collection, Swansea University
Coal Industry National Consultation Council minutes
S.O. Davies papers
National Union of Mineworkers, Annual conference reports
National Union of Mineworkers, South Wales Area minutes
Tŷ Toronto archive

National Library of Wales
Lord Edmund Davies papers
Alun Talfan Davies papers
Diocese of Llandaff papers
Cyril Moseley papers
Eilfryn Peris Owen papers
Lord Morris of Borth y Gest papers
Rev. Evan Wyn Williams papers
Harri Webb papers
I.C. Rapoport photograph collection

II. Interviews and correspondence

Interviews and/or correspondence with the authors, mostly in 1997-9, with most relevant position for their evidence.
Ackner, Desmond (Counsel, APRA)
Bacon, Jenny (Director General, HSE)

Barnes, Kenneth (former Deputy Secretary, Department of Employment and Productivity)

Berkley, J.B. (Disaster Action)

Billnitzer, Dave

Blackshaw, Alan (former private secretary to Richard Marsh [q.v.], Ministry of Power)

Castle, Barbara (former Secretary of State for Employment and Productivity)

Cooksey, A. (HM Deputy Chief Inspector of Railways)

Cuthill, J.M. (Psychiatrist)

Davies, Ron (former Secretary of State for Wales)

Davis, Gerald (former Secretary, Aberfan Disaster Fund)

Dearing, Ron (former Assistant Secretary, Coal Division, Ministry of Power)

Evans, Andrew (Centre for Transport Studies, UCL)

Gates, Terry (HSE Policy Unit)

Hillsborough Families Support Group

Hodgkinson, Peter (Centre for Crisis Psychology)

Howe, Geoffrey (Counsel at Aberfan Tribunal)

Hughes, Cledwyn (former Secretary of State for Wales)

Lang, J.S. (Chief Inspector of Marine Accidents)

Langdon, B. (HM Chief Inspector of Mines)

Leiper, Elizabeth (Psychotherapist)

McKinlay, R.C. (AAIB)

McQuaid, Jim (Director of Science and Technology, HSE)

Marsh, Richard (former Minister of Power)

Morgan, Geoffrey (former Secretary, Aberfan Disaster Fund)

Moseley, Cyril (solicitor, APRA)

O'Connell, Morgan (Consultant psychiatrist)

Parkes, Colin Murray (bereavement consultant at Aberfan)

Sisson, C.H. (former Director of Occupational Safety and Health, Department of Employment and Productivity)

Spooner, Peter (Herald Charitable Trust)

Talfan Davies, Alun (former trustee, Aberfan Disaster Fund)

Taylor, John (Lord Robens' private office)

Thatcher, Margaret (Former Shadow Spokesperson on Fuel and Power)

Tudor, W. & Tudor, J. (Aberfan)

Walker, Harold (former Parliamentary Under-Secretary of State, Department of Employment and Productivity)

Watkin, Hugh (teacher, Aberfan)

Watkins, Tasker (former trustee, Aberfan Disaster Fund)

Wilson, Geoffrey (Assistant counsel for the Miners' Federation of Great Britain, Gresford disaster inquiry)

Aberfan Study [series of interviews]: An unknown spring (1986), South Wales Coalfield Collection, Swansea University
Richards, Emlyn and Elaine. AUD/519
Lewis, Sheila (Mrs). AUD/520
Beale, John. AUD/521
Williams, Howell. AUD/522
Williams, Hetty. AUD/523
Davey, Audrey. AUD/524
Jones, Raymond Gwynfryn. AUD/525
Jones, Mair. AUD/526
Vaughan, Joan and Cyril. AUD/527
Hayes, Kenneth (Rev.), Carpenter, Bryn and Pearson, Doug. AUD/528
Elwyn-Jones (Lord). AUD/530

The authors have also informally spoken to many people involved in differing capacities at Aberfan and other disasters.

III. Newspapers and periodicals

Birmingham Post
British Medical Journal
Colliery Guardian
Daily Express
Daily Mail
Daily Mirror
Daily Telegraph
Financial Times
Independent
Locomotive Journal
Merthyr Express
Private Eye
The *Guardian*
The *Observer*
The *Sun*
The Times
Times Higher Education Supplement
Transport Review
South Wales Argus
South Wales Echo
Sunday People

Sunday Times
Wales on Sunday
Washington Post
West Virginian Gazette
Western Mail

IV. Government and parliamentary publications

British Labour Statistics, Historical Abstract 1886-1968 (Dept of Employment & Productivity: HMSO, 1971).

Charity Commission, *Annual Reports*.

Davies, Edmund (chairman), *Report of the Tribunal appointed to inquire into the Disaster at Aberfan on October 21st 1966*, HL 316, HC 553 (London: HMSO, 1967).

Department of Employment, *The Flixborough Disaster: Report of the Court of Inquiry* (London: HMSO, 1975).

Depart for Business, Energy, and Industrial Strategy, *Historical Coal Data: Coal Production, 1853 to 2015*, at https://www.gov.uk/government/uploads/system/uploads/.../Coal since 1853.xls, accessed 14 November 2016.

Department for Business, Energy, and Industrial Strategy, *Digest of UK Energy Statistics* annual at https://www.gov.uk/government/collections/digest-of-uk-energy-statistics-dukes, accessed 29 November 2016.

Disasters Working Party, *Disasters: Planning for a Caring Response, Part One: The Main Report* (London: HMSO, 1991).

Emergency Planning Society, *Responding to Disaster: The Human Aspects*, Guidance Document, 1998.

Government Response to the Report of the House of Lords Select Committee on the Inquiries Act 2005 June 2014, Cm 8903, at http://www.parliament.uk/documents/lords-committees/Inquiries-Act-2005/Cm8903 Government%20response%20to%20HL%20Committee%20on%20the%20Inquiries%20Act%202005 260614 TSO Print.pdf, accessed 21 November 2016.

Hansard *various dates, available at* https://hansard.parliament.uk

Health and Safety Commission, *Health and Safety at Work etc Act: The Act Outlined*, HSC2, 1994.

— *Annual Reports*

— *Enforcement Policy Statement*, 1995.

Health and Safety Executive, *Reducing Risks, Protecting People*, Discussion Document (London: HSE, 1999).

— *Work-related Deaths: A protocol for liaison* (London: HSE, 1998).

Hidden, Anthony (chairman), *Investigation into the Clapham Junction Railway Accident*, Cm. 820 (London: HMSO, 1989).

Home Office, *Report of the Disasters and Inquests Working Group* (London: Home Office, 1997).

— *Dealing with Disaster* (London: HMSO, 1992 & 1997 edns).

— Press release, 066/98. 18 February 1998.

House of Commons Library Briefing Paper 04358, June 2016: *Legal Aid for representation at an inquest*. At http://researchbriefings.files.parliament. uk/documents/SN04358/SN04358.pdf, accessed 21.11.2016.

House of Lords Select Committee on the Inquiries Act 2005, *The Inquiries Act 2005: post-legislative scrutiny*, HL 143, 2013-14, http://www.publications.parliament.uk/pa/ld201314/ldselect/ ldinquiries/143/143.pdf, accessed 21 November 2016.

Law Commission, *The Actions of Loss of Services, Loss of Consortium, Seduction and Enticement*, Published Working Paper no. 19 (London: HMSO, 1968).

— *Report on Personal Injury Litigation – Assessment of Damages*, Report No. 56 (London: HMSO, 1973).

— *Criminal Law: Involuntary Manslaughter*, Consultation Paper No. 135 (London: HMSO, 1994).

— *Damages for Personal Injury: Non-pecuniary Loss*, Consultation Paper No. 140, (London: HMSO, 1995).

— *Legislating the Criminal Code: Involuntary Manslaughter*, Report No. 237 (London: HMSO, 1996).

— *Claims for Wrongful Death*, Consultation Paper 148 (London: HMSO, 1997).

Local Government in Wales, Cmnd. 3340 (Cardiff: HMSO, 1967).

Lord Chancellor's Department, *Damages for Bereavement: A Review of the Level* (London: Lord Chancellor's Department, 1990).

Leigh, C., *Reports of HM Inspectors of Mines and Quarries (under the Mines and Quarries Act 1954) for 1966, South Western Division* (London: HMSO, 1967).

Stephenson, H.S., *Report of HM Chief Inspector for Mines and Quarries (under the Mines and Quarries Act 1954) for 1966* (London: HMSO, 1967).

Reports of the Charity Commissioners for England and Wales.

Registrar General's Statistical Review of England and Wales for the Year 1966 (London: HMSO 1967).

Robens, Lord, (Chairman) *Safety and Health at Work, Report of the Committee*, Cmnd 5034 (London: HMSO, 1972).

Sheen, Barry, *MV Herald of Free Enterprise: report of Court no. 8074, formal investigation* (London: HMSO for Department of Transport, 1987).

Taylor, Peter, *The Hillsborough Stadium disaster, 15 April 1989: Inquiry by the Rt. Hon Lord Justice Taylor: Interim Report*, Cm 765 (London: HMSO, 1989).

Taylor, Peter, *The Hillsborough Stadium disaster, 15 April 1989: Inquiry by the Rt. Hon Lord Justice Taylor: Final Report*, Cm 962 (London: HMSO, 1990).

V. Law cases

Attorney General v Cory Brothers & Co Ltd [1921] 1 AC 521.

Benham v Gambling [1941] AC 157.

DPP v Kent & Sussex Contractors Ltd [1944] KB 146.

DPP v P&O European Ferries (Dover) Ltd [1991] 93 Cr. App. R. 73.

Frost and others v Chief Constable of South Yorkshire Police and others, TLR, 4 December 1998.

Hicks v C.C.S. Yorkshire [1992] 2 All ER 65.

Moore v Bresler [1944] 2 All ER 515.

Re Gillingham Bus Disaster Fund [1957] 3 WLR 1069.

R. v Cory Brothers and Company, Limited. Feb. 2, Glamorgan Assizes [1927] 1 KB 810.

R v ICR Haulage Ltd [1944] 30 Cr App R 31.

R v Northern Strip Mining Construction Ltd, *The Times*, 2, 4 & 5 February 1965.

Rylands v Fletcher [1868] LR 3 HL 330.

Yorkshire Electricity Board v Naylor [1968] AC 529.

VI. Other published material

Adam Smith Research Trust, *But Who Will Regulate the Regulators?* (London: Adam Smith, 1993).

Allen, D.K., Bourn, C.J. & Holyoak, J.H., (eds.), *Accident Compensation after Pearson* (London: Sweet & Maxwell, 1979).

Allen, Simon, 'Rescuers and Employees – Primary Victims of Nervous Shock', *New Law Journal*, 7 February 1997, 158-160.

American Psychiatric Association, *Diagnosis and Statistical Manual of Mental Disorders: DSMI-IV* (Washington: American Psychiatric Association, 4th edn, 1994).

Anon., 'Disasters', *Which?*, September 1988, 426-9.

— 'Disasters Update', *Which?*, November 1989, 558-60.

— (Editorial) 'Disaster Planning – Fact or Fiction?', *British Medical Journal*, 24 May 1975, 406-7.

— (Editorial), 'Prepared for a Disaster?', *British Medical Journal*, 27 September 1975, 723.

— 'Disasters as a catalyst for civil and/or criminal proceedings', *P&I international*, December 1996, 238-239.

— 'Time to reform railway safety', *Modern Railways*, December 1997, 760.

Arnott, Hilary, 'Justice: Hillsborough's Final Victim?', *Legal Action*, April 1992, 7-8.

Ashworth, William, *The History of the British Coal Industry, Vol. 5, 1946-1982: The Nationalised Industry* (Oxford: Clarendon Press, 1986).

Austin, Tony, *Aberfan: The Story of a Disaster* (London: Hutchinson, 1967).

Bailey, Eric, 'Post-Traumatic Stress Disorder: A Contrasting View', *Disaster Prevention & Management*, 2, 3 (1993), 22-5.

Ballard, Paul H. & Jones, Erastus (eds.), *The Valleys Call: A Self-examination by People of the South Wales Valleys during the 'Year of the Valleys', 1974* (Ferndale: Ron Jones Publications, 1974).

Barton, Allen H., *Communities in Disaster: A Sociological Analysis of Collective Stress Situations* (Ward Lock Educational, 1969).

Bedfordshire County Council, *Picking up the Pieces: Report of a Multi-agency Workshop to Develop Post-major Incident Psycho-social Support Plans* (Bedford, 1996).

Benson, John, 'Charity's Pitfalls: The Senghenydd Disaster', *History Today*, 43, 11 (1993), 5-7.

Benthall, John, *Disasters, Relief and the Media* (London: I.B. Tauris, 1993).

Bergman, David, *Deaths at Work: Accidents or Corporate Crime* (London: WEA, London Hazards Centre & Inquest, 1991).

— 'A Killing in the Boardroom', *New Statesman & Society*, 15 June 1990, 15-6.

— *Disasters: Where the Law Fails: A New Agenda for Dealing with Corporate Violence* (London: Herald Charitable Trust, 1993).

Bohlen, Francis H., 'The Rule in Rylands v. Fletcher. Part I'. *University of Pennsylvania Law Review and American Law Register*, 59, 5 (1911), 298-326.

Bovens, Mark, *The Quest for Responsibility: Accountability and Citizenship in Complex Organisations* (Cambridge: Cambridge University Press, 1998).

Breyer S. and MacAvoy, P.W., 'Regulation and Deregulation', in J. Eatwell et al. (eds.), *The New Palgrave Dictionary of Economics vol 4.* (London: Macmillan, 1987), 128-34.

British Psychological Society, *Psychological Aspects of Disaster* (Leicester: British Psychological Society, 1990).

Brittain, Victoria, 'New Grass in the Valley but Scars on the Mind Remain', *The Times*, 12 October 1971.

Brook, Richard, *An Introduction to Disaster Theory for Social Workers* (Norwich: Social Work Monographs, 1990).

Brown, John H., *The Valley of the Shadow: An Account of Britain's Worst Mining Disaster: The Senghenydd Explosion* (Port Talbot: Alun Books, 1981).

Bryan, Sir Andrew, *The Evolution of Health and Safety in Mines* (London: Ashire Publishing, 1975).

Butt Philip, Alan, *The Welsh Question: Nationalism in Welsh Politics 1945-1970* (Cardiff: University of Wales Press, 1975).

Cairns, Elizabeth, *Charities: Law and Practice* (London: Sweet & Maxwell, 3rd edn, 1997).

Cane, Peter, *Atiyah's Accidents, Compensation and the Law* (London: Butterworth, 5th edn, 1993).

Cannon, Tom, *Corporate Responsibility: A Textbook on Business Ethics, Governance, Environment: Roles and Responsibilities* (London: Pitman, 1994).

Carby-Hall, J.R., 'Health, Safety and Welfare at Work', *Managerial Law*, 31, 1/2, (1989), 1-57.

Castle, Barbara, *The Castle Diaries 1964-70* (London: Weidenfeld & Nicolson, 1984).

— *Fighting all the Way* (London: Macmillan, 1993).

Chesterman, Michael, *Charities, Trusts and Social Welfare* (London: Weidenfeld & Nicolson, 1979).

Claricoat, John & Phillips, Hillary, *Charity Law, A-Z: Key Questions Answered* (Bristol: Jordans, 1995).

Clarkson, C.M.V., 'Corporate Culpability', *Web Journal of Current Legal Issues*, http://webjcli.ncl.ac.uk/1998/issue2/clarkson2.html

Clegg, Francis, 'Disasters: Can Psychologists help the Survivors?', *Psychologist*, April 1988, 34-35.

Cohen, David, *Aftershock: The Psychological and Political Consequences of Disaster* (London: Paladin, 1991).

Colbey, Richard, 'New Look at Disaster Pay-outs', *Guardian*, 11 October 1997.

Coleman, Sheila, Jemphrey, Ann, Scraton, Phil & Skidmore, Paula, *Hillsborough and After: The Liverpool Experience, First Report* (Liverpool: Liverpool City Council, 1990).

Collins, Henry E., *Mining Memories and Musings: Autobiography of a Mining Engineer* (Letchworth: Ashire Publishing, 1985).

Cook, Judith, *An Accident Waiting to Happen* (London: Unwin, 1989).

Couto, Richard A., 'Catastrophe and Community Empowerment: The Group Formulations of Aberfan's Survivors', *Journal of Community Psychology*, 17 (July 1989), 236-248.

— 'Economics, Experts, and Risk: Lessons from the Catastrophe at Aberfan', *Political Psychology*, 10, 2 (1989), 309-24.

Coward, Ros, 'Death Watch', *New Statesman & Society*, 28 April 1989, 12-3.

Crainer, Stuart, *Zeebrugge: Learning from Disaster, Lessons in Corporate Responsibility* (London: Herald Charitable Trust, 1993).

Crenson, Matthew A., *The Unpolitics of Air Pollution: A Study of Non-decisionmaking in the Cities* (Baltimore: John Hopkins University Press, 1971).

Crossman, R.H.S., *The Diaries of a Cabinet Minister. Vol. 2: Lord President of the Council and Leader of the House of Commons 1966-68* (London, 1976).

Dalton, A.J.P., *Safety, Health and Environmental Hazards at the Workplace* (London: Cassell, 1998).

Davis, Howard & Scraton, Phil, *Beyond Disaster: Identifying and Resolving Inter-agency Conflict in the Immediate Aftermath of Disasters*, A Research Report for the Home Office Emergency Planning Division, 1997.

— 'Failing the Bereaved: Inter-agency Relationships in the Immediate Aftermath of Disaster' in *Picking Up the Pieces: Report of a Multi-agency Workshop to develop Post-major Incident Psycho-social Support Plans* (Bedford: Bedfordshire County Council, 1996).

Davison, Gerald C., & Neale, John M., *Abnormal Psychology* (New York: John Wiley, 7th edn, 1997).

Dawson, Sandra, Willman, Paul, Clinton, Alan & Bamford, Martin, *Safety at Work: The Limits of Self-regulation* (Cambridge: CUP, 1988).

De Courcy, Anne, 'A generation was wiped out that day', *Daily Mail Weekend*, 5 October 1996, 10-13.

Deakin, N. (chairman), *Meeting the Challenge of Change: Voluntary Action into the 21st Century*, The Report of the Commission on the Future of the Voluntary Sector (London: NCVO, 1996).

Dimbleby, Jonathan, 'Aberfan: Four Years After', *New Statesman*, 25 December 1970, 862.

Dix, Pamela, 'Corporate Responsibility for Public Safety', *Consumer Policy Review*, 5, 6 (1995), 200-2.

— 'Distress and Redress', *Guardian*, 29 December 1993.

— 'A Hard Crusade', *Guardian*, 25 July 1998.

Doel, Melanie & Dunkerton, Martin, *Is it Still Raining in Aberfan? A Pit and its People* (Little Logaston: Logaston Press, 1991).

Douglas, Mary, *Risk and Blame: Essays in Cultural Theory* (London: Routledge, 1992).

Drabek, Thomas E., *Social Dimensions of Disaster: Instructor Guide* (Emmitsburg: Federal Emergency Management Agency, 1996).

— 'Following Some Dreams: Recognising Opportunities, Posing Interesting Questions, and Implementing Alternative Methods', *International Journal of Mass Emergencies and Disasters*, 15, 1 (1997), 21-46.

Duckham, Helen, *Great Pit Disasters: Great Britain, 1700 to the Present Day* (Newton Abbot: David & Charles, 1973).

Elliott, Sue, Humphries, Steve and Jones, Bevan, *Surviving Aberfan: The People's Story* (Guildford: Grosvenor House Publishing, 2016).

Ellis, Tom, *Mines and Men: The Career of a Mining Engineer* (Reading: Educational Explorers, 1971).

— 'Aberfan: The Real Lesson?, *Planet*, July-August 1999.

Elwyn-Jones, Lord, *In My Time: An Autobiography* (London: Futura, 1988).

England, Edward, *The Mountain that Moved* (London: Hodder & Stoughton, 1967).

Erikson, Kai T., *In the Wake of the Flood* (London: Allen and Unwin, 1979).

Evans, Neil, 'Community, Memory and History', *Planet*, 115, February/March 1996, 47-55.

Evans, R.S., 'The Development of Local Government', in *Merthyr Tydfil: A Valley Community* (Merthyr: Merthyr Teachers Centre Group, 1981).

Eyre, Anne, 'Faith, Charity and the Free Market', in Gee, Peter & Fulton, John (eds.), *Religion and Power, Decline and Growth: Sociological Analyses of religion in Britain, Poland and the Americas* (British Sociological Association, Sociology of Religion Study Group, 1991).

— 'More than PTSD: Proactive Responses Among Disaster Victims', *The Australasian Journal of Disaster and Trauma Studies*, 1998-2, http://www.massey.ac.nz/~trauma/issues/1998-2/eyre.htm

— 'Bridging the Gap: Research-based Emergency Management', *Emergency Management*, Spring 1999, 9.

Follis, Richard, 'Case Review: Davis v Central Health Authority', *AVMA Medical and Legal Journal*, April 1991, 11.

Francis, Hywel & Smith, David, *The Fed: A History of the South Wales Miners in the Twentieth Century* (Cardiff: University of Wales Press, 2nd edn, 1998).

Fritz, Charles E., 'Disaster', in Robert K. Merton & Robert A. Nisbet (eds.), *Contemporary Social Problems* (New York: Harcourt, 1961), 651-694.

— 'Disasters' in *International Encyclopaedia of the Social Sciences*, vol. 4 (New York: Macmillan & Free Press, 1968).

Gist, Richard & Lubin, Bernard (eds.) *Psychosocial Aspects of Disaster* (New York: Wiley, 1989).

Gleser, Goldine C., Green, Bonnie L. & Winget, Carolyn N., *Prolonged Psychosocial Effects of Disaster: A Study of Buffalo Creek*, (New York: Academic Press, 1981).

Gold, Edgar, 'Learning from Disaster: Lessons in Regulatory Enforcement in the Maritime Sector', *Review of European Community and International Environmental Law*, 8, 1 (April 1999), 16-20.

Green, Bonnie L., Grace, Mary C., Lindy, Jacob D., Gleser, Goldine C., Leonard, Anthony C. & Kramer, Teresa L., 'Buffalo Creek Survivors in the Second Decade: Comparison with Unexposed and Nonlitigant Groups', *Journal of Applied Psychology*, 20, 13 (1990), 1033-50.

Green, Bonnie L., Lindy, Jacob D., Grace, Mary C., Gleser, Goldine C., Leonard, Anthony C., Korol, Mindy, Winget, Carolyn, 'Buffalo Creek Survivors in the Second Decade: Stability of Stress Symptoms, *American Journal of Orthopsychiatry*, 60, 1 (1990), 43-54.

Gregory, Robert, 'Political Responsibility for Bureaucratic Incompetence: Tragedy at Cave Creek', *Public Administration*, 76 (1998), 519-38.

Griffiths, Robert, *S.O. Davies: A Socialist Faith* (Llandysul: Gomer Press, 1983).

Habermas, Jürgen, 'Learning from Disaster: A Diagnostic Look Back at the Short 20th Century', *Constellations*, 5, 3 (1998), 307-20.

Haines, Fiona, *Corporate Regulation: Beyond 'Punish or Persuade'* (Oxford: Clarendon, 1997).

Hannon, Patrick (ed.), *Wales on the Wireless: A Broadcasting Anthology* (Llandysul: Gomer, 1988).

Harrison, Paul, 'Aberfan: A Hope of Community', *New Society*, 15 March 1973, 587-9.

Harrison, Shirley (ed.), *Disasters and the Media* (Basingstoke: Macmillan, 1998).

Hattenstone, Simon & O'Sullivan, Tom, 'Those who were left behind', *Guardian Weekend*, 8 May 1999, 23-30.

Herman, Judith Lewis, *Trauma and Recovery: From Domestic Abuse to Political Terror* (London: Pandora, 1994).

Hillman, Judy & Clarke, Peter, *Geoffrey Howe: A Quiet Revolutionary* (London: Weidenfeld & Nicolson, 1988).

Hills, Alice, 'Seduced by recovery: the consequences of misunderstanding disasters', *Journal of Contingencies and Crisis Management*, 6, 3 (1998), 162-70.

Hinton, Peter (ed.), *Disasters: Image and Context* (Sydney: Sydney Association for Studies in Society and Culture, 1992).

Hodgkinson, Peter E., 'Technological Disaster: Survival and Bereavement', *Social Science and Medicine*, 29, 3 (1989), 351-6.

Hodgkinson, Peter E. & Stewart, Michael, *Coping with Catastrophe: A Handbook of Disaster Management* (London: Routledge, 1991).

Howe, Geoffrey, 'The Aberfan Disaster', *Medico-Legal Journal*, 38, 1968, 107-21.

— *Conflict of Loyalty* (London: Macmillan, 1994).

— 'Procedure at the Scott Inquiry', *Public Law*, Autumn 1996, 445-460.

— 'The Management of Public Inquiries', *Political Quarterly*, 70, 3 (1999), 294-304.

Hughes, Maureen (ed.), *Aberfan: Our Hiraeth* (Aberfan: Aberfan & Merthyr Vale Community Co-operative, 1999).

Humphrys, John, *Devil's Advocate* (London: Hutchinson, 1999).

Hutter, Bridget M. & Lloyd-Bostock, Sally, 'The Power of Accidents: The Social and Psychological Impact of Accidents and the Enforcement of Safety Regulations', *British Journal of Criminology*, 30, 4 (1990), 409-22.

Hutter, Bridget M., 'Regulating Employers and Employees: Health and Safety in the Workplace', *Journal of Law and Society*, 20, 4 (1993), 452-70.

— 'Variations in Regulatory Styles', *Law and Policy*, 11, 2 (1989), 153-174.

James, Arnold J. & Thomas, John E., *Wales at Westminster: A History of the Parliamentary Representation of Wales, 1800-1979* (Llandysul: Gomer, 1981).

Jardine, Casandra, 'Aberfan's 'lucky' one', *Daily Telegraph*, 18 October 1996.

Johnes, Martin, 'Disasters and Responsibility: Lessons from Aberfan', *Planet*, 135, June-July, 1999, 13-8.

— '"Heads in the Sand": Football, Politics and Crowd Disasters in Twentieth-century Britain', in Paul Darby, Martin Johnes & Gavin Mellor (eds.), *Soccer and Disaster: International Perspectives* (London: Routledge, 2001), 10-27.

— *Wales since 1939* (Manchester: Manchester University Press, 2012).

Jones, Erastus, 'Working in Aberfan and the Valleys', *Social & Economic Administration*, 9, 1 (1979), 30-40.

— 'Aberfan – The village that refused to be destroyed', *Merthyr Express*, 16 October 1986.

Jones, T. Mervyn, *Going Public* (Cowbridge: D. Brown, 1987).

Jones, Michael Wynn, *Deadline Disaster: A Newspaper History* (Newton Abbot: David & Charles, 1976).

Keller, A.Z., Wilson, H.C., & Al-Madhari, A., 'Proposed Disaster Scale and Associated Model for Calculating Return Periods for Disasters of Given Magnitude', *Disaster Prevention and Management*, 1, 1 (1992), 26-33.

Kemp, David (assisted by Peter Mantle), *Damages for Personal Injury and Death* (London: Sweet & Maxwell, 7th edn, 1999).

Kendell, R.E. & Zealley, A.K. (eds.), *Companion to Psychiatric Studies* (Edinburgh: Churchill Livingstone, 5th edn, 1993).

King, Cecil, *The Cecil King Diary, 1965-1970* (London: Cape, 1972).

Kletz, Trevor, 'Are Disasters Really getting Worse?', *Disaster Prevention & Management*, 3, 1 (1994), 33-6.

— *Learning from Accidents in Industry* (London: Butterworth, 1988).

Knapman, Paul A., 'Hillsborough Lives On', *Justice of the Peace & Local Government Law*, 25 January 1997, 79-80.

Lacey, Gaynor N., 'Observations on Aberfan', *Journal of Psychosomatic Research*, 16 (1972), 257-60.

Lacey, Nicola & Wells, Celia, *Reconstructing Criminal Law: Critical Perspectives on Crime and the Criminal Process* (London: Butterworth, 2nd edn, 1998).

Lee, Laurie, *I Can't Stay Long* (Harmondsworth: Penguin edn, 1977).

Lieven, Michael, *Senghennydd, the Universal Pit Village, 1890-1930* (Llandysul: Gomer, 1994).

Littlewood, Jane, *Aspects of Grief: Bereavement in Adult Life* (London: Routledge, 1992).

Llewellyn, Richard, *How Green Was My Valley* (London: Michael Joseph, 1939).

Llewelyn, Chris, *Learning Lessons from Disasters* (Cardiff: Welsh Consumer Council, 1998).

Luxton, Peter, *Charity Fund-raising and the Public Interest: An Anglo-American Legal Perspective* (Aldershot: Avebury, 1990).

McLean, Iain, 'The Political Economy of Regulation: Interests, Ideology, Voters and the UK Regulation of Railways Act 1844', *Public Administration*, 70 (1992), 313-31.

— 'On Moles and the Habits of Birds: The Unpolitics of Aberfan', *Twentieth Century British History*, 8, 3 (1997), 285-309.

— 'It's not too late to say sorry', *Times Higher Education Supplement*, 17 January 1997.

— 'Memorandum by Iain McLean, Professor of Politics, Oxford University: On not scrapping the Tribunals of Inquiry (Evidence) Act 1921' in House of Commons, Public Administration Select Committee, *Government by Inquiry* HC 51-II, 2005, written evidence pp Ev 44-5.

McLean, Iain and Johnes, Martin, '"Regulation run mad': the Board of Trade and the loss of the *Titanic*', *Public Administration* 78 (2000), 729-49.

Madgwick, Gaynor, *Aberfan, Struggling out of the Darkness: A Survivor's Story* (Blaengarw: Valley and the Vale, 1996).

— *Aberfan: A Story of Survival, Love and Community in One of Britain's Worst Disasters* (Talybont: Y Lolfa, 2016).

Marsh, Richard, *Off the Rails* (London: Weidenfeld & Nicolson, 1978).

Mason, Helen, 'All in a good cause?' *Sunday Times*, 27 September 1987, 59.

Mead, Christine (ed.), *Journeys of Discovery: Creative Learning from Disasters* (London: National Institute for Social Work, 1996).

Miller, Joan, *Aberfan: A Disaster and its Aftermath* (London: Constable, 1974).

— 'Community Development in a Disaster Community', *Community Development Journal*, 8, 3 (1973), 161-8.

Morgan, Alun, 'The 1970 Parliamentary Election at Merthyr Tydfil', *Morgannwg*, 12 (1978), 61-81.

Morgan, K.O., *Rebirth of a Nation: Wales, 1880-1980* (Cardiff/Oxford: Oxford University Press & University of Wales Press, 1981).

— 'Welsh Devolution: The Past and the Future' in Taylor, Bridget & Thomson, Katarina (eds.), *Scotland and Wales: Nations Again?* (Cardiff: University of Wales Press, 1999).

Morgan, Louise, Scourfield, Jane, Williams, David, Jasper, Anne and Lewis, Glyn 'The Aberfan disaster: 33-year follow-up of survivors', *British Journal of Psychiatry*, 182 (2003), 532-6.

Napier, Michael, 'Medical and Legal Trauma of Disasters', *Medico-Legal Journal*, 59, 3 (1991), 157-84.

— 'Zeebrugge: the way forward', *Law Society's Gazette*, 40, 7 (1990), 2.

Newburn, Tim, *Making a Difference? Social Work after Hillsborough* (London: National Institute for Social Work, 1993).

Newburn, Tim (ed.), *Working with Disaster: Social Welfare Interventions During and After Tragedy* (London: Longman, 1993).

Nilson, Douglas, 'Disaster Beliefs and Ideological Orientation', *Journal of Contingencies and Crisis Management*, 3, 1 (1995), 12-7.

Nightingale, Benedict, *Charities* (London: Allen Lane, 1973).

Nossiter, Bernard D., 'Aberfan: Tragedy Molds New Spirit', *Washington Post*, 27 May 1973.

Nunn, Charles, 'The Disaster of Aberfan', *Police Review*, 16 October 1987, 2069-71.

Parker, Dennis J., & Handmer, John, *Hazard Management and Emergency Planning: Perspectives on Britain* (London: James & James, 1992).

Parkes, Colin Murray, 'Planning for the Aftermath', *Journal of the Royal Society of Medicine*, 84 (1991), 22-5.

— *Bereavement: Studies of Grief in Adult Life* (London: Routledge, 3rd edn, 1996).

Parkes, Colin Murray & Black, Dora, 'Disasters', in Colin Murray Parkes & Andrew Markus (eds.), *Coping with Loss: Helping Patients and their Families* (London: BMJ Books, 1998), 114-125.

Payne, Christopher F., 'Handling the Press', *Disaster Prevention & Management*, 3, 1 (1994), 24-32.

Paynter, Will, *My Generation* (London: Allen & Unwin, 1972).

Peltzman, S. 'Toward a more general theory of regulation', *Journal of Law and Economics*, 19 (1976), 211-40.

Picarda, Hubert, *The Law and Practice Relating to Charities* (London: Butterworth, 1977).

Pimlott, Ben, *Harold Wilson* (London: HarperCollins, 1992).

Prochaska, Frank, *The Voluntary Impulse: Philanthropy in Modern Britain* (London: Faber & Faber, 1988).

Raphael, Beverley, *When Disaster Strikes: A Handbook for the Caring Professions* (London: Unwin Hymen edn, 1990).

Rhodes, Gerald, *Inspectorates in British Government: Law Enforcement and Standards of Efficiency* (London: George Allen, 1981).

Richardson, Bill, 'Socio-Technical Disasters: Profile and Prevalence', *Disaster Prevention and Management*, 3, 4 (1994), 41–69.

Ridley, Ann & Dunford, Louise, 'Corporate Killing – Legislating for Unlawful Death?', *Industrial Law Journal*, 26, 2 (1997), 99-113.

Robens, Lord, 'Mine Disasters', *Advancement of Science*, June 1969, 391-394.

— *Ten Year Stint* (London: Cassell, 1972).

Roberts, Ken, *The Reconstruction of 'Community': A Case Study of Post-disaster Aberfan* (Coventry: Warwick Working Papers in Sociology, 1985).

Robertson, E.H., *George: A Biography of Viscount Tonypandy* (London: Marshall Pickering, 1992).

Robins, L.N., 'Steps towards evaluating Post-traumatic Stress Reaction as a Psychiatric Disorder', *Journal of Applied Social Psychology*, 20 (1990), 1674-7.

Rosenhan, David L. & Seligman, Martin E.P., *Abnormal Psychology* (New York: W.W. Norton, 3rd edn, 1995).

Scraton, Phil, *Hillsborough: The Truth* (Edinburgh: Mainstream, 1999).

— 'The Lost Afternoon', *Observer*, 11 April 1999.

Scraton, Phil, Jemphrey, Ann & Coleman, Sheila, *No Last Rights: The Denial of Justice and the Promotion of Myth in the Aftermath of the Hillsborough Disaster* (Liverpool: Liverpool City Council, 1995).

Scraton, Phil, Berrington, Eileen & Jemphrey, Ann, 'Intimate Intrusions? Press Freedom, Private Lives and Public Interest', *Communications Law*, 3, 5 (1998), 174-82.

Shader, Richard I. & Schwartz, Alice J., 'Management of Reactions to Disaster', *Social Work*, 11, 2 (1966), 98-104.

Shearer, Ann, *Survivors and the Media* (London: Broadcasting Standards Council, 1991).

Siddle, H.J., Wright, M.D., Hutchinson, J.N., 'Rapid Failures of Colliery Spoil Heaps in the South Wales Coalfield', *Quarterly Journal of Engineering Geology*, 29 (1996), 103-132.

Simpson, A.W.B., 'Legal Liability for Bursting Reservoirs: The Historical Context of *Rylands v. Fletcher*', *Journal of Legal Studies* 13, 2 (1984), 209-64.

Slapper, Gary, 'Crime without conviction', *New Law Journal*, 142, 14 February 1992, 192-93.

— 'Corporate Manslaughter: An Examination of the Determinants of Prosecutional Policy', *Social and Legal Studies*, 2 (1993), 423-43.

— 'Crime without punishment', *Guardian*, 1 February 1994.

— 'Corporate Crime and Punishment', *The Criminal Lawyer*, March/April 1998, 6-7.

— 'Cost of Corporate Crime', *The Times*, 22 June 1999.

— 'Corporate homicide and legal chaos', *New Law Journal*, 9 July 1999, 1031.

Slapper, Gary & Tombs, Steve, *Corporate Crime* (London: Longman, 1999).

Smith, Dai, 'The Valleys: Landscape and Mindscape', in Prys Morgan (ed.), *Glamorgan County History vol. VI: Glamorgan Society 1780-1980* (Cardiff: Glamorgan County History Trust, 1988), 129-49.

Spooner, Peter, 'Developing the Corporate Mindsets which will Help to Reduce Man-made Disasters', *Disaster Prevention & Management*, 1, 2 (1992), 28-36.

Stigler, G., 'The Theory of Economic Regulation', *Bell Journal of Economics and Management Science*, 2, (1971), 3-21.

Suddards, Roger W., *Administration of Appeal Funds* (London: Sweet & Maxwell, 1991).

Taylor, Ian, 'English Football in the 1990s: Taking Hillsborough Seriously?', in: Williams, John & Wagg, Stephen (eds.), *British Football and Social Change: Getting into Europe* (Leicester: Leicester University Press, 1991).

Teff, H., 'Liability for Psychiatric Illness after Hillsborough', *Oxford Journal for Legal Studies*, 12 (1992), 440-52.

Thatcher, Margaret, *The Downing Street Years* (London: HarperCollins, 1993).

— *The Path to Power* (London: HarperCollins, 1995).

Thomas, George, *Mr Speaker: The Memoirs of the Viscount Tonypandy* (London: Century Publishing, 1985).

Thomas, Wyn, *Hands Off Wales: Nationhood and Militancy* (Llandysul: Gomer, 2013).

Tombs, Steve, 'Law, Resistance and Reform: "Regulating" Safety Crimes in the UK', *Social and Legal Studies*, 4 (1995), 343-65.

Walter, Tony, 'The Mourning after Hillsborough', *Sociological Review*, 39, 3 (1991), 599-625.

Walters, David & James, Philip, *Robens Revisited: The Case for a Review of Occupational Health and Safety Legislation* (London: Institute of Employment Rights, 1998).

Watkins, Hugh, '"From Chaos to Calm" The Diary of the Gordon-Lennox Education Centre, Nixonville, Aberfan from Thursday November 3rd, 1966 to Thursday, December 1st, 1966', *Merthyr Historian*, 7 (1994), 58-69.

Wells, Celia, 'Inquests, Inquiries and Indictments: The Official Reception of Death by Disaster', *Legal Studies*, 11 (1991), 71-84.

— *Corporations and Criminal Responsibility* (Oxford: Clarendon, 1993).

— *Negotiating Tragedy: Law and Disasters* (London: Sweet & Maxwell, 1995).

— 'Cry in the Dark: Corporate Manslaughter and Cultural Meaning', in Ian Loveland (ed.), *Frontiers of Criminality* (London: Sweet & Maxwell, 1995).

— 'Corporate Manslaughter: A Cultural and Legal Form', *Criminal Law Forum*, 6, 1 (1995), 45-72.

— *Corporations and Criminal Responsibility* (Oxford: Oxford University Press, 2001).

— 'Corporate criminal liability: a ten-year review', *Criminal Law Review*, 12 (2014), 849-78.

Welsby, Catherine, '"Warning her as to her future behaviour": The Lives of the Widows of the Senghenydd Mining Disaster of 1913', *Llafur*, 6, 4 (1995), 93-109.

Whitham, David & Newburn, Tim, *Coping with Tragedy: Managing the Responses to Two Disasters* (Nottingham: Nottinghamshire County Council, 1992).

Williams, R.M., & Murray Parkes, C., 'Psychosocial Effects of Disaster: Birth Rate in Aberfan', *British Medical Journal*, 10 May 1975, 303-304.

Wilson, Harold, *The Labour Government 1964-70: A Personal Record* (Harmondsworth: Penguin, 1974).

Wood, Bruce, *The Process of Local Government Reform, 1966-74* (London: George Allen, 1976).

Woolf, Anthony D., 'Robens Report – The Wrong Approach', *Industrial Law Journal*, 2 (1973), 88-95.

Wolfenstein, Martha, *Disaster: A Psychological Essay* (Glencoe: The Free Press, 1957).

Woolfson, Charles, Foster, John & Beck, Matthias, *Paying for the Piper: Capital and Labour in Britain's Offshore Oil Industry* (London: Mansell, 1996).

Woolfson, Charles & Beck, Matthias, 'Deregulation: The Contemporary Politics of Health and Safety', in McColgan, Aileen (ed.), *The Future of Labour Law* (London: Cassell, 1996).

Wright, Kathleen M., Ursano, Robert J., Bartone, Paul T., Ingraham, Larry H., 'The Shared Experience of Catastrophe: An Expanded Classification of the Disaster Community', *American Journal of Orthopsychiatry*, 60, 1 (1990), 35-42.

Yehuda, Rachel & McFarlane, Alexander, 'Conflict between Current Knowledge about Posttraumatic Stress Disorder and its Original Conceptual Basis', *American Journal of Psychiatry*, 152, 12 (1995), 1705-13.

Yule, William, 'The Effect of Disasters on Children', *Bereavement Care*, 9, 2, (1990).

— 'Work with Children following Disasters', in Martin Herbert (ed.) *Clinical Child Psychology: Social Learning, Development and Behaviour* (Chichester: John Wiley, 1991).

VII Other unpublished material

Aberfan Tribunal of Inquiry, transcripts of oral evidence.

Akers, David J., *Overview of Coal Refuse Disposal in the United States*, Coal Research Bureau, West Virginia University, Report No. 172, January 1980.

Cuthill, James M., *The Aberfan Disaster – A Study of the Survivors*, Unpublished, no date.

Davis, Gerald, *The First Report of the Management Committee of the Aberfan Disaster Fund*, 1968.

Disaster Action, *Newsletters*

— *Response to the Law Commission Involuntary Manslaughter Consultation Paper (LCCP No. 135)*, 1994.

Elliott, Dominic Paul, *Organisational Learning from Crisis: An Examination of the Football Industry, 1946-97*, Ph.D. thesis, University of Durham, 1998.

Eyre, Anne, 'Calling for a Disasters Study Group: A Proposal', Paper given at British Sociological Association Conference, 1999.

Morgan, C. Geoffrey, *The Second Report of the Aberfan Disaster Fund*, 1970.

Park, W.R. et al., *Interim Report of Retaining Dam Failure, No. 5 Preparation Plant, Buffalo Mining Company, Saunders, Logan Country, West Virginia*, no date.

Slapper, Gary, *Law and Political Economy: Legal Responses to Deaths at Work*, LSE, Ph.D. thesis, 1995.

VIII Select broadcasts

Aftermath: Zeebrugge, ITV, 4 March 1988.
Disaster [series], BBC2, March 1999.
Lockerbie: A Night Remembered, Channel 4, 29 November 1998.
File on Four, BBC Radio 4, 16 February 1999
Hillsborough: The Legacy, BBC1, 11 April 1999.
Survivors – Evil Acts, Partners in Motion (Canadian television broadcast)
Timewatch: Remember Aberfan, BBC2, 15 October 1996.
Wales this Week, HTV Wales, 25 October 1996
Surviving Aberfan BBC4, 14 October 2016
Cantata Memoria by Karl Jenkins, with performance by Ynysowen Male Voice Choir and others, premiere, Wales Millennium Centre, October 2016: S4C and Classic FM.
Aberfan: the fight for justice, produced and directed by Iwan England, presented by Huw Edwards. BBC1, October 2016.
Aberfan: Yr Ymchwiliad, produced and directed by Iwan England, presented by Huw Edwards. S4C, October 2016.

Index

NB. Job titles in [square brackets] are those held on 21 October 1966, or other material time.

Williams, Howell [teacher] 5-6, 24, 27

Williams, James [victim of 1909 Pentre slide] 40, 55

Wilson, Harold (Lord Wilson of Rievaulx) [Prime Minister] x, 35-6, 43, 49, 51, 64-5, 144-5, 175

Wright, Thomas [Area General Manager, No. 4 Area, South

Western Division, NCB] 31-2, 40

Wynne, Thomas [manager, Merthyr Vale colliery] 40

Year of the Valleys (1974) 110

Ynysowen Primary School 159

Zeebrugge, see *Herald of Free Enterprise* disaster (1987)

Lightning Source UK Ltd.
Milton Keynes UK
UKHW020036011121
393173UK00007B/34